NON AD PERNI-CIEM

In Memory Of

Carl W. Altenburg '41

Dedicated by the
Carleton College
Alumni Association

*Fighting Sail on Lake Huron
and Georgian Bay*

Fighting Sail on Lake Huron and Georgian Bay

~

THE WAR OF 1812 AND ITS AFTERMATH

Barry Gough

Naval Institute Press
Annapolis, Maryland

Naval Institute Press
291 Wood Road
Annapolis, MD 21402

Library of Congress Cataloging-in-Publication Data

Gough, Barry M.

    Fighting sail on Lake Huron and Georgian Bay : the War of 1812 and its aftermath / Barry Gough

      p.   cm.

    Includes bibliographical references (p.) and index.

    ISBN 1-55750-314-1 (alk. paper)

    1. United States—History—War of 1812—Naval operations. 2. Great Lakes Region—History, Naval—19th century. 3. Huron, Lake, Region (Mich. and Ont.)—History, Naval—19th century. 4. Georgian Bay Region (Ont.)—History, Naval—19th century. I. Title.

E360.G68 2002

973.5'25—dc21

2001059630

Printed in the United States of America on acid-free paper ∞

09 08 07 06 05 04 03 02   9 8 7 6 5 4 3 2

First printing

*To my colleagues and students at
Wilfrid Laurier University*

Contents

Preface and Acknowledgments
〜

*T*he age of fighting sail lives only in historical memory. The sight of a man-of-war moving under a spread of canvas is a majesty not now to be beheld. These days aircraft carriers, submarines, frigates, and minesweepers are the vessels of naval war: since the era of John Paul Jones and Horatio Nelson, technology has supplanted all predecessor forms of gun-carrying platforms. An age of wood and wind has given way to something entirely different and certainly more lethal to the course of human affairs.

In this book our minds are called back to an earlier time. Only seven years after Nelson's remarkable victory over gallant French and Spanish fleets at Trafalgar, ships and men trained in similar navies began fighting for control of those inland seas, the Great Lakes of North America. The War of 1812 invokes memories of suffering and endurance, of injured pride and quickening patriotism, and of folly as well as bravery. The war was not one of Canada's choosing, but 1812 became a sign of solemn import to Canadians: an example and a warning. For Americans, the war brings to mind memories of a desperate struggle against the Royal Navy and British military forces in North America, mainly on Canadian soil. It is also a testament to the necessity of maintaining fidelity to the Union. For the British, 1812 is the forgotten war, a quarrel almost, against an upstart young nation. The military lessons were of mighty portent, and the struggle led eventually to an easing of tensions on the northern borders of the United States. In all, the War of 1812 marks the first, perhaps necessary, phase in the resolution of numerous difficulties. From these, great partnerships were to emerge between and among Canada, the United States, and the United Kingdom.

In 1812 Britain was engaged in a titanic contest. Almost singlehandedly that nation had resisted the combined powers of Europe, headed up by France with its exorbitant expectations. The war in Europe was a stupendous struggle, pinning down and nearly exhausting British resources. By means of blockade the British sought to control Napoleon, and the naval necessities or requirements to do this were enormous. The War of 1812, by contrast, was a struggle for the control of Canada, specifically the borderlands of Lakes Champlain, Ontario, Erie, Huron, Michigan, and Superior. This history is the story of how sea power, and maritime strategies of respective nations (and empires), came to be projected into the continental heartland. For the last time in this old order of fighting sail, the shape of territorial gains, commercial prizes, and Indian alliances were being formed, even determined, by men-of-war.

The war had many consequences. Most notably, it established by subsequent convention the Canadian-American border as far as the Rocky Mountains, set in place the Great Lakes as a waterway to be shared by two nations (neither of which could establish a primacy in the continental interior), and, of tragic consequence, ended any dream held by Indian peoples of North America for a separate, sovereign homeland or homelands. In short, that which was on offer as a prize was immensely valuable to the nascent United States, to the ever-expansive Great Britain, to the emerging colony of the Province of Upper Canada (and all trade based upon Montreal), and to many native nations now fighting their last great struggle for independence. Far from this being, as has been imagined, an unnecessary war, or one which had no lasting consequences, this conflict set in place significant factors for the next to last phase of the struggle for the international boundary to the Pacific Ocean.

This book brings together two personal passions, one professional, the other vocational. Much of my career as a historian has been in researching and writing naval and imperial history, with a focus on how sea power has shaped the affairs of the Americas. Much of my spare time has been devoted to sailing. This book tells of inland waters that I have sailed, from the St. Clair River (where Lake Huron drains into waters flowing to Lake Erie), to Lake Huron and north of the Bruce Peninsula, and then again into Georgian Bay, particularly into Penetanguishene. This last-named place is the mooring place for my sloop. Almost without exception the scenes and locales of this book have been visited by me. This vast and complicated landscape, with all its marine challenges, has provided further cause of wonder to me as a historian. Acquired knowledge of waterways and hazards has enriched my understandings of the difficulties of navigation in those seas. Without the aid of charts, pilots, sailing directions, radar, and Global Positioning System, mariners of the War of 1812 made their way safely. This is a tribute to the sea-keeping capabilities of the brigs and schooners built for these waters as well as to the skills of the officers and men who sailed them.

It is true that a very large literature already exists on the War of 1812. To date much has been written about single-ship engagements, about privateering, and about the British blockade of the Chesapeake—to give but a few examples. Even so, little is known about the history of naval warfare and amphibious operations in the northern theater of the North American war. Two recent books have illuminated, as case studies, naval warfare on two of the Great Lakes. These are Robert Malcomson's *Lords of the Lake: The Naval War on Lake Ontario, 1812–1814* (1998) and David Curtis Skaggs and Gerard T. Altoff's *A Signal Victory: The Lake Erie Campaign, 1812–1813* (1997). Rich in detail and analysis, these works examine individual lakes, so to speak, against the larger naval history of the continental heartland. This book has a parallel focus and theme. It tells the story of Lake Huron and Georgian Bay: 1812 might be called the war for the upper lakes and hinterland. Of necessity my work describes the larger themes, and where necessary (as in the struggle for control of Lake Erie, which had such direct results for waters upstream) goes over somewhat familiar ground. As will be seen, the history of Lake Huron and Georgian Bay is intricately related to that of Lake Erie.

This account involves a number of competing forces: the U.S. Navy and U.S. Army on the one side and the Royal Navy and various British and Canadian military units on the other. It also involves the North West Company, a Montreal fur-trading concern, and, of particular significance (though often neglected in the recounting and analysis), the native peoples, or Indians, of the continental interior and the Great Lakes fighting to retain their resources, lands, and political power. This is an account of how three powers—American, British, and Indian—fought for primacy and influence. In the upper Great Lakes the British and Canadians and their native allies retained possession, despite heavy military pressure from increasingly preponderant American forces. In the telling, this unfolding drama brings to light all the failures and foibles of war, and I have sought to retain absolute fairness, and lack of bias, in recounting particulars of a terrible war in which national and racial hatreds raised themselves to fervent pitch.

This book is above all an inquiry into the nature of naval operations in that hitherto little-known backwater of the war: Lake Huron and its annex, Georgian Bay. That classic age of fighting sail is noted for its grand fleet actions and great single-ship encounters. But naval warfare on the upper Great Lakes was of comparative diminutive scale. Men-of-war were not large, heavily gunned ships-of-the-line. Rather, they were brigs, schooners, sloops, and even bateaux and canoes—in fact, almost anything that could float. Canadian and American brigs and schooners on these inland seas carried in their holds the business of emerging western empires and native alliances. For the nature of that war in northern lakes and forests—and the desperate campaign British and Canadian forces fought alongside their native allies—was one of unusual expediency. At another level, this work is an example in military history in which both powers were fighting a long way from home bases. Equally significant to the reading and recounting is that this was a war in which an indigenous North American trading corporation, aided and abetted by Indian support and manpower, had imperial intentions of consolidation and expansion. This is an account of the problems of a logistical nightmare of fighting a campaign deep in a frontier territory. Exposed flanks, tenuous alliances, precarious food supplies—all these and more made the war a series of thrusts and counterthrusts often fragmentary in their impact on the course of the war.

In those hazardous days, fur posts, garrisons, and forts changed hands according to the fortunes of war. From the British perspective, at the outset of the war Detroit and Michilimackinac were in American hands. Amherstburg, Sault Ste. Marie, and St. Joseph Island were in danger of so becoming. The Canadian fur post at Prairie du Chien on the Upper Mississippi River, key to the interior trade, was likewise in jeopardy. At stake was not only the Canadian hinterland but also the Indian alliance upon which so much hinged. In the circumstances, the imperial allies fought on desperate terms, their goal being to keep the Indian alliance, to protect trade and shipping upon which this alliance and the fur trade depended, and to fight rear-guard, irregular actions against the enemy.

On their part, forces of the United States were highly advantaged in number of personnel, strength of materiel, and quality of supplies. Initiative gained after the buoyant success of Commodore Perry's fleet at Put-in-Bay in late summer 1813 could be sustained at the Detroit River and waters upstream but only if the British could be found and engaged in combat. Despite such advantages as the Americans possessed, the ultimate prize—control of Lake Huron— eluded them. How a small party of armed men accomplished the negation of American advantages in these waters is one of the subjects of this inquiry. It is a choice example in history of small-boat and amphibious operations as undertaken by joint naval and army commanders.

Of related importance in this book, and of fascination to many students of history and Canadian-American relations, is how, in consequence of the diplomacy that ended the War of 1812, an equilibrium was established between two powers along this international boundary that divided Lake Huron. For some years after the Peace of Ghent (1814) the two powers eyed each other with guarded suspicion. The present-day "myth of the unguarded frontier," as Canadian military historian Col. Charles P. Stacey put it cogently, has blinded students of history to the realities of decades of border-defense history after 1814. The British, so as to secure their northern dominion, kept up a sizable naval and military establishment at Penetanguishene on the shores of Georgian Bay. Penetanguishene did double duty: it formed the bulwark for defense against American attack and served as a base for amphibious operations against the potential enemy. This sheet-anchor of empire, so to speak, at the northwestern extension of the great military road Yonge Street, which linked York (Toronto) on Lake Ontario with channels of trade and communication north to Sault Ste. Marie and Fort William near Thunder Bay, Lake Superior, enjoys a history perhaps small in the large scale of international affairs, war, and diplomacy. Yet it is an insightful one, instructive about naval administration and shipbuilding as well as difficulties of fortification and defense.

At Penetanguishene, for two decades and more, the British government kept men-of-war and a garrison. Here no gun was fired in anger. Here men, acting on instructions issued from faraway York, Kingston, Montreal, and London, planned for another War of 1812. Peace remained precarious. However, by the early 1830s diplomatic successes by London and Washington made active military preparations on the Great Lakes redundant. In consequence, the base at Penetanguishene was wound down and then closed. The small fleet of schooners and gunboats—sad remnant of British fighting sail there—fell to the fortunes of the auction block. Thus ended the preliminary chapter in a larger story of how British forces in subsequent decades were to withdraw in turn from Kingston, Quebec, Esquimalt, and Halifax. Such were the processes of the imperial recessional, all beginning on what had become sleepy Georgian Bay and Lake Huron. For a time, however—the era spanned by this book—war, or fear of war, dictated every action in those waters.

So that the reader may more readily follow the time line of this account and place each event in relation to others of importance I have included, following this preface, a chronology of the war on Lake Huron and adjacent waters.

Many remarkable persons present themselves in this historical canvas—Navy and Army officers and men, patriot chiefs, Indian agents, shipbuilders, and strategists. Many are otherwise unknown to history. The upper Great Lakes offered a field of opportunity for professional soldiers and sailors. In large measure this was a young man's war, with many of the commanders in their early twenties. It was a field in which to build or lose a reputation. Two future presidents of the United States parade across this historical landscape: William Henry Harrison and Zachary Taylor. A future secretary of state, Lewis Cass, plays a prominent part. Of immense significance is Tecumseh, last great hope for an Indian sovereign territory. Virginia and Kentucky play prominent roles in the interior war, and a congressman from Kentucky, Richard Johnson, we find leading mounted riflemen into Canadian territory. Oliver Hazard Perry, previously unknown, becomes a hero. Commo. Arthur Sinclair on Lake Huron finds himself under a dark cloud. The British naval commander Robert Heriot Barclay faces near-ruin but is exonerated. His Army counterpart, Henry Procter, finds himself removed from his command, for blunders not fully of his own responsibility. New faces make their appearance. Accordingly, in the text I have drawn character sketches of the most important of them. These may serve as an added dimension to a book that describes the campaigns and the struggle for the control of the interior heartland of North America. I am aware that the voices of the common sailor and soldier are almost silent in these pages. This is not for want of looking but because of the paucity of material in manuscript and print. I have used what I could find; and in particular the account of American seaman David C. Bunnell has proved a boon to details of the taking of the *Tigress* and *Scorpion*. Bunnell had enlisted in the U.S. Navy, thinking it an honorable duty to do so and having "no children to mourn my fate." He joined to give "an opportunity to settle some small *accounts* with *John Bull*." It was a war in which patriotism ran deep.

This book begins with the British master stroke, or preemptive strike: the taking of Michilimackinac and the fall of Detroit. It then moves to the Battle of Put-in-Bay and its consequences to British possibilities, which had become bleak and nearly proved fatal. The story of this battle has been told many times, and with this in mind I have given the essence of the encounter but with specific reference to its consequences for the land campaign and the struggle for Lake Huron, Georgian Bay, and Lake Superior. My narrative then takes up the story of that doughty little schooner *Nancy*, pressed into His Majesty's Service as a transport vessel. Without men-of-war imperial forces were obliged to take unusual measures, as told in the tridimensional chapter entitled "The Water Rats." Fort Willow (and its companion Nottawasaga), Michilimackinac, Prairie du Chien—these three form together an ingenious western military design concocted by British military planners. Subsequently, the narrative shifts to an inquiry of U.S. naval strategy and operations under the ill-starred Commo. Arthur Sinclair. Then follows discussion of small boat operations of Lieutenant Worsley's little war. These resulted in the British regaining their naval ascendancy through the seizure of two U.S. armed schooners, the *Tigress* (renamed by the British *Surprize*) and *Scorpion* (renamed *Confiance*). The defense of Michilimackinac against amphibious American assault and the British campaign to recapture Prairie du Chien constitute, together, the last phase of this northern war. The year 1814 closed with the British in command of the upper Great Lakes and, at the same time, the British realization that a naval base had to be founded on Lake Huron. Penetanguishene became that naval base. The ships maintained there, and the workings of that yard, form the material for the next to last chapter. Steam supplanted sail, and iron replaced wood, and so the age of fighting sail passed for all time on the upper Great Lakes. This constitutes the last chapter, which tells how diplomatic relations between Britain and the United States solved many of the border problems that the War of 1812 had been fought over, with such phenomenal cost and so little gain to either party except the natives, who suffered grievously. Included here are details of the various schooners and other vessels that feature in the later stages of this narrative. There are two appendixes: (1) Lt. Miller Worsley's little-known letter to his father dated 6 October 1814 detailing his recent action against the U.S. Navy at Nottawasaga, and (2) Worsley's 1831 appeal that the monarch, William IV, recognize his great feats in the Royal Navy.

A special, unqualified word needs to be said about the use of the place name *Michilimackinac*. Readers should note that Fort Mackinac, on Mackinac Island, is sometimes referred to as Michilimackinac. Indeed, throughout this book the terms are used interchangeably. This is not all: they are not to be confused with Mackinaw City, a settlement on the northeastern reaches of the Lower Michigan Peninsula adjacent to Mackinac Island. Nowadays the main passage leading by these locations between Lake Michigan and Lake Huron appears on the chart as Strait of Mackinac. Further particulars about these place names are given in the text. No matter how it is spelled, advise travel guidebooks, it is pronounced Mack-in-naw, not Mack-in-ack. Also, I connote imperial forces to mean British, Canadian, and Indians together in their alliance. Except when quoting from original texts I have used contemporary spellings; for example, St. Marys River, Sault Ste. Marie. Tecumseh's name is generally spelled that way, and I have followed that convention here. Note, however, that the British schooner-of-war named for that great patriot chief was spelled HMS *Tecumseth,* a spelling I have used here. The Ottawa chief Newash (or Naywash or Neebish) also lent his name to one of HM schooners, spelled *Newash,* and is spelled herein that way. An additional point needs to be mentioned. Numerical strength of fighting forces and size of battle losses are always difficult to report with certainty, and frequently they are twisted or adjusted for propaganda purposes. I cannot vouch, therefore, for the accuracy of all the details included here on these matters, but I have attempted to come up with reasonable figures on the basis of the evidence available.

NOTE ON BRIGS AND SCHOONERS

A *brig* is a vessel with two masts, fore and main, both of them square-rigged but having a large gaff mainsail known as a brigsail. The fore-and-aft brigsail is secured to a boom. A brig also carries several fore and aft sails and a spanker. A brig is a flush-deck vessel. Because of its square sails and yards, it required a crew of necessary size to be able to bend on and take off sails from the yards. A brig would be of one hundred tons burden upward to five hundred tons. The mast of a brig consists of three sections: lower, top, and topgallant mast. The main mast of a brig is always taller than the foremast. A brig is a deep-waisted vessel, with a deep draft; even so, a brig often lacked displacement and stability for heavy armament. The bulwarks were too high and heavy. The rig was large and the ship top-heavy. Hence the ship was dangerous, and many of them were lost. Such a vessel could carry up to sixteen guns. The Royal Navy had a class of them to suppress slavery: they carried ten guns and are referred to as the "coffin class." During the War of 1812 and after, these brigs, carrying additional boats and an added quarterdeck, became increasingly unstable. In 1817 these brigs were altered by increasing the sheer forward, thus giving many of them an extended life.

A *schooner* is a vessel with fore and aft sails on two or more masts. Strictly speaking, schooners have just two masts, the main taller than the fore. Schooners with seven masts have been built, but those of the 1812 war had two masts. A topsail schooner would carry one square sail aloft on the foremast. With its two main sails and its foresails, a schooner could work closely to the wind. Because the square sail cannot be trimmed efficiently to the wind, a brig had difficulty working to windward in the fashion that the schooner could more easily do. Also, schooners required fewer hands, for their sails could be worked efficiently from the deck. In a schooner, too, the windage and leeway were lessened. Thus the schooner was always more economical in use. Schooners had excellent qualities for the coasting trade and fishing, especially on the Grand Banks, as they required few crew and could sail to weather relatively well. On the Great Lakes during the War of 1812 schooners were constructed of seventy to one hundred tons.

By and large, the brig, with relatively wide beam, was a more stable platform for carrying guns, assuming the vessel to be ballasted properly. Schooners were more prone to "turning turtle" and sinking altogether, especially if poorly ballasted and sailing in seas with great squalls. If guns were carried on deck this would accentuate the risk, as James Fenimore Cooper tells in his story *Ned Myers*. Brigs could be similarly tender, and the Royal Navy, as noted, had its "coffin-brigs." In order to increase stability and prevent calamities, guns of schooners would be stowed below deck and raised and positioned for action when necessary.

NOTE ON SOURCES

This book rests on a large body of documentation from British, Canadian, and American archives, both in manuscript and printed form. For the first time in the writing of the War of 1812 in the continental hinterland of North America, full use has been made of Admiralty papers, particularly in-letters, or reports of proceedings. These supplement British War Office and Colonial Office manuscripts. Also I have exploited papers of Viscount Melville and Commo. Sir Robert Hall in the British Library, the manuscripts of Adm. Sir John Boase Warren in the National Maritime Museum, and those of Commo. Robert Barrie in the Royal Military College of Canada. Papers of the U.S. Navy and Secretary of War have been used for the reconstruction of American strategy and force deployments. I have aimed for a balance between British and Canadian sources on the one hand and American sources on the other. Wherever possible, I have used the original documents and have cited them in the notes. A full inventory of materials used, including various histories and special studies of the war and its aftermath, is given in the bibliography.

I have used various collections of documents: William Wood's *Select British Documents on the Canadian War of 1812* and William S. Dudley's *Naval War of 1812: A Documentary History.* Of related value to this study are two collections of documents compiled by Ernest A. Cruikshank, *The Documentary History of the Campaign upon the Niagara Frontier* and *Documents Relating to the*

Invasion of Canada and the Surrender of Detroit. For the amphibious operations of British imperial forces, including North West Company personnel serving in militia regiments, also including the Royal Newfoundland Fencibles, I have benefited from the Bulger Papers printed in the *Wisconsin Historical Collections* and other items from that series. Problems of American military operations in Michigan, 1814 and 1815, are available in printed form in Clarence Carter, ed., *The Territorial Papers of the United States,* vol. 10, *The Territory of Michigan, 1805–1820.* All of the above printed collections I have used as supplementary to the unpublished sources.

In researching this book I amassed many debts. Chris Johnson drew the maps. Peter Rindlisbacher provided many fine paintings for reproduction. I thank Parks Ontario (Wasaga Beach Provincial Park); Penetanguishene Public Library; Discovery Harbour, Penetanguishene, and the Marine Heritage Association; Archives of Ontario; Parks Canada; National Archives of Canada; Marine Museum of the Great Lakes in Kingston, Ontario; Marine Museum of Upper Canada in Toronto; Royal Ontario Museum; Toronto Reference Library; Hamilton Public Library; the Library of the Royal Military College of Canada in Kingston, Ontario; Royal Canadian Military Institute Library; Fort Malden National Historic Site; Erie Maritime Museum; Toledo Museum of Art; Clements Library, University of Michigan; Naval Historical Center, United States Department of the Navy; Mariners' Museum, Newport News, Virginia; Special Collections, University of California–San Diego Libraries; Boston Athenaeum; Rhode Island Historical Society; Public Record Office, Kew, Surrey; National Maritime Museum, Greenwich; and Department of Manuscripts, British Library. In particular, I thank John Polacsek, Jeff Seiken, Rob Bromley, Maurice Smith, Fred Drake, William S. Dudley, Michael Crawford, Reginald Horsman, David Skaggs, Graeme Mount, Grant Head, James Seay Dean, M. J. Mulloy, Chris Wittick, Jean Morrison, John Mellor, Keith Widder, Gordon Hafner, Maurice D. Smith, Chris Anderson, Don Withrow, John Docker, Claudia Jew, Ann Skene Melvin, John Gibson, A. J. McLaughlin, Brian Leigh Dunnigan, Bob Garcia, Dennis Carter-Edwards, and Suzanne Stark. I am grateful to my students in naval history at Wilfrid Laurier University (and elsewhere that I have lectured) who listened with interest and sometimes wonder at how such a war, that of 1812, should have been fought at all between and among peoples now among the best of friends and allies.

Chronology of the War on Lake Huron and Adjacent Waters

~

1811

7 Nov.   General Harrison leads attack on joint Indian force in Battle of Tippecanoe, Indiana Territory

1812

19 June   President Madison proclaims war

27 June   Canadians captured the *Commencement* near Black Rock, Niagara River, in first encounter after U.S. declaration of war

30 June   *Nancy,* recently taken into British service, sails from Amherstburg to Fort Erie

2 July   *Cuyahoga Packet* captured by British near Grosse Island, Detroit River

12 July   General Hull's army invades Upper Canada at Sandwich

17 July   British and Indian (Dakota, Menominee, Winnebago, Ottawa, and Ojibwa) forces under Captain Roberts force U.S. surrender of Michilimackinac

16 Aug.   U.S. forces under General Hull surrender Detroit, capital of Michigan Territory

4 Oct.   *Nancy* eludes American capture in St. Clair River

9 Oct.   Americans capture the *Caledonia* and sink the *Detroit* near Fort Erie

13 Oct.   Battle of Queenstown Heights; death of Maj. Gen. Isaac Brock

1813

18 Jan.   Americans force British and Indians to withdraw from Raisin River

27	April	Major General Dearborn and Commodore Chauncey capture York
27	May	American forces capture Fort Erie
31	July	Captain Barclay lifts blockade of Presque Isle
1–4	Aug.	Commodore Perry takes his fleet out of Presque Isle
10	Sept.	Battle of Lake Erie; British fleet under Captain Barclay captured; U.S. Navy gains dominance on upper Great Lakes.
26	Sept.	British evacuate Detroit
27	Sept.	Major General Procter begins retreat from Fort Malden
5	Oct.	Battle of the Thames (Moraviantown); General Harrison routs British and Indians under General Procter; death of Tecumseh; Indian town destroyed
10	Dec.	American forces burn Newark, Ontario
19	Dec.	British capture Fort Niagara

1814

4	March	American victory on Upper Thames River at Longwood
1	May	Gen. William Clark proceeds from St. Louis to establish post at Prairie du Chien
15	May	Americans burn Port Dover, Lake Erie
18	May	Col. R. McDouall's relief expedition reaches Michilimackinac
2	June	U.S. forces under Clark establish post at Prairie du Chien
28	June	Maj. William McKay's expedition quits Michilimackinac destined for Prairie du Chien
3	July	British again capitulate to Americans at Fort Erie
12	July	U.S. warships and land forces under Commodore Sinclair and Major Croghan sail north into Lake Huron
14	July	Encounter along St. Marys River; Americans raid North West Company post Sault Ste. Marie
20	July	British and Indian (Dakota, Menominee, Ojibwa, Winnebago) forces capture U.S. post Fort Shelby on the Upper Mississippi (Prairie du Chien) and rename it Fort McKay
20	July	U.S. fleet with army units anchors off abandoned British post on St. Joseph Island and destroy remains
24[?]	July	U.S. Navy under Sinclair captures North West Company's schooner *Mink* and interrogate captives
4	Aug.	U.S. naval and land forces anchor off Mackinac Island
4–5	Aug.	Croghan's attack on Fort Mackinac beaten off by British

13	Aug.	USS *Niagara, Scorpion,* and *Tigress* anchor off mouth of Nottawasaga River
14	Aug.	Loss and destruction of the *Nancy* and blockhouse
18	Aug.	Lieutenant Worsley proceeds from Nottawasaga River for Michilimackinac
3	Sept.	British forces seize the *Tigress* off Drummond Island
6	Sept.	British forces take the *Scorpion*
15	Nov.	British reoccupy Fort Erie after American withdrawal
24	Dec.	Peace of Ghent ends Anglo-American War

1815

	Feb.	British begin construction of naval base and arsenal at Penetanguishene, Georgian Bay
19	June	Captain Bulger, who had burned Fort McKay (Shelby), 24 May, returns to Michilimackinac with the Michigan Fencibles
24	June	British choose site for Fort Collier, Drummond Island
27	June	1st/81st Regiment of Foot sent down from Michilimackinac to York, with units to follow
1	July	Fort Niagara returned to British hands
18	July	U.S. forces occupy Fort Mackinac, a treaty stipulation
18	July	Fort Malden returned to Great Britain, a treaty provision

Fighting Sail on Lake Huron
and Georgian Bay

Introduction

~

THE WESTERN FRONTIER

O
n 19 June 1812 the president of the United States, James Madison, in accordance with an act of Congress, proclaimed a state of war with Great Britain and the British Empire. The House of Representatives voted for war by seventy-nine to thirty-nine; the Senate likewise, by nineteen to thirteen. Announcement that a state of hostilities existed between two powers previously at peace for a generation came as no surprise to the parties involved. It brought on an armed struggle that ranged on the North American continent, along the Atlantic seaboard, and on distant seas. Heavily armed American frigates, more powerful than their corresponding British cruisers, were quickly sent to sea to attack British shipping. Soon the invasion of Canada was commenced.

Various circumstances had compelled the president to announce a state of war. The proclaimed reason was that of maritime rights. For many years the U.S. government had been incensed over the impressment of American seamen by British men-of-war. In 1807 the British two-decker *Leopard*, hovering off the Virginia coast, had attacked the U.S. frigate *Chesapeake*, taken off four British deserters, and nearly touched off war. British orders-in-council had been passed for the purpose of giving British commanders powers of stopping neutrals from trading with the enemy, the French. Beginning in 1793 Britain had become locked in deadly struggle with Napoleon Bonaparte and France. In such straightened circumstances, British policy was invariably one of expediency, and that meant pushing aside the tender interests of American maritime rights. Technically speaking, the Americans fought their 1812 war on the issue of impressment, and on this issue the British would not budge.

However, another cause of war, one more deeply seated than the maritime issue, lay like a festering sore on the American arm of statecraft. Unrest on the frontier constantly worried political leaders and was a matter of serious concern to George Washington. "There are combustibles in every State, which a spark might set fire to," he warned at the time of Shay's Rebellion. He was quick to point the finger at Britain. "That she is at this moment sowing the seeds of jealousy and discontent among the various tribes of Indians on our frontier admits of no doubt, in my mind. And that she will improve every opportunity to foment the spirit of turbulence within the bowels of the United States, with a view to distracting our governments, and promoting divisions, is, with me, not less certain."[1] The real clue to the 1812 U.S. declaration of war against England, in fact, is to be found in the urgent circumstances of the American western frontier.

In his message President Madison referred to the renewal of warfare by Indians "on one of our extensive frontiers." He went on to describe such warfare as one "which is known to spare neither age nor sex, and to be distinguished by features particularly shocking to humanity." The British and Canadians were to be blamed for this state of affairs, he charged, for it was difficult to account for various activities of traders and native peoples without concluding that the hostility of the latter was connected with various British garrisons on the Canadian frontier. "Such is the spectacle of injuries and indignities which have been heaped on our country," concluded Madison. Forbearance and conciliation would now no longer do to deal with "these progressive usurpations, and these accumulated wrongs."[2]

To secure possession of the Old Northwest (as it is known in American history), that area lying beyond the Alleghenies and on the southerly side of the international boundary dividing British America from the United States, and to remove the ever-present Indian "menace"—these two potent impulses furnished intertwining reasons for beginning the war. In 1811, at Tippecanoe and elsewhere deep in Indiana Territory, events confirmed American fears of British trade and Canadian infiltration. When Gen. William Henry Harrison, governor of Indiana Territory, during a punitive expedition, fell into a battle with the Indians, under Tecumseh and the Prophet, at Tippecanoe, and suffered great losses, British arms and ammunition were found on the natives. English guns had been supplied to Indians. Tecumseh's plans to create an Indian confederacy and to stay the flood of American settlement through an armed rising seemed undeniably to be traceable to a Canadian source. "Within the last three months the whole of the Indians on this frontier have been completely armed and equipped out of the King's stores at Malden," wrote Harrison. "The Indians had, moreover, an ample supply of British glazed powder. Some of their guns had been sent to them so short a time before the action, that they were not divested of the list covering in which they are imported."[3] Such evidence seemed conclusive to those minds who proposed to secure the western frontier by force and reprisal. The "war hawks" intensified their cries.

In addition, American land hunger also formed a motivation for the prosecution of this war. From New Hampshire to Kentucky, frontier voices called for an expulsion of the British from Canada, and this complimented southern calls for the addition of Florida, to be captured from Spain. Such land hunger, anticipating Manifest Destiny, found itself dramatically stated in the oft-quoted words of John Randolph delivered in the House of Representatives on 16 December 1811:

> Sir, if you go to war it will not be for the protection of, or defence of your maritime rights. Gentlemen from the North have been taken up to some high mountain and shown all the kingdoms of the earth; and Canada seems tempting in their sight. That rich vein of Gennesee land . . . is said to be even better on the other side of the lake than on this. Agrarian cupidity, not maritime right urges the war. Ever since the report of the Committee on Foreign Relations came into the House, we have heard but one word—like the whip-poor-will but one eternal monotonous tone—Canada! Canada! Canada! Not a syllable about Halifax, which unquestionably should be our great object in a war for maritime security.[4]

What Madison or the War Hawks had not counted on was the rapid and firm development of the Province of Upper Canada, established 1791. Its founding governor, John Graves Simcoe, was very much the mastermind of its new imperial quest. A veteran of British forces fighting American patriots during the Revolutionary War, he was well aware of expansionist zeal south of the line. The great peninsula of Ontario he imagined as heartland for the British Empire in America. He put it this way, in giving advice to the Colonial Office in London:

> I conceive the peninsula surrounded the waters of the Great Lakes (a kind of lesser continent) to be the most favourable situation in nature for a British colony. It is

3

the country in which Champlain, the founder of Canada, intended to have made great establishments, but which has been since neglected except by the casual erection of a few posts. There are but a very few Indians who inhabit within it, the greater part of the soil has been purchased and the whole ought to be before it will become of value, as the Indians will not want for suggestions to enhance its price. I consider this country to be of immense value, whether it be regarded in respect to its *immediate advantages,* the future *prospect of advantage,* or the probable grounds for supposing that it will remain the most *permanent foreign possession* of Great Britain.[5]

To effect these purposes the governor suggested that a special corps of troops be raised, consisting of four companies, each about one hundred men strong. Such a force could be trained to operate naval vessels on the Great Lakes (the future Provincial Marine of Upper Canada) and would preserve the security of the infant colony against American expansion on the one hand and Indian attack on the other. Thus as of 1812 Upper Canada's defense rested on a scheme developed by Simcoe, which consisted of a consideration that the Ontario peninsula was a strategically located bastion, one that would limit American expansion and win back to Britain and the Empire some of its lost lands and citizens. Naval arsenals were to constitute the first line of defense on the Great Lakes, with a system of linked interior posts transforming the continental hinterland into a central fortress. "Such a system," Simcoe had written with an eye to the future, "comprehensive, regular and unalterable in its design is most necessary . . . and calculated to protect this great Country in its infant Establishment, and gradually build it up with that solidity and permanence that may display its many advantages and render it a most important Part of the British Empire."[6] In effect, Simcoe's model was that of the Roman military colony. Military personnel, military installations, and roads were designed to promote an adherence to the British Empire.

To Simcoe and his successors the Indian alliance continued to be of paramount concern. In the Old Northwest the British found themselves facing fearful odds. Many Indians considered that King George had abandoned them in the peace arrangements of 1783 and placed them, south of the line, unmercifully at the hands of Washington and the "Long Knives." To counter such sense of betrayal as the Peace of Paris induced in native minds, and to safeguard imperial interests in commerce and defense, British statesmen saw merits in a novel idea—a neutral Indian state, a barrier, so to speak, lying between Upper Canada and the American-held Old Northwest. The concept of a neutral native zone rested as much in self-serving requirements as in altruism. Yet for all its possibilities, as we shall see, it died on the peace table ending the War of 1812. With it expired the last fading vision of an Indian empire of the upper Great Lakes.

After the American War of Independence, which ended in 1783, Britain had retained certain frontier posts—to secure the interior trade, to cultivate the alliance with the Indians, and to necessitate American good faith in payment of prewar commercial debts. British statesmen thought it important to mediate for the Indians in any diplomatic relations with the Americans, and this they did in 1794 and again in 1814. The reason, said Lord Hawkesbury, of the Board of Trade, was that such a measure would show the Indians that they had not been wholly abandoned. "The Indians will charge us with treachery," he warned. "They may massacre all the English now settled among them, and the war which they now wage against the Americans may be turned into an Indian war against us." As the North West Company agents were anxious to point out to government, unless a just and proper peace be forged between the Americans and the Indians, with mutual guarantees for protection of the subjects of the other, the natives would conclude that the British had abandoned them and in resentment would destroy all the traders in the country and fall violently on the defenseless inhabitants of Upper Canada.[7]

Even so, Canadian traders held the Old Northwest as their own special fur preserve. Their secret weapon was the British-nurtured Indian alliance.[8] After Jay's Treaty, in 1794, these posts were surrendered to American hands. After 1794 British agents bountifully supplied native allies with food, clothing, arms, ammunition, and presents. They had also conquered the territory in their beds. Throughout present-day Michigan and Wisconsin French Canadian and Scottish traders had established many tender ties with native females. Blood ties linked Montreal with such places as Michilimackinac, Prairie du Chien, Grand Portage, and Fond du Lac. In short, the Canadians had what might be termed an informal empire south of the line, one which posed challenges to American troops, traders, and settlers alike.

The merchants of Montreal, smarting under successive limitations to their commercial empire in the continental interior, saw a future war as a way of regaining Canada's lost territories and of retaining a sphere of trading influence endangered by Jay's Treaty. Their commerce, they claimed, had been cut in the Old Northwest by the American factory system. The Louisiana Purchase of 1803, they also bemoaned, had enlarged United States dominium near the headwaters of the Mississippi and elsewhere. Boston ships sailing by way of Cape Horn to the Columbia River mouth and along the Northwest coast indicated a rising tie of American empire there, a place where British traders had first been preeminent. The Montreal merchants, with true continental aspirations, viewed as a just cause the military conquest of American posts, including Detroit, Michilimackinac, and Prairie du Chien—each of them watchtowers or keys to trade and navigation.

At the commencement of hostilities in 1812, the United States had the sovereignty of Detroit and the young Michigan Territory (created in 1805). In 1796, in conformity with Jay's Treaty, U.S. forces had occupied Detroit and run up the Stars and Stripes on land acknowledged as American since 1783, by the Articles of Peace ending the American War of Independence. This ended a British occupancy dating from 1760, when Britain supplanted the French at this strategic choke point of the St. Lawrence River system. Detroit had been very much like a challenge cup, the prize of contending nations. Three flags had flown at Detroit in the span of half a century. French policy had been to adhere closely to Indian interests, and the British were quick to learn the same lesson. The Indians were self-interested in the struggles going on at Detroit, but they were also unfortunate pawns in a gigantic struggle for control of the interior heartland. They were prone to circumstances dictated by European war. As William Henry Harrison said in 1810, "These remote savages have felt their full share of the misfortunes which the trouble in Europe have brought upon the greater part of the world."[9]

The North West Company, partners with the Indians in the fur business and known as Nor'Westers, understood that a war on Lake Erie would force upon them a new strategy of interior communications. The customary lifeline by way of Detroit and the St. Clair River would be hazardous and subject to American interdiction. Therefore, they proposed enhancing a hitherto little-known route, though one used for a century or more by the Iroquois and other natives. This was from York, north to Gloucester Bay on Georgian Bay, thence to Michilimackinac via Lake Huron's northern passage, the North Channel, and ultimately through Sault Ste. Marie to Lake Superior, to Grand Portage, and to the great hinterland beyond. The Nor'Westers worried that American forces would cut them off at Sault Ste. Marie if means were not taken to prevent them. What they proposed, therefore, was shifting the British garrison from Fort St. Joseph, which provided no apparent protection to trade, to Sault Ste. Marie. There, they reasoned, a stout position might be made to secure this choke point of trade and communication. Northward, therefore, shifted the course of Canadian empire and defense strategy.

These merchants of Montreal, patriotic as well as self-interested, prepared to offer their services and join in common cause with the British War Department. To them war and trade went hand in hand. They proposed to lend all their Great Lakes vessels for the martial tasks of the government. They had a vessel of 120 tons on Lake Superior that could be armed with six guns. They had another, of 60 tons, on the same body of water, and this vessel could be run down the Falls of St. Marys, or Sault Ste. Marie, to be made use of on Lakes Huron and Michigan. They also had two vessels at Moy, or Sandwich, across from Detroit. These last were the *Caledonia* and the *Nancy,* each carrying four guns. The traders likewise proposed assigning two companies of their servants as troops, each company headed by a lieutenant colonel, and they imagined that several hundred traders would take up arms for the imperial cause.

The Nor'Westers did not stop there. The company proposed deploying as many voyageurs and natives as they could muster—they calculated about three hundred of each—to be used as auxiliary forces. These would work in concert with the Post Regulars, so-called, those British troops stationed at St. Joseph Island, who would go forward on frontier expeditions. The Nor'Westers also reasoned, rightly as it turned out, that their officers ought to be given military commissions, so that they would be given added influence with their native allies and, of importance to their own personal security, not be treated as "freebooters," or plunderers, should they fall into enemy hands. "They have tendered all their Vessels for the Service of Government if the exigencies of the war should make it necessary to call for them," wrote Capt. Andrew Gray, deputy quartermaster general at Montreal. "In short they are full of Loyalty and Zeal, and manifest a degree of public spirit highly honorable to them."

Gray was much taken by the Canadian viewpoint. He put the value of the Nor'Westers as follows: "By means of these Companies, we might let loose the Indians upon them [the Americans] throughout the whole extent of their western frontier, as they have a most commanding influence over them." In keeping with the above-mentioned suggestions the Montrealers even had devised their own war plan. As a first step they proposed capturing Michilimackinac and effecting the removal of the British garrison from St. Joseph Island to Sault Ste. Marie. They further proposed a war of their own: to act with the forces at Sault Ste. Marie in offensive measures on Lake Superior. The outcome, they believed, would "dislodge the enemy from any position he may take upon the

Lake and in short exclude him entirely from any participation in the naviga-tion or Commerce of Lakes Superior, Huron and Michigan."[10]

As to the defense of Upper Canada, that large peninsula surrounded or flanked by the St. Lawrence River system and Great Lakes, military planners faced a logistical nightmare. Everything of a defensive nature had to be im-ported or concocted on the spot. Whereas the British, as noted, crafted a pol-icy to hold Indians as allies, they were bound to project their own military power into the Canadian heartland. They had to fight a war in which their flank was protracted and vulnerable. In prewar strategic analysis the Quartermaster General's Office in Quebec knew the nuts and bolts of the matter. It would be a mistake, so Capt. Noel Freer of that office reasoned, to assume the defensive: to let the Americans carry the war into Canada against British arms. What was needed for a consistent plan of defense was to assume the offensive with a bold plan of operations. The object would be to carry the war into the enemy's coun-try and do him all the harm in his power. Among the first objects would be to sack and destroy American naval establishments wherever found, leaving noth-ing that would give them any capabilities to cope with British forces. Detroit was to be taken, and refortified, as chief post for that frontier and as grand ren-dezvous of the Indians. "With the possession of Detroit," he argued, "we could have full command of the communications leading to Kentucky, and prevent any force from that quarter approaching or establishing themselves upon our frontiers." The south shores of Lake Ontario and Lake Erie were to be scoured, forcing the enemy on the defensive. The object would be to give "confidence to our friends and spread terror and distrust amongst our Enemies." Canadian fur traders would be valuable to the prosecution of this species of warfare. The whole was intended for a preemptive strike before the enemy had time to pre-pare his means.

Against such reasoning stood no agreeable benefit. The British would have to withdraw from the Detroit frontier, bring shipping and stores to Long Point, Lake Erie, and try to take up a position somewhere on that shore. With the enemy pen-etrating the Niagara frontier, the western defense would eventually fall back upon York, "where it is presumed the last stand will be made, and where the remnant of our force will concentrate itself. It is hoped measures are taken by this time, for removing the Naval depot and stores to York." Only one year's campaign would suffice to complete the destruction of Upper Canada, Freer warned.[11]

In the end, Freer's plan (as enhanced and modified by Lt. Gen. Sir George Prevost, the British officer commanding in Canada) held firm. Quebec, the only permanent fortress in Canada, was the key to the whole defense, an effective counterweight to anything the Americans might throw at it. Quebec was the door of entry of all sustenance. And throughout the war, London's directions called for encouraging forward movements into the interior of American territory so long as the safety of such force remained beyond doubt. The object of such operations was to protect His Majesty's possessions in America, and this could be effected by the destruction of American establishments at Sackets Harbour and the naval establishments on Lake Erie and Lake Champlain. The occupation of Niagara and Detroit areas would ensure the protection of Upper Canada. This then was the general plan: not a defensive war, but a thrust into the heartland of North America, to dominate the waterways so as to secure the vital points of control.

At the outset of the war, Maj. Gen. Isaac Brock commanded the military forces in Upper Canada. He also administered, on a temporary basis, the civil government of the province. To repeat, the Canadian boundary to be defended was long and vulnerable. Brock had few troops at his disposal. Only one British regiment of the line was stationed in Upper Canada: the 1st Battalion of the 41st (later the Welch) Regiment. A detachment of the 10th Royal Veteran Battalion was there, too, and another of the Royal Newfoundland Fencibles, the oldest regiment in British America, members of which were chiefly employed as marines on the Great Lakes. A few artillerymen were in Upper Canada to complete the military establishment. A provincial militia, largely untrained and consisting of men of military age organized in paper battalions, stood behind or beside the regular forces. In Lower Canada were five battalions, roughly fifty-four hundred troops, fit to be considered as regulars. With the sixteen hundred regulars in Upper Canada the military defenses of the Canadian provinces were not only feeble, they tottered precariously. In such circumstances, Brock had cause to worry, and he went quickly about the business of deploying these forces to best advantage and giving his commanders broad instructions to act as they saw fit.

British expense of carrying on the war in North America was enormous. With the bulk of the effective Canadian population engaged in transporting naval and military supplies, the Canadians could neither defend themselves nor provide for the food requirements of the British Army. Provisions came from England and Ireland and were transported a thousand miles upriver to the Niagara frontier. As one officer stationed near Fort Wellington on the River St. Lawrence remarked, "Every kind of Military and Naval Stores, every bolt of canvas, every rope yarn, as well as the heavier articles of guns, shot, cables, anchors, and all the numerous etceteras for furnishing a large squadron, arming forts, supplying arms for the militia and the line had to be brought from Montreal to Kingston . . . exposed to the shot of the enemy." Had American forces stationed four field guns along the St. Lawrence and a corps of riflemen covering them they could have cut off communications to Upper Canada. "If they had done so with any kind of spirit," recollected Tiger Dunlop, a British soldier, "we must have abandoned Upper Canada, Kingston and the fleet on Ontario included, and leaving it to its fate, confined ourselves to the defence of such part of the Lower Province as came within the range of our own empire, the sea."[12] Quebec City and Montreal formed fulcrums of British defense for the St. Lawrence and Great Lakes. Here, accordingly, the British amassed their troops. Sound principles of military strategy should have obliged the Americans to concentrate their operations against Montreal and thereby acquire the means of cutting the communications to the Great Lakes. The defense of Upper Canada rested solely on this essential line of communication.

To American expansionists, and others, such as Thomas Jefferson, the taking of Canada would be a mere matter of marching. "The conquest of Canada is in your power," stated Henry Clay, of Kentucky. "I trust I shall not be deemed presumptuous when I state that I verily believe that the militia of Kentucky are alone competent to place Montreal and Upper Canada at your feet."[13] However, the Americans chose to chop at the upper branches of the two rather than striking at the trunk or roots.[14] Fortune thus favored the defenders of Upper Canada at the outset of the war. Even so, the first shock of the American attack had to be met by British forces then in feeble strength and numbers. The United States could draw on a heavy reservoir of manpower. Much has been made of the unreliable nature of the American militia in this war, but in such a continental war preponderance in numbers can play a decisive role. At the outset of the war, U.S. regular troops counted about thirty-five thousand. Far fewer, perhaps only thirteen thousand, served in the field. They had, in fact, only a marginal advantage in numbers over the regulars defending the Canadian provinces.

The invasion of Canada had to be made via rivers and lakes, and thus sea command was essential. Maintaining sufficient naval strength on the Great Lakes thus became the vital task of the contenders. As the Duke of Wellington was frequently fond of saying, no success could be achieved by British forces unless there was held a naval superiority on the Lakes. Both powers knew this at the outset, and to build fleets on either shore became the requirement of the belligerents. The Americans used their greater and more accessible resources and manpower to steady advantage, thus exerting escalating pressure on the Canadian frontier. By 1813 the struggle for command of the Great Lakes reached new heights, and by 1814 the shipbuilding war there had reached intense proportions. A large ship-of-the-line, HMS *St. Lawrence,* was built by the British, and even some frigates were built. "The contest became almost farcical," observed Theodore Roosevelt in his history of the war, "for it was one of shipbuilding merely, and the minute one party completed a new ship, the other promptly retired into harbour until able to complete a larger one."[15] This shipbuilding contest was confined almost wholly to Lake Ontario and, to a lesser extent, to Lake Champlain and Lake Erie.

At the commencement of hostilities Canadian defenders possessed one decided advantage over the Americans: superior naval forces on the Great Lakes. During the American War of Independence the Royal Navy had kept a small naval establishment on Lake Erie and were running supplies to their posts at Detroit and Michilimackinac.[16] A local sea militia called the Provincial Marine of Upper Canada had a number of armed ships quite superior to anything the Americans had. The Provincial Marine, essentially a transport service, answered to the quartermaster general's Department of the Army. Despite its apparent inefficiency, in the first year's campaign the Provincial Marine kept Upper Canada from falling to American arms. The Provincial Marine gave the Army its mobility, for in those days the colony's roads were primitive in the extreme or nonexistent. Given the advantages of sea mobility and virtual command of Lakes Ontario and Erie, the British deployed troops and supplies at will.

However, against this stood one decided disadvantage. Upper Canada was heavily populated by recent United States immigrants. Officials could not expect that these persons of dubious loyalty would happily answer a call to imperial arms. In fact, the opposite was anticipated. "A country defended by Free Men," said Brock, in rallying Canadians to arms, "enthusiastically devoted to the cause of their King and Constitution, can never be conquered."[17] Such a call met with little response. "My situation is most critical, not from anything the enemy can do, but from the disposition of the people," Brock wrote the adjutant general at headquarters in Lower Canada. "The population, believe me is essentially bad. A full belief possesses them all that this Province must inevitably succumb. . . . What a change an additional regiment would make in this part of the Province."[18] By August another regiment, the 49th, was on its way to reinforce the western frontier.

Brock refused to be dogged by defeatist Canadian attitudes. Garnering all the strength at his disposal, he took the offensive, following an ancient maxim of British arms. He assumed a vigorous local offensive, indeed a preemptive strike designed to crush the enemy at Detroit. Meanwhile, with the British enjoying naval supremacy on Lake Erie, military planners concluded that they could deploy troops and supplies in the interior country at will.

That first year of the war saw the United States stun England with a string of victories on the high seas. Especially annoying to British observers was the fact that the Americans sailed, as the *Times* of London put it dismissively at the time, "a few fir-built ships, manned by a handful of bastards and outlaws."[19] The British underestimated both American ships and American sailors. However, until such time as the British could bring their more than a thousand men-of-war to bear on the course of American fortunes, the twenty-three ships of the U.S. Navy tormented their opponent.

While American victories at sea seemed resplendent and continuing, in the early stages of the war the land campaigns went badly for the United States. The editor of the influential *Niles' Weekly Register* of Baltimore, pondering this surprising paradox, remarked, sympathetically, that the American war against the Barbary pirates had given American sailors an opening for their genius. In the Army, by contrast, except at the smashing battle of Tippecanoe in the Indiana Territory, not one in five hundred soldiers had seen a real fight. Nearly thirty years of peace since the American War for Independence had led to a lapse in martial capabilities. Theory had replaced practice. "Our enemy, whose military fame, however, is not of the highest grade, has powerful advantages in this respect over us," remarked the same well-informed editor, "for of her troops in *America* a majority of the regulars have 'seen some service,' and many of them, indeed, are ranked as *veterans*. In a little time we, also, shall learn how to fight on the land; and, as there are as brave spirits in the army as the navy can boast of, (and we gladly give our tars their full due) it cannot be doubted that as brilliant achievements are in store for this portion of the national force."[20]

The U.S. government intended that the Army to be used in the Lake Erie campaign should be composed exclusively of regular troops, and no less than seven thousand were called for. Gen. William Harrison, headquartered at Upper Sandusky, Ohio, worried about many matters. Nothing caused him greater concern than quality of troops, which to his way of thinking was more important than their numbers. Besides which, such a large force would have to be supplied adequately, and to keep them in waiting for a campaign would consume all available means of support. He needed two regiments of ten companies each plus one hundred men for field platoon and musical duties.[21]

Projecting this American military power inland to the Great Lakes necessitated use of primitive roads and unimproved waterways. All ships of war would have to be constructed on Lake Ontario and Erie shores. Shipwrights and carpenters, guns and nails, sail and rope—all these, and more, would have to be carried overland. Blockaded on their Atlantic shore the U.S. government, out of necessity, shifted its focus of naval operations to the continental heartland.

By contrast the Canadians had demonstrated their military power on the Great Lakes since the days of Frontenac, Cadillac, and LaSalle. In the War of 1812 they fought on well-known ground, using forces built or based at several naval yards and arsenals. As a defense problem, Canada remained a nightmare: the duke of Wellington classified it as "all frontier and nothing else."[22] Even so, across the Niagara Peninsula improved water communications from York to Burlington Bay and by way of portages and river courses to Long Point, Lake Erie, facilitated movement of trade goods and military supplies. At Sault Ste. Marie the North West Company had bypassed rapids with locks. Canadian local knowledge as well as alternate northern passages—by various rivers hitherto unknown except to native, fur trader, or missionary (the French and the Ottawa) and by land (from York via Yonge Street to Nottawasaga on Georgian Bay)—gave imperial forces advantages in that unusual brand of war they were obliged to fight in 1812: *la petite guerre.*

I

~

The Rowboat War

MICHILIMACKINAC

ake Huron, unheralded inland sea of 1812 history, ranks second only to Superior in size. Huron forms the hub of the Great Lakes: through it must transit, or cross, all waterborne commerce of the upper Great Lakes. Today, ships from such "lakeheads" as Green Bay and Chicago on Lake Michigan or Grand Portage, Duluth, and Thunder Bay on Lake Superior must use Lake Huron. In terms of military geography, Lake Huron's two strategic choke points are its interior extremity, where waters from Michigan and Superior flow separately into it, and its outpouring into the St. Clair River.

Georgian Bay, Lake Huron's annex, lies northeast of the main body of water and is separated from it by two vast lands—Bruce Peninsula and Manitoulin Island—as well as by various islands and shoals. In length 110 miles, in width 48 miles at its extremity, Georgian Bay might well be called the sixth Great Lake.[1] Sailors who know its shores notice pronounced differences between its western and eastern extremities, for the former, sheltered by the Bruce Peninsula and Manitoulin Island, embrace large, deep bays while the latter, hard against the Canadian shield, house a seemingly unending collection of islets and reefs that are exceedingly hazardous to navigation. This eastern maze of passages is now charted and marked by navigation aids, but in 1812 it was known only to the native and the voyageur. It is an intriguing fact for students of Canadian history, who ponder how the Canadian shield has shaped the character of

Lake Huron and Georgian Bay 1812 – 1814
(Boundaries As Determined In 1818)

Surrounded by waterways, the Province of Upper Canada, a British colony founded in 1791, became a battleground during the War of 1812. The naval and shipbuilding bases and military establishments, many of which are shown here, played key roles in the struggle for the heartland of America.

national northern progress, that this vital waterway for the defense of Canadian and Imperial interests during the War of 1812 should have provided a critical link with the Indian and fur-trading alliance.

Champlain, explorer and founder of New France, was much taken with Georgian Bay and called it "the sweetwater sea." On its shores lived native peoples crucial to the French future in North America, and of these none was as important in the early seventeenth century as the Huron, who lived in the heartland that was to become during the War of 1812 the means of naval defense and amphibious attack against American forces. In the intervening years, from the days of the Huron mission to the War of 1812, the Huron had been dispersed, cut down by the Iroquois or wasted by various lethal diseases, and had been replaced by various Anishnabe, or Algonquian-speaking persons. Iroquois used the route from Lake Simcoe, north of York, to the mouth of the Nottawasaga River (at the south end of Lake Huron) and to the great fur-bearing forests of the North and West. Georgian Bay still remained a native homeland in 1812 and had not one settler cabin or lighthouse on it. It was the domain of various Indian peoples—and of those agents of government, the church, or the fur trade based in Montreal that entered the realm of the continental interior of which Lake Huron was the hub.

North-northwest of Detroit 255 miles, at the northwest extremity or corner of Lake Huron, stands a famous island. The French referred to it as Michilimackinac. Its shortened name, Mackinaw, now in universal use, is a truncated form of Michilimackinac, meaning "place of big lamed person" or "place of big wounded person," and this owes its origin from the now-extinct native place name Mishinimaki or Mishinimakinagog. Many contend that the name signifies "place of the Great Turtle."

The island, measuring some three miles long and two wide, lies in the Straits of Mackinac between the Lower and Upper Peninsulas of Michigan. Here the gray waters of Lake Michigan enveloped by silver mist rush through the passage to join blue Lake Huron with its clear air. Not far northward from the Upper Peninsula, Lake Superior's waters join Lake Huron through straits and passages of St. Marys River, or Sault Ste. Marie. At Michilimackinac the grand waters of the continent seem to intermingle. From the remarkably clear waters of Lake Huron, Mackinac Island rises in the most part in prominent limestone cliffs. Well wooded, the island also has glens and ravines as well as some caverns rich in native associations.

Michilimackinac seems first to have been occupied by Ojibwa. It was later, though only for a short time, settled by some Huron, who arrived there after

Iroquois expelled them from the southern shore of Lake Huron in 1649. Iroquois and European traders based on Albany visited there in 1670. Subsequently, the Ottawa had a village there. Gradually the island became a gathering place for various tribes who revered the island risen from the straits.

"It is the key and the door for the people of the South," observed the Jesuit Claude Dablon in 1670, who chose the island for a mission, "as the South is the key for the people of the north."[2] The celebrated Jesuit Jacques Marquette, there the next year, brought refugee Huron and Ottawa to the straits and then moved the mission to the north side, establishing St. Ignace. French commercial and missionary expansion had gone boldly hand in hand until 1705, when Governor Cadillac forced the zealous Black Robes out of the mission field. Cadillac thought Mackinac Island to be the watchtower of the straits.

As early as 1712 the French had put up a trading post on the south side of the straits, near where Mackinaw City stands today. In 1761 the French surrendered this post to the British, who in turn kept a small guard to regulate trade and keep order. Sooner or later all the great trading tribes of present-day Wisconsin, Illinois, Michigan, and Ontario would frequent the place. "Michilimackinac was a crossroads," observed the historians of the place in the age of the American Revolution. "This fortified trading village of only a few hundred winter residents was the center of a complex fur trading industry which reached far north of Lake Superior, west across the Mississippi River, south into the Illinois Country and along the wooded shores of Lake Michigan."[3]

In 1783, by a new boundary between British dominions in America and the United States, sovereignty of Michilimackinac passed to the hands of the young Republic. The boundary cut through Lakes Ontario, Erie, Huron, and Superior.

This boundary also cut through the heart of Ojibwa country. The Ojibwa, or Chippewa, controlled the northern shores of Huron and Superior from Georgian Bay to Manitoba. Four groups are apparent in the historical record: the Ojibwa of Lake Superior, the Mississauga of Manitoulin Island, the Ottawa of Georgian Bay, and the Potawatomi of the west shore of Lake Huron, who moved in the eighteenth and nineteenth century to its east shore. After the demise of Iroquois power the Ojibwa entered an era of remarkable ascendancy. In the west they made gains at the expense of Sioux and Fox. In the southeast they overran the peninsula between Lakes Huron and Erie. Trade in guns and ammunition enriched them. British determination to make the Ojibwa keen allies in the Old Northwest, south and west of the newly established 1783 boundary, meant that they were subject to special diplomacy, care, and consideration. If the colonial wars of North American history had given the Ojibwa only marginal notice because of northern remoteness, the War of 1812 gave them a prominence hitherto unknown.[4]

For two decades the British garrison kept the lonely watch at Michilimackinac. The lieutenant governor and superintendent of Michilimackinac, Patrick Sinclair, a soldier as well as ship captain of great ability, held strong views that the fort was so exposed to assault as to be virtually defenseless. Accordingly, and not waiting for London's approval, in 1779 he ordered the garrison removed from the mainland to Mackinac Island. There he chose the site for the fort, drew working drawings for a blockhouse, and surveyed the island.

Fortunes of this island fortress rested on steady importation of rum, food, and supplies. The "milk" of British friendship flowed even more freely now. Regularly the king's vessels *Wyandot* and *Welcome* brought precious gifts from Detroit and Fort Erie for the Indians. Sinclair boldly, if a little unwisely for his career prospects, ran up the Indian Department's bills.[5] Auditors scratched their heads and then found themselves appalled by the size of the Indian Department's payroll. However, the fact of the matter remained that the alliance gave the garrison its much-needed mercenary arm. Sinclair left in 1782 to face questions about rising costs. Not much changed, however. The next commandant continued the necessary work of nurturing native fidelity to the imperial cause and of encouraging the trade of the inland seas.

After 1783, with a guarded eye to the future, the British Indian Department sought to counter any feelings of abandonment on the part of Indians. From Quebec, Governor Frederick Haldimand sent a message to the western Indians that the king, George III, still considered them his children and that he would continue to protect them. His message explained why His Majesty had permitted the Americans to establish a new nation. The flow of Indian presents to Michilimackinac was not stopped.[6] British traders continued to maintain posts on United States territory, much to the annoyance of American rivals and politicians.

Jay's Treaty, signed in 1794, required that the British evacuate the interior posts by 1 June 1796. That October, in conformity with this arrangement, American troops arrived at Mackinac Island and ran up the Stars and Stripes on U.S. soil. "Our fort at Michilimackinac," wrote a visiting inspector in his report to the U.S. secretary of war,

> from every consideration is one of the most important posts we hold on our western frontier. It . . . is an irregular work partly built with a strong wall and partly with pickets; and the parade ground within it is from 100 to 125 feet above the surface of the water. It contains a well of never failing water, a bomb proof used as a magazine, one stone barracks for the use of the officers, equal if not superior to any building of the kind in the United States; a good guard house and barracks for the soldiers and convenient storehouse for provisions, with three strong and convenient blockhouses. This post is strong both by nature and art, and the possession of it has great influence with the Indians in favor of the United States.[7]

British official policy after Jay's Treaty gave every encouragement to the Indians so that they would not feel abandoned by the British withdrawal from Detroit, Michilimackinac, and elsewhere. The governor of Canada, Lord Dorchester, had instructions to build posts on the Canadian side of the line to facilitate commercial intercourse with the natives and make the evacuation of the old posts as little felt as possible.[8]

One of these key new posts was Fort St. Joseph, not far from Michilimackinac and on a lonely island to where the British had been forced, grudgingly, to relocate after Jay's Treaty. To this post went a British Army officer, Capt. Charles Roberts, who might have wished for more peaceful employment in the wilds of northwestern Canada. Fate had dealt him a nasty hand in the long and dutiful service of King George. Ten years soldiering in the Caribbean tropical heat, mainly in Trinidad, had sapped his health. Fever-ridden, he had escaped the lot of so many military personnel who had become a fatality to "yellow jack." By age thirty-four he was obliged, as were many of his kind, to "seek for ease in a Veteran Battalion," an innovation of the British War Department designed to make units of a nonregimental sort out of meritorious soldiers who on account of wounds, infirmity, and age had become unequal to more active duties of regular infantry. Promise of two hundred acres of Canadian bush (said suitable for agriculture) offered additional inducement to Captain Roberts. He shipped for Quebec in 1807 as a captain in the 10th Royal Veteran Battalion. Perhaps in these northern climes a long stint of slumbering garrison duty could be expected for Roberts. Such was not to be, for saber-rattling on the southern frontier led his superiors to send him first to Saint-Jean on the Richelieu River and then, all the more urgently, to Fort St. Joseph, at St. Joseph Island, in the northwesterly wilds of Lake Huron.

Roberts, age thirty-nine at the outbreak of the conflict, had been well trained in the arts of war. Years of campaigning in the West Indies among garrison troops accustomed to amphibious operations had given him a sure military knowledge about how to mount an expedition to take Michilimackinac, that thorn in the side of the British. Small-boat expeditions were second nature to him. In his hands, such wide discretionary powers as Maj. Gen. Sir Isaac Brock, president and administrator of Upper Canada, gave him would not be wasted. Perhaps Roberts thought the moment for which he had waited so long had arrived at last. In any event, once Brock's orders reached him, on 15 July, confirming that a state of war existed, he took steps to grab the American prize.[9] The news was brought to him by Capt. William McKay in a canoe. McKay had rushed three thousand miles from Montreal to deliver advance word that the United States had declared war on Great Britain, and that Roberts ought to take whatever actions or precautions he thought necessary to this new state of affairs.

As commandant at Fort St. Joseph, Roberts pondered this intelligence. He knew that the Americans intended to reinforce Michilimackinac as soon as possible—and to do so in heavy numbers. Any day now, he imagined, U.S. men-of-war, or supply schooners such as the *Erie* and *Freegoodwill*, would arrive to land reinforcements of men and supplies. Those natives who had been collected at Fort St. Joseph were not only ready for action, but had become impatient—indeed, dangerously so. Roberts feared that he would be abandoned by his native allies if he did not strike quickly. In other words, all requirements of his situation led him to the conclusion that he must take the American post before it could be reinforced. Mustering his native support, he determined to act prudently, as indeed Brock had instructed, and without loss of time attack Michilimackinac.

Roberts had what so many good commanders possess: a sense of timing. It is instructive to read in his report of proceedings that he realized that taking the initiative could be his only option. Indeed, he noted, his existing situation at Fort St. Joseph was "totally indefensible."[10] He went to Michilimackinac because he could not remain at Fort St. Joseph. As an early historian of this campaign expressed it with undeniable military logic, "The best defence always is attack, whenever the attackers can destroy the enemy's means of destroying them."[11]

To this point in time, Fort St. Joseph had served the interests of crown and company with equal measure. Geographical position gave it unique authority. Fort St. Joseph stood handsomely on a beautiful rise of ground, where the soil was promising for cultivation. And it lay at the end of the peninsula at the southern end of St. Marys River. Visitors there thought it a desolate location, and troops regarded it as nothing less than a Siberia. Such indeed was the case, for deserters would perish in the winter's frozen cold or suffer severe frostbite. It was an island abounding in rocks. It did double-duty as a North West Company post and a British military establishment. First used by British troops about the year 1763, here the Nor'Westers kept a depot for building canoes. Guardian of the North Channel's entry to Georgian Bay, the post acquired enhanced status in 1796, when the British enlarged their military post to replace recently relinquished Michilimackinac. Fort St. Joseph also marked where the Ottawa River route of supplies and trade joined that coming by way of the lower Great Lakes. From this nexus both routes completed their westernmost portions, following a track past Sault Ste. Marie and thence through Lake Superior to the Nor'Westers' Fort William, near Thunder Bay. The Ojibwa of the St. Joseph Island area depended heavily on the economy of canoe building, and, indeed, the business of the place was related to transportation and communication—and to the defense of both. The European inhabitants there gave one visitor the impression of people living in exile. "Coin of this Country [is] call'd Whisky," remarked a trader who called there in 1807, and he wished he had taken much more with him.[12]

Nine hundred miles from Montreal and forty-five from Mackinac Island, Fort St. Joseph, this most westerly outpost of the British Empire, could not sustain an assault in force, Captain Roberts knew. But as a key link in the Indian alliance and fur trade communications it was superb. This post counted not so much as a place of general trade but as a location where most if not all Indians came for no other reason than to receive their annual bounty from the Crown. Most of these natives came from the American side of the line. A few Algonquins came from faraway French River. The Americans, to their cost, paid scant attention to the Indians. Indeed, observed the noted trader and traveler Sir Alexander Mackenzie, who visited the place many times, the Americans blithely told the Indians that they kept possession of their country by right of conquest. They went even further and said that American traders would come to them only if they deserved attention by industrious habits.[13] The Americans, indeed, operated on the basis of a hard-nosed reality.

Subsequent events were to prove the merit of cultivating the native alliance in this entryway between Superior and Huron. Correct also was Captain Roberts's decision that he could not resist an American assault there but should employ the adage "the best defence is attack" and gather all possible resources for an assault on Fort Mackinac.

From the beginning Captain Roberts planned a stealthful operation. Against such superiority in numbers as the Americans possessed, surprise tactics and loyal followers counted for everything. Roberts possessed intimate local knowledge of the islands and waters, including the geography and defenses of Mackinac Island. Fur traders and Indians alike provided up-to-date intelligence of American preparedness and means of resistance. Roberts enjoyed splendid support of the Indian Agents, who were in the employ of the British Military Department. From all quarters (and from both sides of the international boundary) the Indians gathered at Fort St. Joseph for the attack. They did not have to be coaxed into joining the Imperial cause.

Once ready, the force constituted an irregular little army. With Captain Roberts were 47 redcoats of the 10th Royal Veteran Battalion. Three artillerymen—a sergeant and 2 rank-and-file of the Royal Regiment of Artillery—accompanied the expedition. They zealously guarded two 6-pounders that had been carefully loaded and ballasted in their water craft. There were, besides, 180 volunteers— mainly Canadian—engagees, and others gathered from Fort William, Sault Ste. Marie, and other Nor'Wester establishments. No fewer than 400 Indians, the largest component, were ready to fall upon the enemy. All told, the British force numbered about 630 men.

Roberts came into possession of Brock's instructions on 15 July. The following day, by ten in the morning, he embarked his men, the Canadians, the Indians, and the two guns in the boats. They left St. Joseph Island and headed toward Mackinac Island. Roberts had the advantage of intelligence that a state of war existed. His counterpart at Michilimackinac was still in the dark.

Following carefully prepared plans, and with every assurance of success, they landed at Mackinac Island under cover of darkness, moved to the interior of the island, scaled the cliffs using a number of ladders, and placed themselves so as to command the enemy who lay sleeping 150 feet below. Unknown to the Americans, the imperial forces kept their watch atop the hill in total quietness, awaiting the arrival of one of the unwieldy cannon that had to be wrestled up the slope. Once the one gun had been brought up to a height commanding the garrison, effected by about ten o'clock, Roberts sent a summons to the post demanding its surrender and suggesting it was useless to shed such blood as was likely to follow, given the size of the British force.

The U.S. officer commanding, Lt. Porter Hanks of the U.S. Regiment of Artillery, had sixty-one men under his command, and many of them were sick or otherwise unfit for service. He acted wisely in the circumstances. The

American capitulation followed, and Roberts immediately took possession of the fort. At twelve noon the Stars and Stripes were hauled down and those of His Majesty raised.

In reporting his success to his superior officers, Roberts was careful to give credit where credit was due. He said the greatest praise was due to every individual employed in the expedition. To his own officers he was particularly indebted for their diligence in carrying out all his orders. He praised the French Canadians for their swift and steady paddling of canoes. Then he came to the remarkable native contribution. The episode, he noted, was "a circumstance I believe without precedent." What he had in mind was the role of the Indians in the affair, and, equally important, those who had managed their activities. The trader John Askin, commanding the Indians assembled for the assault, concluded that it was a fortunate circumstance that the fort capitulated without firing a single shot, for had the Americans resisted, he firmly believed that not one of them would have been saved from an Indian raid. He credited his son, and three others, who rendered him great service in "keeping the Indians in order," as he put it, "& executing from time to time such Commands as were delivered to me by the Commanding Officer.—I never saw so determined a Set of people as the Chippawas & Ottawas were. Since the Capitulation they have not drunk a single drop of Liquor, nor even killed a fowl belonging to any person (a thing never known before) for they generally destroy every thing they meet with." The British commander held a similar view. "Although these people's minds were much heated," said Roberts, "yet as soon as they heard the Capitulation was signed they all returned to their Canoes, and not one drop either of Man's or Animal's blood was Spilt, till I gave an Order for certain number of Bullocks to be purchased for them." The North West Company's officers, too—"the Gentlemen of St. Joseph's and St. Marys"—had also been of invaluable assistance.

By this preemptive strike Roberts and his men had got possession of Michilimackinac. In closing his report to Brock he deferred to the cautious requirements of his superior: "I trust, Sir, in thus acting I have not exceeded Your Instructions, for be assured that prudential measures of the first necessity demanded the Step which has put me in possession of this Island."

The Articles of Capitulation signed between Captain Roberts on the one hand and Lieutenant Hanks on the other, not only called for the immediate surrender of "the Fort of Michilimackinac" but also contained other provisions. The U.S. garrison would march out with the Honors of War, lay down their arms, and become prisoners of war, and were to be sent to the United States by the British and not serve in the war until regularly exchanged for other prisoners. All merchant vessels in port, with their cargoes, were to remain in possession of their respective owners. The fur business would continue, and shipping be allowed to carry on provided military duties were not undertaken. Private property should be held sacred as far as was in the power of the captain commanding, Roberts. Lastly, all citizens of the United States not choosing to take the oath of allegiance to the king were to depart from the island with their property within one month of the date of the Capitulation. In a supplement to the Articles of Capitulation, signed 17 July, Hanks agreed that the captains and crews of the two transport vessels, *Erie* and *Freegoodwill,* were to be included in the category as nominal prisoners of war. Indeed, the officers in question had pledged their word and honor that they would not take part in military activities—in short, they were not to trade for the Americans or undertake any measure against the British.

The capture of the "Gibraltar of the Straits" had immense value to imperial forces, and nowhere was this more important than in the native alliance. "This acquisition, with the noble motives by which Tecumseh was actuated, secured us the friendship of all the western Indians."[14] So wrote Capt. W. H. Merritt, veteran of the Upper Canada campaigns.

Captain Roberts, it has been argued, deserves a place in the pantheon of military heroes. Except for the recorded details of this expedition he would be lost in the sea of arcane data. Canadian historians have shamefully neglected him. It took an American, distinguished Harvard scholar Edward Channing, to proclaim Charles Roberts among the trio of warriors who saved Canada for the British Empire in this war. The others were Sir George Prevost, who masterminded defense strategy and, out of necessity, ordered prudent measures for Canada's protection,[15] and Brock, the administrator of Upper Canada, who evolved a scheme of "flank companies"—that is, small, motivated and highly trained militia. In judging Roberts's victory, Channing concluded that the American disaster turned the Indians of the Northwest away from the United States. "It was, therefore," he noted of the fall of Michilimackinac, "one of the decisive events of the war; but, as far as is known, no notice of this important service of Charles Roberts was ever taken by the British government."[16] Prevost, in fact, acknowledged Roberts's abilities.

No laurels were showered upon Captain Roberts. The demands of the Michilimackinac expedition and occupation reduced the state of Roberts's health even further, and the requirements of his command failed to diminish.

Roberts worked tirelessly to maintain the garrison and, with a strategic view to the west, to establish a company of Canadians called the Michigan Fencibles. Roberts found himself engulfed by worry and anxiety. He thought his Veteran Battalion soldiers "debilitated and worn down by unconquerable drunkenness." He suffered greatly from "debility of the Stomach and Bowels," and accordingly he requested relief from his duties. Once word of this reached him, he went down to Montreal. There he requested retirement on full pay (which, too, was eventually granted). He spent his last days in England, and died there, in London, in May 1816. So ended the life of the stealthful conqueror of Michilimackinac Island. To others would fall tasks of keeping what had been so surprisingly and so effectually bought by military genius.

The actions of Captain Roberts and his impromptu little army had important consequences to the American fur trade at Michilimackinac. At that time the powerful New York trader and merchant John Jacob Astor owned the goodly portion of the Mackinaw Company, rival to the Nor'Westers. Roberts's action brought the American business to a standstill and had the additional effect of chasing Indian business into British hands. This, in turn, gave the British added allied military power against Detroit. Many Michilimackinac traders were indebted to Astor, and he sent his famous emissary Ramsay Crooks to do what he could to rescue the American trade. However, only the North West Company business remained profitable during the war, that at Michilimackinac having been hit on the head. Inadequate American supplies for distant posts was one problem. Further, U.S. Navy Department officers carrying private property on their vessels—merchandise or furs—discouraged another means of importation.

At Michilimackinac piles of furs lay awaiting shipment. Astor desperately need a vessel to carry away these peltries. He not only secured one vessel, the schooner *Union*, but also got the recognition from British authorities at Montreal that if she, or other such vessels, were to fly a flag of truce they would be free from seizure. Thus such vessels were permitted to proceed to the pre-arranged port of convenience—Isle du Bois Blanc, hard by Michilimackinac—and there take on fur packs already awaiting shipment for market. This explains why Roberts had not taken American commercial vessels captive but instead had allowed them to run free.[17] Obtaining new furs was a different proposition: that depended on native labor and expertise. Accordingly, the British took measures to secure the monopoly of the fur business, and to bring all the trade to the French River and thence east. Throughout the war the Canadians kept up their million-dollar-a-year business, with furs coming via Fort William on Lake Superior through St. Marys River and thence across Lake Huron to the French River and then east to Montreal. Lake Huron's North Channel was the safe conduit of trade. In wartime such communications were tenuous and insecure. However, the northern traders, with bulldog persistence, kept to their business: they nurtured their native allies with whom they had many tender ties and even, as one by one Nor'Wester schooners fell into American hands or were otherwise destroyed, the Canadians kept up their legendary enterprises by canoe.

From the outset of the war, British generals kept to their well-devised plan. Prevost had a comprehensive knowledge of every British post, starting with the most vulnerable, Fort St. Joseph at the head of Lake Huron, then Fort Amherstburg on the River Detroit (in present-day Ontario), the dockyard and marine arsenal for the upper lakes, then Forts George and Erie on the Niagara frontier, then York, best adapted for depositing military stores and as a marine arsenal, and then Kingston, at the head of boat navigation of the St. Lawrence, though exposed to sudden American attack but indispensable to all measures to hold Upper Canada.[18] To his commanders he issued instructions to take the initiative, though always at their discretion, and to press against the enemy's defenses.

The British, not the Americans, made the first conquests and gathered the spoils of war. William Hull, the governor of Michigan Territory, who had been appointed a brigadier general, would have liked to have taken the village of Amherstburg, with its fine port and shipbuilding capabilities, and the military post of Malden. However, his invasion of Upper Canada fizzled out, and his war plans and instructions were all lost when the schooner *Cayahoga Packet* carrying them fell into enemy hands.[19] Brock, who had come to the Detroit frontier to offset attempts by Hull to win Canadians to the cause of the Stars and Stripes, scared Hull into the surrender of Detroit without a shot being fired. Hull, who knew the British had collected a sizable number of Canadian militia and Indians, worried that he could not defend Detroit against such a force. He was correct in doing so: as of 16 August, therefore, the British had feet on both sides of the Detroit River and could now press their advantage. Hull's army, consisting of twenty-five hundred men and twenty-five pieces of ordnance, was no more. The officers of the American Army were so mortified by having had to surrender without fighting, a British officer noted in his journal of the proceedings of that day, that they were indifferent about the American colors still flying. Once the Americans had marched out (after some preliminary confusion on the British part) the British units, including the Grenadiers and the 41st Regiment, "marched into the Fort, with Drum & Fife to the tune of the British Grenadiers—I must say that I never felt so proud, as I did just then." Once the British were inside the fort, the Stars and Stripes were taken down and the Union Jack hoisted, and "the Indians when the Salute was fired with the Cannon gave an Indian yell every shot."[20]

The Right Division of the British Army, under Maj. Gen. Henry Procter, was now able to strike deeply into American lands, thrusting south and southeast along Lake Erie's shores, forcing the Americans to hurry their defenses on the River Raisin, Sandusky River, and Maumi River. This was war on the old frontier pattern, with a violence exhibited on both sides unbecoming to more civilized modes of war. But as this first phase closed of the 1812 campaign, Britain had demonstrated the advantages of forward strategy. And with Detroit's capture came into British hands the brig *Adams,* mounting six guns. She was renamed *Detroit.* As of that date the British possessed complete mastery of the upper Great Lakes.

Before leaving this aspect of the history of this preliminary campaign it is important to note what Brock said about the native peoples he found at Amherstburg. There were some "extraordinary characters" among the Indians, he told the prime minister, Lord Liverpool, and he remarked that some of them had come from a very long way for this war. "He who attracted most my attention was a Shawnee chief, Tecumseh [Shooting Star], brother of the Prophet, who for the last two years has carried on (contrary to our remonstrances) an Active Warfare against the United States." Brock said this about his native opposite: "A more sagacious or a more gallant Warrior does not I believe exist." And he continued: "He was the admiration of every one who conversed with him: from a life of dissipation he is not only become, in every respect, abstemious but has likewise prevailed on all his nation and many of other Tribes to follow his example. They appear determined to continue the contest until they obtain the Ohio for a boundary." He went on to cite the reasons for Indian anxiety. What was at issue was a war for lands, a war that Tecumseh and his kind could not afford to lose, worried as they were about being removed beyond the Mississippi River.[21]

And what did Tecumseh think of Brock? "I observed him [Tecumseh] looking narrowly at the General [Brock]," recorded a civilian who was present on 13 August, after Brock had arrived by boat and was being greeted by Col. Matthew Elliott, the superintendent of Indians, and was presented to Tecumseh.

To this he remarked to his confidant Elliott, as they were returning to the meeting house: that "the General was a brave man, deserving of all confidence."[22]

Two great warriors, Brock and Tecumseh, from entirely different walks of life, had found themselves campaigning together on the Detroit frontier. They held each other in high regard, and it is said that when Brock entered Detroit in triumph Tecumseh rode beside him, and that Brock gave him his sash as a mark of respect. Tecumseh honored Brock by naming him war chief. Tecumseh was, as his opponent General Harrison remarked, "one of those uncommon geniuses which spring up occasionally to produce revolutions."[23] In the struggle for the Great Lakes hinterland that revolution was to be crushed, but for the interim Brock and Tecumseh were the cornerstone of the British-Indian relationship.

II

~

The Battle of Lake Erie

NAVAL SUPERIORITY ON
THE LAKES IN THE BALANCE

At the commencement of the war, the British held the prized possession of Lake Erie. With five armed ships plus the *Adams* captured at
Detroit, the British could strike at American forces and posts at will.
Obtaining such command would have undoubted benefits to the United States.
Troops could be ferried to distant locations for garrison duties or frontier expeditions and be resupplied as required. The enemy could be prohibited from
doing the same. Accordingly, upon control of these inland seas rested the
defense of Upper Canada and, from the American point of view, the tempting prospects of enlarging the United States' sphere of influence and stamp-
ing out the Indian menace.

The strategic requirements of both nations embraced the concept of the
command of Lake Erie and waters above. Brock had put the matter thusly, the
year before hostilities commenced: "From Amherstburg to Fort Erie my chief
dependence must rest on a naval force for the protection of that extensive coast.
. . . But considering the state to which it is reduced, extraordinary exertions and
great expense will be required before it can be rendered efficient. At present it
only consists of a ship and a small schooner, the latter of a bad construction,
old, and in want of many repairs yet she is the only King's vessel able to navigate Lake Huron, whilst the Americans have a sloop and a fine brig capable of
carrying twelve in perfect readiness for any service."[1] As the war grew in intensity and became more concerned with continental as opposed to maritime, or

oceanic, issues, so too did rival military planners work strenuously to achieve dominance on the inland seas.

Niagara Falls interposed itself between the lower and the upper Great Lakes. Accordingly, Lake Erie, being closest to Lake Ontario and thus the material resources of the eastern seaboard from whence came its sustenance, grew as the focal point of shipbuilding for the upper lakes campaign. At Fort Erie, on the Canadian shore, stood a small arsenal and naval yard, and one of its functions was to serve as transshipment point for supplies destined for Amherstburg, where the British had a military outpost and yard for naval construction and repair. Fort Erie formed the beachhead for all water communications of the Imperial forces stretching north and west via Lakes Erie, St. Clair, Huron, and beyond to Michigan or Superior. Another supply route existed for the British across the Niagara Peninsula: from Burlington Bay at the head of Lake Ontario across lowlands and river courses to Long Point, Lake Erie.

At about the same time that Brock was urging the necessity of command of the lakes, the American secretary of war, Dr. William Eustis, received advice from Gen. John Armstrong, soon to succeed him, that if the United States were to complete the conquest of Canada, command of the lakes would be mandatory. "Resting, as the line of Canadian defence does, in its whole extent on navigable lakes and rivers," Armstrong advised, "no time should be lost in getting a naval ascendancy on both . . . the belligerent who is the first to obtain this advantage will (miracles excepted) win the game."[2]

Commo. Isaac Chauncey, commanding U.S. forces on Lake Ontario, knew of British preparations to create a superior fleet. He proposed to destroy the enemy's squadron as soon as convenient and (ever alive to the merits of surprise) to take out the enemy at its source. As the next task he made plans to assault the yard at Kingston and put a torch to any vessels he could find—those in the water or any building on the stocks.

In contrast to the British, who had been in the business of shipping on Lake Erie since taking up imperial duties from the French in 1763, the Americans were new to the field. It is true that at Detroit the Americans built ships for commercial purposes and at Black Rock on the Niagara River, three miles below Buffalo, had a naval yard. But at the outset of the War of 1812 they had no fixed naval station of consequence for Lake Erie.

With these matters in mind, during the winter of 1812–13 Chauncey inspected the eastern end of Lake Erie. He found Black Rock precariously close to the Canadian frontier and a tempting goal for a British raid. He therefore

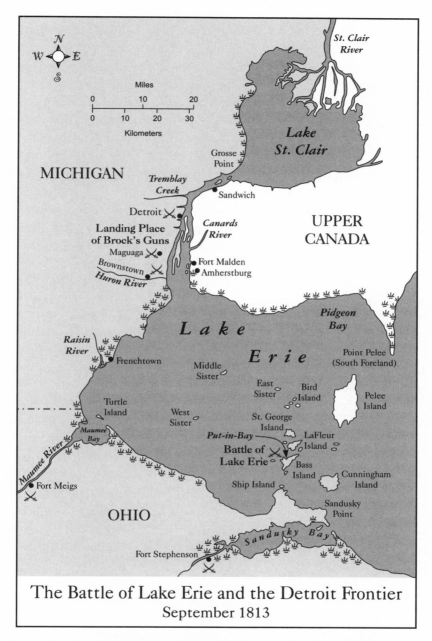

The Battle of Lake Erie and the Detroit Frontier
September 1813

Commodore Barclay's British squadron sailed from Amherstburg and fought U.S. naval forces under Perry at the Battle of Lake Erie. The loss of British command of these waters forced the British Army to withdraw from the Detroit frontier, and by mid-October 1813 it was fighting desperately to maintain control of the western district of Upper Canada.

concluded it unsuitable as a base for the squadron. Presque Isle (present-day Erie, Pennsylvania), then wilderness, could be more easily supplied from Philadelphia by way of Pittsburgh. Although the entrance to Presque Isle was shallow, the port was well protected. Accordingly, Chauncey ordered the shift westward.

Meanwhile, a different kind of war had been waging—one of cutting out expeditions. On the night of 9 October 1812, Lt. Jesse Elliott led a raid against Fort Erie. From Black Rock he gathered seamen and pistols and crossed the Niagara River in two boats, fifty men in each. They took the sleeping British by surprise. Right from under British noses (and the fort's guns) Elliott and his commandos snatched two vessels. The attack was partly successful because those vessels were considered "under cartel" and manned by skeleton crews that were transporting American prisoners from captured Detroit. One of the vessels was the *Detroit* (the former American gunboat *Adams*), the other the North West Company's *Caledonia*. Elliott says they were both brigs. The former, unfortunately for Elliott and his men, grounded and stuck fast. The Americans put the torch to the *Detroit*, for if the vessel could not wear the Stars and Stripes, it could not fly any flag. The *Caledonia* was towed by rowboat to the safety of Black Rock. There the *Caledonia* joined the four merchant vessels Elliott had gathered together. The action had important consequences, for the *Detroit* had had five guns mounted and six others stored below plus a large quantity of muskets and ammunition.[3]

In Washington, the secretary of the navy, William Jones, echoed Chauncey's calls for decisive, forward action. "It is impossible to attach too much importance to our naval operations on the Lakes," he wrote in January 1813. He added, in this letter to Chauncey, "The success of the ensuing campaign will depend absolutely upon our superiority on all the lakes—every effort, resource, must be redirected to that object." Jones trusted that Chauncey could oppose the passage of any British naval supplies and gunboats across the Niagara Peninsula. To counter every urgent British preparation, Jones authorized Chauncey to build a force at Presque Isle "sufficient to assure our ascendancy on the whole of the upper Lakes."[4]

Jones grasped the role sea power could play in Lake Erie operations both afloat and ashore. He was anxious to seize the trident of Neptune on that inland sea. He knew that control of communications would give mobility of arms and thereby allow American forces both freedom of movement and range of action that could facilitate the capture of Upper Canada. Jones put the advantages of "command of the Lake" this way: "This force would facilitate beyond calculation the operations of General Harrison's Army, & in the event of the fall of Malden & Detroit, would enable you to detach a part of your force to Lake Huron, to take the post at the mouth of French River on the N.E. side of Lake Huron, where you will intercept the supplies for the western Indians, which are sent up Grand River to this post, as soon as the waters of these Rivers are navigable, & from them distributed through the waters of Huron & Michigan to the tribes, even beyond the Mississippi. It is this commanding position which gives to the Enemy the absolute control of the Indians. This force would also enable you to take Michilimackinack & command the waters of Lake Michigan." Jones knew the Americans must counter any squadron the British might put on Lake Erie. "Whatever force the Enemy may create," he stressed once more, "we must surpass; & with this view it will require all your vigilance to penetrate their designs."[5]

Washington's directions for an enhanced war on Lake Erie had strategic consequences that were far-reaching. Orders coming from successive secretaries of the navy deflected attention from the St. Lawrence River waterway and valley. "It is possible," concludes the authority on the Lake Erie campaign, David Curtis Skaggs, "that, had Chauncey shown the enterprise expected of him, the emphasis on Lake Erie would have proven productive; Detroit could have been retaken and the troops released for duty to the east before the British had time to react. Granted the advantages of good leadership, dependable troops, and interservice cooperation, the American strategy might have succeeded; but none of these prerequisites was present. Even so, the British operated on an extremely narrow margin of error."[6]

Chauncey's arrangements cut right across the bow of Elliott's well-intended course. At that time the yard at Black Rock had vessels for the Lake Erie fleet, with Elliott in charge.

In May 1813 Perry visited Black Rock en route to Lake Ontario for a consultation with Chauncey. His purpose was to hasten the arming and outfitting of the merchant vessels, then numbering five. On his way back to Presque Isle, he took with him from Chauncey's fleet a few men. From the Army he borrowed two companies of men, and with these he manned the vessels and sailed them to Presque Isle. Of this episode, recounted surgeon Usher Parsons, "It was a herculean labor to drag these vessels by land up the rapids at Black Rock into the Lake, and required nearly a week with two hundred men, who warped them with ropes over their shoulders." These vessels narrowly escaped detection and capture. Perry made active preparations to resist the enemy reported to be near "and to board the enemy should he come near us." It was a close affair, apparently. "Fortunately we were not discovered," said Parsons, "and on the evening of the next day our little squadron entered Erie in safety."[7]

Meanwhile, at Erie, or Presque Isle, the Americans went about the business of this shipbuilders' war largely unnoticed by the British. The shift away from Black Rock did not appeal to Elliott, who opposed such a move, and was in any event out of keeping with what he thought should be done in the circumstances, which was to convert existing merchant vessels into gunboats. Elliott had a falling out with Capt. Daniel Dobbins, the seasoned Great Lakes mariner who had lobbied Washington strongly with a view to building a new fleet, one capable of sweeping the British from these waters. Elliott opposed this civilian's idea and thought it impossible. Quite likely his opposition turned to resentment, and this provides a clue as to his tardy, even dilatory, conduct during the pending battle.

At Presque Isle shipwrights made steady progress in building gunboats, and by January 1813 had two such, each fifty feet in length, completed for the coming season. An indifferent flow of provisions and stores hindered their progress, and in the new year a strange malady "lake fever," or "the sickness," as it was generally referred to, made widespread appearance. Desertions became more frequent, and Dobbins called on Washington to supply more shipwrights and carpenters. That winter, too, master shipwright Noah Brown came to Lake Erie and provided substantial help for Dobbins—and for the new direction for the Lake Erie fleet that was to be floated and armed that spring. We return to that theme presently.

These developments caught the British unawares. In command headquarters in Montreal, Governor Prevost remained in the dark concerning British fortunes on Lake Erie. He had reason to be satisfied that that quarter was well served. No storm warnings were reaching him from the far western rim of empire. In fact, news from Kingston indicated sufficient naval and military forces for the western campaign. At the outset of the war, content with the existing force on Lake Erie—the *Queen Charlotte*, mounting twenty 24-pounders, the *Hunter*, ten 12-pounders, the *Prevost*, fourteen 9-pounders, the *Nancy*, eight 6-pounders, the *Caledonia*, eight 6-pounders, and *Detroit* (the former *Adams*), still building—Prevost had ordered the construction of only one new vessel, a schooner to carry twelve guns.[8] Both the *Caledonia* and *Detroit* were lost to American arms early in the 1812 campaign, as we have seen. Prevost showed no great fear about American preparations or capabilities. He seems to have been indifferent to numerous pleas for additional guns and manpower to fight a maritime war on the upper lakes. From Gen. Henry Procter commanding the Right Division that had by this time struck deep into Ohio, at Raisin River and elsewhere, came appeal after appeal for more materiel and more trained seamen.

Thus from the Army came the plea for more men-of-war. Up and down the various chains of command, as well as between the War Office and the Admiralty and their commanders on the spot, the request passed. Meanwhile, at the naval base of Bermuda in March 1813, a young lieutenant, Robert Heriot Barclay, found himself without a ship to command or without any prospects for service. He would not have to wait long. His arrival at Bermuda coincided happily with the commander in chief's requirement, based upon the pressing needs on the upper lakes, for a senior officer to take over in those waters. At Bermuda, the commander in chief, Adm. Sir John Borlase Warren, who had spent most of the war establishing the blockade of American ports and hunting down U.S. merchantmen, quickly seized on Barclay's unemployed status and decided to use him for the benefit of the service. He issued orders for Barclay to travel to Kingston, Upper Canada. There he would take command as senior naval officer of Royal Navy vessels on the upper lakes with the rank of acting commander.[9]

Barclay came directly from the Nelsonic mode and was formed in the heroic style. Naval warfare had shaped his life. He had entered the Navy at the same age as Nelson, twelve, and through dint of perseverance and success in arms had risen to commissioned rank, lieutenant, on the eve of Trafalgar. Like the great Nelson, Barclay was the son of a minister, but in his case one of the Church of Scotland. In King's Kettle, Fife, he had attended a school where John Strachan, later the Upper Canada clergyman and educator of prominence, held classes. Barclay had fought at Trafalgar: as a midshipman he was in the thick of things in the seventy-four-gun *Swiftsure*. He saw the prize *Redoubtable* surrender to the merciless sea, and, although he was instrumental in saving some of the crew of this prize, he witnessed the tragic loss of her officers and crew. Three years later, in 1808, off the Biscay coast in the frigate *Diana*, he fought an action against an enemy convoy. Barclay took a ball from an enemy swivel gun that nearly tore off his left arm. The surgeon left a stump below the shoulder. For the loss of this limb Barclay was awarded a pension.[10] A change of naval administration delayed his advancement in the service, but in 1812 he was serving as a first lieutenant of the frigate *Iphigenia*, all the time waiting for his own command. It was at this stage that Warren appointed him to "the Lakes."

Barclay sailed from Bermuda for Halifax, and with him went other acting commanders, all junior to himself, Daniel Pring and Robert Finnis. They then went overland, from Halifax to Saint John, upriver by boat, then across the height of land to the St. Lawrence. Pring went to Lake Champlain, Finnis to Lake Erie. Great prospects lay before them: a chance to grapple with the American Navy. And were not some toasts of the day "a bloody war or a sickly season" and "a willing foe and sea-room"? These men were inured to battle, anxious for action. And great expectations were held for these officers. They were pressed on to their respective assignments "as their judgment and experience are essential to the completion of our preparations for ensuring our ascendancy on Lake Ontario," as Prevost put it in his letter to Earl Bathurst, the secretary of war.[11] Barclay's deployment to Kingston accorded exactly with the Navy taking charge of warships on the lakes and all establishments ashore. The Navy took over from the Canadian sea militia. All officers of the Provincial Marine, though keeping the same salaries as before, were to be reduced to lesser ranks. "The Brave Soldiers of Upper Canada," proclaimed Prevost's general order of 22 April, "will greet with heartfelt joy, the arrival of a Gallant Band of British Seamen." Barclay and Pring reached Kingston in late April. Barclay took command of the corvette *Wolfe,* mounting twenty-three guns, and Pring the *Royal George.*

At Kingston, Barclay was now at the mainspring of Upper Canada's defense establishment. There, besides his own command, he found three British men-of-war and a sizable naval yard and arsenal at Point Frederick. Barclay thought the vessels as fine as any he had seen, a worthy compliment. Of the officers of the Provincial Marine Barclay recognized their hurt feelings at having been supplanted in their influence and authority by the Royal Navy. He turned his hand to dockyard improvements and upgrading the readiness of the small fleet.

On 15 May Barclay was superseded by Commo. Sir James Lucas Yeo, who arrived that day in Kingston as flag officer for the Royal Navy on the Great Lakes. Yeo had come directly from England with a draft of a dozen noncommissioned officers and four hundred seamen. Yeo had now to decide who should be sent to Lake Erie, and Cdr. William Mulcaster (also recently arrived on station), who was senior to Barclay, was offered this command. He declined it on grounds, Barclay later testified, "of its ineffectual State and Sir James Yeo refusing to send Seamen." Barclay then got the nod and was ordered to quit Kingston for Lake Erie, going by way of York. Thus, from being commandant at Kingston and flag officer for all HM vessels on the Lakes, Barclay found himself shunted farther west to an altogether different set of circumstances.

Barclay took with him what he regarded as a ragamuffin crowd of men: "I was ordered to proceed to that Lake with three lieutenants, one surgeon, a purser, a master's mate, and 19 men, 12 of these were Canadians who had been discharged from [Commodore Yeo's] own Squadron on Lake Ontario, the others were the most worthless Characters that came from England with him."[12] En route to Lake Erie, Barclay and his men dodged various American war parties and worked along the shore to Burlington Bay and then across the height of land to Long Point, Lake Erie. There a handful of armed schooners of the Provincial Marine lay at anchor. Barclay took the *Lady Prevost* as his flagship, a tolerably nice vessel, and ran up his broad pendant. The other vessels, the *Chippewa* and *Mary,* were fine, too.

Barclay's woes mounted in earnest, for he was in want of good seamen ready for war. He put it this way in his early request, dated 1 June, to Yeo:

> Thus you may observe that the state of the Squadron on Lake Erie is by no means so well manned and equipped as you were led to believe from report and candidly (with the exception of about 10) the men which I brought with me are but little cal-culated to make them better. Those men on board the *Lady Prevost* and *Chippewa* I have mustered and examined. Some even cannot speak English, all are Canadians with very few exceptions. . . . I hope you will see the necessity of sending me a rein-forcement of *good* Seamen that by mixing them with these I may be able to perform any service with honor to ourselves and advantage to the Country.[13]

On 2 June Barclay sailed from Long Point with the contingent he had brought from Kingston. He must have readied the ship's crew with remarkable haste, because he hoped to have a peek at the American shipyard at Presque Isle. Winds were not in his favor, and accordingly, he steered for his new home port, Amherstburg. History might have been remarkably different had he struck first at the American yard at that early date. Barclay was at Amherstburg on the sixth and later sailed back to Long Point to reassess the situation. From the begin-ning he realized his disadvantages. These were two in number: first, the poverty of the fighting condition of his ships and sailors and, second, the gathering robustness of the American force across the lake. The American naval com-mander Perry (whom we meet presently) had arrived in late March, fully ten weeks in advance of Barclay, and he had arrived with a goodly supply of offi-cers and seamen to equip a strong flotilla. That ten weeks advance time could not be made up, particularly given the size of the American war preparations.

Thus when he arrived on Lake Erie, Barclay, with justifiable reason, joined the new chorus calling for urgent reinforcements. Contrary to Prevost's perspective, the British worked from a severe disadvantage. All around them their defenses were hard-pressed. The campaign for control of the Niagara

Peninsula was in full swing. British neglect of bases for the Lake Erie campaign doomed the fortunes of their fleet. Fort Erie was barely adequate and was, in any event, at the wrong end for the coming operations. It was, besides, liable to American cross-border raiding. In fact, Fort Erie, like a challenge cup, passed to and fro from one power to the other at the time of the Battle of Lundy's Lane fought nearby. At the other end of Lake Erie, Amherstburg lay prone and open to attack from Detroit (if in American hands) or subject to raids from elsewhere on the lake. Historian A. T. Mahan linked the vital ties of bases to a fleet: "In a sea war, as in all others, two things are from the first essential—a suitable base on the frontier . . . from which the operations start, and an organized military force, in this case a fleet, of size and quality adequate to the proposed operations."[14]

Hard-pressed Fort Erie could not be, in any event, much value to lonely Amherstburg and Fort Malden situated at the western extremity of the lake. In such circumstances, and given the great surging of American military might overland from the Atlantic seaboard, British naval strategy ought to have been entirely defensive. To preserve the fleet could have been Barclay's goal. The traditions of Nelson, intimately known to young Barclay, called for something entirely different. Barclay chose a forward strategy of engaging the enemy, one entirely in keeping with his times and the service. He miscalculated. Whatever naval intelligence he had ought to have indicated clearly that some other measure than a general fleet action would be advisable. Indeed, early in the campaign of 1813 he addressed to his superior another option—taking the emergent American naval force out at its base of operations: "On my taking command here [Barclay advised Prevost on 16 July 1813], I instantly reconnoitered the Enemy's naval stations, and on finding so great a force getting ready at Presqu'isle, I judged that an immediate attack by Land and the Lake would decidedly be the best mode of annihilating their naval equipments at once. Under that impression I wrote to Genl. [John] Vincent for a sufficient body of regulars, to join what Genl. Procter could bring with him from Amherstburg, and a body of Indians (which he could at all times command) to enable me to attack Presqu'isle at once."

Barclay's request to Vincent yielded the promise of some of the 41st Regiment, and from Procter came a similar agreement to bring his troops and Indian allies in support of the scheme. The whole design was overturned from on high, from Maj. Gen. Francis de Rottenburg, Procter's superior, who said in no uncertain terms that such an operation could not be supported, for there were insufficient numbers to make it likely of success. But Barclay sailed: "I left Amherstburg with all the vessels that I could employ as men of war—and manned with the former Canadian crew, strengthened by 50 of the 41st. Regt.—but our actual force being so much inferior to that of the Enemy when they get equipment for them renders the situation of this squadron in a most hazardous situation." Barclay intended to blockade Presque Isle. But he admitted the impossibility of this if seamen and ordnance were not sent to him from Lake Ontario, together with stores of every description. "If the Enemy do gain the ascendancy on this Lake, all supplies must necessarily be cut off," he declared. Should the British naval force be obliged to retire, that is face defeat, "the whole line under Genl. Procter must lay open to the Enemy."

In surveying his future prospects, as of mid-June, Barclay knew that he had insufficient armament and means of resupply. Even the new vessel, his intended flagship *Detroit* (named for the vessel captured from the Americans at Detroit but lost to them at Black Rock), ready to launch at Malden on 20 July, could not be enough. There was insufficient ordnance, ammunition, and other stores, and not a man to put into her, he said. Defending the Canadian province required him to use the *Detroit* and the rest of his fleet, he admitted. At the same time he was not sanguine about the result, although he did expect that the Americans might not yet have a decided advantage. He called upon Yeo for 250 to 300 seamen "to render His Majesty's Squadron perfectly effective."[15]

To this urgent plea General Prevost gave this solemn, blood-chilling reply: although he was well aware of Barclay's difficulties, Barclay would have no choice but to "obtain your Ordnance and Naval Stores from the Enemy." He told Procter the same thing. All that he could say, cheerily, was that he too had pressed upon Yeo the necessity of sending, immediately, a supply of petty officers and seamen. Yeo promised to do so without delay. All existing circumstances pointed to the necessity of an early attack on Presque Isle—before the enemy flotilla could venture out. Barclay, however, could make no military strike. All he could do was cruise back and forth in a distant blockade, and when on 5 August he penned his next report of proceedings to Yeo, he made clear that the scales were tipping against him. "The time is now come which I have so long feared," he wrote, "that of being obliged to withdraw from this without supplies." The American fleet was now outside, over the bar. Now the American vessels could prey upon British supplies coming from Long Point. British seamen being sent from Fort Erie and Long Point were liable to capture. Getting the promised guns for the *Detroit* could not now be effected. The only alternative was to take the ordnance from the batteries at Amherstburg, and perhaps, with this defense, run to Long Point to take delivery of the Burlington-transferred guns.

Of the enemy, Barclay reported his expectations: "They have not as yet made any shew of following us: but if they were not ready for Service they would hardly venture over the bar, although under the protection of their Batteries, and I think it more probable, from the great addition to their Military Strength at Presque Isle that their first attempt will be to reinforce Harrison and cut off Genl. Procter's retreat but it is to be hoped from the length of time that he has been there that he may have effected his purpose."[16]

On the eve of battle, General Prevost seems to have had a last-minute change of heart. He had come to realize how perilous was Barclay's position. Already, Prevost knew, the U.S. Navy had acquired a temporary ascendancy on the lake by virtue of numbers and materiel. He knew that the Americans could now check the British flow of supplies for their troops to maintain their present, advanced positions. From news reaching him from Amherstburg, he knew that the state of distress for British arms was now acute. Barclay, he told Commodore Yeo, must make an attempt to gain the ascendancy and he even advised Yeo to send a large number of officers and men from the troopship *Dover* to York and thence Lake Erie.[17] Too little, too late. Yeo remained coldly distant to Barclay's entreaties and seems to have been consumed by problems facing him on Lake Ontario, which were considerable.

Barclay's brilliant opposite was Commo. Oliver Hazard Perry, age twenty-eight. Perry came from a seasoned seafaring family, and as a midshipman he had sailed in a U.S. ship-of-war, the *General Green,* built and commanded by his father. The younger Perry went through the great United States naval command school of that era—contending with Barbary pirates. Immensely patriotic, courageous, and dedicated to duty, Perry, a surveyor as well as ordnance officer, found himself in the early stages of the War of 1812 as master commandant employed in charge of a flotilla of gunboats at Newport, Rhode Island. With the British blockade strangling every opportunity, he welcomed employment with the naval forces of Commodore Chauncey on the Great Lakes. In March 1813 he hurried to Lake Erie under orders. His duties included training men in the use of small arms, exercise of the great guns, and every warlike service on shipboard.

With Perry to Presque Isle had come 149 officers, men and boys, most of them like himself from Rhode Island. Others were to follow. The Navy Department arranged provisions for 500 men for the campaign. Ten weeks to ready a fleet for war service seems an impossibly short interval. In these American efforts skill and resolution were measured in matched proportion.

And nature offered every resource: white and black oak and chestnut from nearby woods furnished the frames for the vessels. The planks were of oak, the decks of pine. Ironware was garnered from local smithies, and blacksmiths were brought from Philadelphia or taken from militia called out as a guard. Additional resources came from Pittsburgh: canvas, muskets, small guns, shot, and ball. Artificers were brought to Lake Erie as required.

From the stocks at Presque Isle there arose two new brigs, *Lawrence* and *Niagara*, each 260 tons burden, 141 feet in length, and pierced for twenty guns. They were ready for launch 23 May. Other vessels were captured by raids. Preparations of the American fleet continued.

Barclay's flagship the *Detroit* was intended to be 244 tons and mount as many as eighteen guns. Barclay gathered his forces, taking up guns from shore batteries as best he could, arranging gunnery drill, assigning his sparse supply of able-bodied sailors as well as possible. Lt. Jesse Elliott, who peeked in to Amherstburg with the U.S. fleet on a dangerous reconnaissance, gave this brazen assessment of the strength of the British: "We had the satisfaction to discover our opponents at anchor under their batteries at Malden with a force equal to ours. The new ship is all a taunto, and what keeps them in God only knows, for they have a third more guns. We have twice stood in, hove about and laid our topsails to the mast; waited two hours with the wind off the Malden shore. John Bull is not generally quick of comprehension, and I assume on this occasion will plead that as an excuse. Our desire was obvious."[18]

The impatient Elliott would have rushed upon the British but Perry had no such intention. What he had in mind was a decisive blow. Perry declined to attack the British when they were unprepared. Seaman David Bunnell explains: "'No,' said our brave and generous commander, 'I will take no advantage of them, but wait until they get in readiness, and meet them fairly and openly on the lake. I feel the utmost confidence in my crew and officers, and know they can fight and do believe that we can beat the enemy without taking any dishonorable advantage of them.'"[19]

Elliott did not know how poorly Barclay thought of his sailors. "I am sure, Sir James," Barclay wrote to Commodore Yeo that same day, "if you saw my Canadians, you would condemn every one (with perhaps two or three exceptions) as a poor devil not worth his Salt."[20] However, Barclay made every possible preparation and set sail from Amherstburg to engage the enemy.

On the evening of 9 September, Perry, then lying at anchor with his fleet at Put-in-Bay among the islands of western Lake Erie, summoned his commanders and gave them their written instructions. He intended to fight the enemy at close quarters, and for the *Lawrence* to take as its opponent the *Detroit,* and the *Niagara* the *Queen Charlotte.* In fact, his instructions called for him to "engage each of your designated adversary in close action, at half cable-length." He showed his commanders the flag of blue bunting upon which were painted Capt. James Lawrence's last words: "Don't give up the ship." It has been written by an early biographer of Perry that as they parted on that moonlit summer night, each to return to his vessel, their young commander gave them the last injunction in the words of Nelson: "If you lay your enemy close along-side, you cannot be out of your place."[21]

At sunrise next day, the tenth, Barclay spotted his opposite's force. The American got underway in light southwest winds and stood for the British fleet. At ten in the morning the breeze shifted to southeast, giving Perry's squadron the precious tactical advantage of being upwind of the British. Perry's ships formed line of battle and bore down on the enemy. At a quarter to twelve the British men-of-war commenced firing. Ten minutes later the U.S. ships returned the fire.

At the outset, British weapons, particularly their celebrated long guns, proved very effective, especially in hitting Perry's flagship, the *Lawrence.* Accordingly, Perry decided to close on the enemy and to get in tight. The *Lawrence,* under relentless bombardment from the *Detroit, Queen Charlotte,* and *Chippewa,* was soon rendered useless as a gun-carrying platform. Two hours of canister fire had put her guns out of action, riddled the hull and rigging, and killed or wounded 80 percent of the crew. The enemy's brilliant gunnery had wrought savage results. The *Lawrence* was put completely out of action.

In the circumstances, Perry acted prudently: he decided to shift his flag to the *Niagara* when convenient and to leave a young lieutenant, John Yarnall, to guard the *Lawrence.*

A change now came over the waters. At two in the afternoon the dilatory Jesse Elliott decided to bring his vessel, the brig *Niagara,* into close action. Perry shifted to the *Niagara* at this point. Soon a signal was put up for "close action." The *Niagara,* little damaged in previous fire, bore up *Niagara*'s helm so that he could head more downwind in order to cut the British line. He passed the British vessels, and in doing so opened a raking fire on them from the starboard guns. British vessels were so close on the port side that the Americans fired pistols at them. The smaller American vessels, now hard upon the *Niagara,* opened a deadly grape and canister fire. The power of the American guns was overwhelming. The two British ships, a brig, and a schooner and a sloop attempted to escape.

They did so in vain. Barclay was badly injured, his first officer killed, and his guns put out of action. Captain Finnis of the *Queen Charlotte* was killed. The commanding officer of the *Hunter* was injured. All of the British men-of-war were damaged or drifted out of action because of rudder damage or other difficulty. The *Little Belt,* for instance, withdrew from battle. The British fate was sealed when the *Queen Charlotte* collided with the *Detroit.* The *Niagara,* right in the middle of the action, was able to train port guns on the *Chippewa* and *Lady Prevost* and starboard guns on the *Hunter, Queen Charlotte,* and *Detroit.*

"What a glorious day to my country," proclaimed Seaman Bunnell, who saw the British squadron surrender in line. "We took as many prisoners as we had men when we commenced the action." The carnage was massive in Barclay's flagship: "The English Commander's ship *Detroit* looked like a slaughter-house," said Bunnell.[22] A total of fifty-two casualties were aboard the *Detroit,* forty-two aboard *Queen Charlotte,* twenty-eight aboard *Lady Prevost,* and much fewer aboard the others.

By half past two in the afternoon silence descended over the summer waters of Lake Erie. The battle had been fought with "great fury" for nearly five hours. The fighting had indeed been ferocious, and it knows no parallel in North American naval history. Its specific uniqueness was not lost on victor and vanquished.

The British had suffered total loss of their fleet. Never before had a full British squadron of armed ships been made the prize of an enemy. "We have met the enemy; and they are ours," wrote the triumphant Perry on 10 September 1813 aboard the *Niagara* off the Western Sister, the head of Lake Erie. This brief declaration, addressed to the governor of Indiana, Maj. Gen. William Henry Harrison, at Seneca on the Sandusky River, announced the establishment of American naval command of that lake. Five enemy men-of-war had been captured. Now they wore the Stars and Stripes. Their British bunting was sent to Washington (and now is proudly on display in the Naval Academy at Annapolis).

By one masterful stroke, remembered in history as the Battle of Lake Erie, or more specifically the Battle of Put-in-Bay, as U.S. Surgeon Usher Parsons called it, American ascendancy on this lake and its tributary waters lying above had been achieved. The situation ashore was changed "as if by magic." To that point in time the British military commander could land where and when he liked—this control had, Mahan said, "hung over the frontier like a pall, until finally dissipated by Perry's victory."[23] With this loss of such preeminence went the British freedom to deploy troops and artillery at will, to cut out enemy parties, and to intercept enemy communications, supplies and trade.

In sum, the British had lost two ships, one brig, two schooners, and a sloop. Together they were smaller in tonnage, guns, and men than the nine vessels under Perry's command, built and outfitted for the service on the lakes. The U.S. ships had a superiority in guns, too. For every fifteen hundred pounds of metal that Perry's ships hurled at the enemy, Barclay's six vessels, though of superior tonnage, could only reply with six hundred. As long as Barclay's long guns could be trained to bear the Americans remained at a disadvantage. Once close combat became a possibility the advantage went to the United States vessels. Only the USS *Lawrence* had been removed as a fighting unit. The British loss in killed and wounded was unimaginable, said Perry, who added with understatement, "It must however have been very great."[24] The casualties were high on both sides: 123 Americans killed and 145 British killed.

Some indication of the severity of the wounds suffered in this encounter is given by Surgeon Parsons, who kept a diary. "The action terminated shortly after 3 o'clock; and of about one hundred men, reported fit for duty in the morning [in the *Lawrence*], twenty were found dead, and sixty one wounded," he reported. Parsons attended to victims with artery wounds and, except where amputation was required, had them all secure before dark. Without an assistant he would have to leave amputations till the morning; in the interim opiates and tourniquets had to suffice. From daylight to eleven in the morning he amputated. "The impatience of this class of the wounded to meet the operation, rendered it necessary to take them in the same succession in which they fell." Then he attended to compound and simple fractures, then dislocations, lacerations, and contusions. He stopped work at midnight. The next day he shifted to the *Niagara* and found the surgeon sick in bed "with hands too feeble to execute the dictates of a feeling heart." Parsons took over, and by the end of his round had tallied up his numbers: twenty-five cases of compound fracture, four simple fracture, three grapeshot wounds, four canister, thirty-seven splinter and lacerated wounds, large and small. There were two cases of concussion of the brain, three of the chest, and two of the pelvis. There were ten contusions and six sprains. Three men died from wounds, all involving fractures (shoulder, lower limbs, skull). Parsons remarked that there were not more than two very singular wounds, or "such as would be unlikely to occur in a sea engagement": grape shot and canister shot that lodged in unusual places. The surgeon marveled at the great recovery of the wounded. He attributed this to various factors: purity of the air (the patients were on deck under awnings), abundant supply of fresh food (fowl, meat, milk, eggs, and vegetables—made available through the kindness of Ohio farmers), "the happy state of mind, which victory occasioned," and the commodore's solicitous aid for all the wounded.[25]

Wrote George Bancroft, former secretary of the navy and secretary of war, with a touch of sentimental reverence,

> An opening on the margin of Put-in-Bay was selected for the burial-place of the officers who had fallen. The day was serene, the breezes hushed, the water unruffled by a wavelet. The men of both fleets mourned together; as the boats moved slowly in procession, the music played dirges to which the oars kept time; the flags showed the signs of sorrow; solemn minute-guns were heard from the ships. The spot where the funeral train went on shore was a wild solitude; the Americans and British walked in alternate couples to the graves, like men, who in the presence of eternity, renewed the relation of brothers and members of one human family, and the bodies of the dead were likewise borne along and buried alternately, English and American side by side, and undistinguished. The wounded of both fleets, meeting with equal assiduous care, were sent to Erie, where Barclay was seen, with tottering steps, supported between Harrison and Perry, as he walked from the landing-place to his quarters.[26]

Indeed the fighting had been furious, the casualties significant, the damage to ships severe. In a nighttime gale in the harbor of Put-in-Bay a few days after the battle, nature completed what the U.S. Navy had begun: *Detroit* was completely dismasted and *Queen Charlotte* partly dismasted.

As Perry had remarked with sympathy just after the battle, the Americans took in many more prisoners than they had men on board their ships. Perry ordered the prisoners landed at Sandusky, and he asked General Harrison to have them marched to Chillicothe to be looked after. The *Lawrence* appeared "so entirely cut up" that she had to go over the Presque Isle bar and into the safety of Erie Harbor as soon as possible. Meantime, riding at anchor outside, two of the captured ships, heavily injured, had lost their masts, and they too were hastened to places of security.

Surveying his captures, Perry had reason to be proud. The *Detroit* seemed a remarkably fine ship—stoutly built and a good sailer. The *Queen Charlotte* was better than advertised. The *Lady Prevost,* another fine prize, was a large schooner. In the history of North American waters no victor could claim a greater haul. And what of the vanquished? Perry reported that Barclay was "*dangerously* wounded" and accordingly decided to parole him and put him ashore on the Canadian side as near Lake Ontario as possible. Barclay must have been in a state of mortification: suffering severely from his wounds and conscious of his absolute defeat at American hands. He was under the impression, said Perry with the sympathy characteristic of a great victorious commander, that his life could only be saved by leaving that part of the country, by which is meant that his injuries were so severe that he must get medical aid. As to the Canadians, Perry remarked that many of them had families who would mourn their loss or welcome their return. Magnanimous in victory, Perry intended to minimize the suffering of the defeated.[27]

On reflection we can now see that the American victory derived from a truly remarkable naval buildup. Ship carpenters had completed in only five months two great brigs, the *Lawrence* and *Niagara*. This may have been a shipbuilders' war but it was also a war of vessels taken up from trade. The *Somers* had been taken up from the merchant service. The *Caledonia* had been captured from the British. The *Ariel, Scorpion, Tigress,* and *Porcupine* had been readied by Noah Brown, manned or floated over the bar at Presque Isle, and brought into deep water. Elliott had gathered five vessels from the yard at Black Rock in early June. Thus, while the British had blockaded Presque Isle and other ports Perry had, with Brown's ingenuity and assistance, put together his battle fleet. "The amount of work that Brown accomplished with about 200 men, without power tools, and in a wilderness during the worst winter months," wrote the great authority Howard Chapelle, "makes some of the modern wartime productions feats something less than impressive. The man was tireless and ingenious."[28] Not only had the Americans gathered and built a fleet, they had put up a blockhouse, guardhouse, mess building, blacksmith shop, barracks, and office and built four camels or floats to get the brigs over the bar. All gun carriages had been built, too. The rigging and sailmaking had been done by the crews being collected by Perry.

Perry was true to Chauncey's calling: he had won personal honor and enhanced the reputation of his country and its navy. Later a rivalry would develop between Perry and Elliot as to tactics employed during the Battle of Lake Erie, and more especially the apparent reluctance of Elliot to join battle. This controversy, which simmered for years, has no interest to the theme of this work.[29]

"The British officer ought to be cashiered for permitting our fleet to get out," observed Baltimore's *Niles' Weekly Register.* The same authority observed that given the superiority of the British fleet, its American opposite could have nothing to hope for in battle and might therefore run from the enemy. Sources even charge that Barclay was more concerned with keeping dinner dates in Canadian ports than maintaining the blockade. Just at the time the American fleet slipped to sea Barclay was out courting.

As to the battle itself, Barclay could not contend with superior guns and gunnery. He had insufficient numbers of seamen. He was outgunned and short-handed. The lower deck was a mixed bag of sailors, soldiers, artisans, and laborers. Neither did the unfolding of events favor the British, rather the reverse. Barclay was dangerously wounded—a shattered thigh and smashed shoulder—and was taken down to his cockpit. All his chief officers and their seconds in command were killed or put out of action. His best ship was "shattered very much."

What led to this calamity? The problem, recounted Lt. George Inglis, who took over command of the *Detroit* from Barclay, was that the *Detroit* and *Queen Charlotte* became so incredibly entangled that their fighting capacity became negligible. Inglis recounts events in his letter dated 10 September to Barclay:

> On coming on the Quarter Deck, after your being wounded, [I saw] the Enemy's second brig [*Niagara*], at that time on our weather beam, shortly afterwards took a position on our weather bow, to rake us, to prevent which in attempting to wear to get our Starboard broadside to bear upon her, as a number of the Guns on the Larboard broadside being at this time disabled, fell on board the *Queen Charlotte*, at this time running up to Leeward of us. In this situation the two ships remained for some time. As soon as we got clear of her, I ordered the *Queen Charlotte* to shoot ahead of us if possible and attempted to back our Fore Topsail to get astern, but that Ship laying completely unmanageable, every brace cut away, the Mizzen Topmast and gaff down, all the other Masts badly wounded, not a Stay left forward, Hull shattered very much, a number of Guns disabled, and the Enemy's Squadron raking both Ships ahead and astern, none of our own in a situation to support us, I was under the painful necessity of answering the Enemy to say we had struck, the *Queen Charlotte* having previously done so.[30]

In analyzing the reasons for the loss, Commodore Yeo, at Kingston, was perfunctory at best when he said in one single sentence: "It appears to me, that though his majesty's squadron were very deficient as to seamen, weight of metal, and particularly long guns, yet the greatest misfortune was the loss of every officer, particularly Captain Finnis, whose life, had it been spared, would, in my opinion, have saved the squadron."[31] Want of effective leadership in the midst of battle is a sorry thing for a force. So it was, implied Yeo, for the British at Put-in-Bay, as they called it. Thus closed Yeo's assessment of what he called "the ill-fated action on Lake Erie."

Commodore Yeo would not leave the matter there. He never held back his punches, and expressed dissatisfaction with Barclay's actions: "The orders I had given Captain Barclay were to cooperate with Major General Procter, against the enemy, according to his judgment, the wishes of the General, and his means, which I know were very inadequate to meet the far superior and well appointed squadron of the Enemy." In other words, Barclay, had he followed instructions, should have taken evasive action and kept his fleet in being, employing vessels as required in support of Procter's Right Division. Yeo, undeniably seeking to shift the blame to his junior, confessed he remained completely in the dark as to the reasons why Barclay had risked an action before reinforcements of seamen arrived. Barclay acted, said Yeo in his report to the commander in chief, Adm. Sir John Borlase Warren, "under the impression that if successful, he had everything to gain, and if not, little to lose." In other words, Yeo classified Barclay as reckless. Not only that, the action was costly to the war effort. Barclay's action had obliged Procter to destroy grain supplies to prevent them from falling into enemy hands. Procter could not be blamed for urging Barclay to act, Yeo continued. He concluded this damning report on his fellow naval officer: "I am therefore of opinion that there was not that necessity for General Procter to urge Captain Barclay to *so hazardous and unequal a contest.*" And again, Barclay was rash and foolish, and certainly "not justified in seeking a contest the result of which he almost foresaw would prove disastrous."[32]

And further up the chain of command flowed the Navy's disappointment about Barclay's disaster. Knowing Yeo's opinion, Warren could speculate that Barclay acted out of urgent necessity, being unable to run he was obliged to fight. "I am sorry that the war in Canada seems not to have assumed that decided character I was in hopes it would have done before this time," Warren wrote the first lord of the Admiralty, Viscount Melville, on 9 November, from Halifax, "but I hope the reinforcements sent from hence and England will prevent any further disaster in that country." He added: "I am concerned to state that no other account relative to the Flotilla upon Lake Erie under the command of poor Captain Barclay has reached me. . . . I much fear the measure of engaging the American force was perhaps urged by the wants of General Procter's army; and before Barclay's Squadron was properly equipped."[33]

These matters could only be dealt with by further inquiries and a court-martial. These would lie in the future and would await investigation. In that flamboyant age charges and countercharges were a way of life in matters military and naval. Fortunately for Barclay he survived to tell his tale, and he got a good hearing in court.

While speculation mounted in Kingston, Halifax, and London, it is note-worthy to see what happened subsequently to the British commander of the ill-fated British fleet on Lake Erie. His captor, Perry, released him, allowing him to return to Quebec, where Barclay believed he could get proper medical treatment. At Terrebone, Quebec, a village south of Montreal, he was warmly welcomed. A dinner and ball were held in his honor on 20 April 1814. Many toasts were given on that fabulous occasion. None was more comforting than that to "this gallant, but unfortunate officer." To which Barclay replied to his foe with equal generosity: "Commodore Perry, the gallant and generous enemy." The inhabitants of Quebec (that is to say, their governors) and the Canada merchants of Montreal and London (the fur-trading lobby) presented Barclay with two splendid pieces of silver plate, calculated to be worth five hundred pounds sterling. These pieces bore an engraved inscription that reported the "exalted courage and heroic valour" of officers, seamen, sailors, and marines of the flotilla in an action against a greatly superior enemy "when the presence of a few additional seamen was only wanting to have effected the total discomfiture of the hostile squadron." It concluded, lovingly and with all the sentiments of that age, that although Barclay "did not command victory he nobly deserved it."[34]

Barclay had to take the heat from the press. When word of the fleet's capture reached London, news was circulated under the heading " 'Tis pitiful—'tis wondrous pitiful." And from a Halifax, Nova Scotia, paper came a sardonic commentary on the British loss. The informant in this case took some weary consolation in the fact that the British flotilla in question "was not any branch of the royal navy; but was solely manned, equipped and managed by the public exertions of certain Canadians, who had formed themselves in a kind of lake fencibles. It was not the royal navy; but a local force; a kind of mercantile military."[35]

August of 1814 found Barclay in London urgently awaiting court-martial. The matter hung heavily over him and was a constant cause of worry. In consequence of his wounds becoming more painful, and his general health worsening, he appealed to the lords of the Admiralty to allow him to remove to a place of convalescence, the town of Worthing, which was highly regarded by those who could afford it as an excellent place for rest and repair. Daily he scanned the papers, anxious to see news of arrival of the Quebec convoy that would bring to London officers who had been under his command at Put-in-Bay. And until the court-martial could be held Barclay's pay was suspended; moreover, their lordships could not fix a pension for his battle wounds until a trial was held. "I am most anxious to have an opportunity of vindicating my conduct," he wrote the secretary of the Admiralty, who replied with bureaucratic ease that the court-martial would be ordered when the officers were available.[36]

On 9 September, on board HMS *Gladiator* at Portsmouth, a court-martial, presided over by Rear Adm. Edward Foote, assembled to inquire into the cause and circumstances of the capture of Barclay's squadron. The court had before it Barclay's letter of proceedings dated 12 September 1813 detailing the particular circumstances. But they were particularly interested in the "very defective means Captain Barclay possessed" to equip the squadron, the want of enough able seamen "whom he had repeatedly and earnestly requested to be sent to him," and the "very great Superiority of the force of the Enemy to the British Squadron." They were also aware that there had been an "unfortunate early fall of the superior Officers in the Action." The court also knew that Commodore Yeo was exceedingly critical of Barclay's actions, which Yeo classified as rash. It is a matter of record that Army records were submitted that gave noteworthy evidence of the difficulties under which Barclay was working.

The court found that Barclay had appeared to make the greatest exertions in equipping and getting into order HM vessels, and that he was "fully justified under the existing circumstances in bringing the Enemy into Action." His judgment and gallantry were highly conspicuous, entitling him to the highest praise; indeed, the conduct of all the officers and men was judged to have been of "the most gallant Manner." This qualified Barclay, his surviving officers and men to be fully and honorably acquitted, which they were.[37] And let Barclay have the final word on this. "That I had little to lose I never can admit as I had not only my Character as an Officer to support but also to uphold the honor of the British Navy which on this occasion I felt was committed to my charge," he declared. To this he added the telling remark: "Had I not risked an action the whole disgrace of the retreat of the Army would have been attached to me, and I should have been justly involved in the shocking imputation of Cowardice."[38]

Barclay remained at the rank of commander for ten years, with discussion of the Lake Erie affair and prospects of other trials of Prevost and Yeo pending, and this, says Barclay's memoirist, prevented his promotion to post rank at the close of the war. Barclay's last command was to the insignificant bomb vessel *Infernal* for a cruise to the Mediterranean, a cruise cut short on the amicable termination of the war against Algiers. Advancing by seniority, he was made captain 14 October 1824, ten years after his court-martial.[39]

We now return to the field. The sweeping American victory at Put-in-Bay placed British land forces in dire straits. All waterways would soon see enemy gunboats and raiding parties. British military installations were ripe places for American amphibious plucking. Perry's victory closed Lake Erie as an effective line of British retreat or supply. The British might escape by only one safe exit from Lake Huron—by way of French River to Montreal. In fact, this ancient voyageur highway of the north served as a route by which some of the people of Malden and Amherstburg could send their most precious possessions to safety.

Lake Huron, or so it seemed to one American newspaper, was now a U.S. field of control. In consequence of the fall of Malden, Lake Huron "must own the sovereignty of *the striped bunting*,' as the English in derision call our flag." The illustrious periodical, *Niles' Weekly Register* of Baltimore, ever hungry for victory in northern lands and waters, similarly imagined great gains to be forthcoming in the upper lakes in consequence of Perry's victory: "The reader will easily imagine the entrance of some part of our squadron into Lake Huron, immediately on the capture of Malden; and in his mind's eye behold them scouring the whole shore of that lake and of Michigan, breaking up all the posts and factories of the white enemy and chastening his red allies, with a celerity and perfection of vengeance that belongs to their crimes." Michilimackinac would soon pass, automatically, into American hands. St. Joseph Island and garrison, too remote for communications or succor, would likewise be given up to U.S. forces. All places for the resupply of the Indians would be destroyed. Indian allies of the British, so dependent on gifts and supplies from Canada, would perish by the thousands for want of food and clothing. The North West Company, "a mighty mercantile establishment, of critical importance to Canada, and of great consideration with the Mother Country," would be knocked on the head. In the next four weeks all these things might conceivably be accomplished. The tide of American military power in the continental heartland was rising quickly.

In consequence of Perry's predominance, Procter and the Right Division fell back from his advanced position. With him Procter had no more than eight or nine hundred regulars, including many who were ill or otherwise unfit for service.

In making his preparations for retreat Procter was embroiled in controversy with Tecumseh and other Indians, who could not be appeased. Tecumseh knew that a great naval battle had occurred on Lake Erie but remained in the dark as to its outcome. Receiving no official information about the loss of the British fleet he was left to draw his own conclusions. To him the failure of the British men-of-war seemed ominous. Native informants brought him news of Procter's downcast appearance and of his preparations to retreat.

At this juncture, on 12 September, Procter knew that the American fleet and Army, then reported among the islands in Lake Erie, would soon make their appearance at Fort Malden. He made hurried preparations to leave Amherstburg. Forces at Detroit and Malden needed time to quit their posts in safety, leaving nothing for the enemy soon to cross the Detroit River. The situation all around him was deteriorating on a daily basis. On the twenty-second Procter ordered the burning of the dockyard at Amherstburg. With his army he marched to Sandwich, opposite Detroit. He retired from all his strongholds. Everything was destroyed or taken away by the British in the course of their withdrawal.

Six days after learning of Barclay's defeat Procter met Tecumseh in council. Procter informed Tecumseh of the outcome of the battle, confirming what the patriot chief already knew. Procter warned that a large army under General Harrison was preparing to invade Upper Canada. Procter's plan was to abandon Detroit, Sandwich, and Amherstburg, to withdraw from this exposed frontier, which Procter knew was so poorly protected with forts and ordnance, and to draw back to the Niagara Peninsula to join with other British forces. Procter called upon Tecumseh and his followers to keep the alliance. And he told them to effect the withdrawal.

The angry and determined Tecumseh, imagining his great and heroic quest for a pan-Indian state disappearing before his very eyes on the field of battle, urged Procter in the name of all Indian chiefs and warriors to fight directly and aggressively. He pleaded, in what is regarded as one of the most celebrated speeches of any patriot chief, for the British to make a joint stand. He did not stop there, so passionate was he in his beliefs. He declared that the Indians would stay and fight alone even if the British decided to retreat.

Major John Richardson, present for the occasion, recorded the intensity of the event, one of the poignant moments in the western frontier war:

> The scene altogether was of the most imposing character. The council room was a large, lofty building, the vaulted roof of which echoed back the wild yell of the Indians [in dismay of Procter's news]; while the threatening attitude and diversified costume of these latter formed a striking contrast with the calm demeanor and military garb of the officers grouped around the walls. The most prominent feature in the picture, however, was Tecumseh. Habited in a close leather dress, his athletic proportions were admirably delineated, while a large plume of white ostrich feathers, by which he was generally distinguished, overshadowing his brow,

and contrasting with the darkness of his complexion and the brilliancy of his black and piercing eye, gave a singularly wild and terrific expression to his features. It was evident that he could be terrible.

"Father—listen!" Tecumseh urged. "Our fleet has gone out; we know they have fought; we have heard the great guns." The Indians knew nothing of what had happened to Barclay, "our father with one arm." Further, "our ships have gone one way, and we are much astonished to see our father tying up everything and preparing to run away the other [way], without letting his red children know what his intentions are." And again: "Listen, Father! The Americans have not yet defeated us by land; neither are we sure that they have done so by water: we therefore wish to remain here, and fight our enemy, if they should make their appearance. If they defeat us, we will *then* retreat with our father."[40]

Tecumseh challenged the British to hold the ground, to face head-on the advancing U.S. forces. Procter had no such predilection. The disgust of Tecumseh was unconcealed. This last speech by the great Shawnee orator illustrated the desperation of the Indian cause at that moment.

By quiet diplomacy held in private quarters Procter convinced Tecumseh of the reasonableness and necessity of retiring. Only that way could the little army be extricated from its perilous dilemma. Indian agent Col. Matthew Elliot was there with Tecumseh, and a map of the country was produced to show that sooner or later the imperial forces would be surrounded and cut off. Tecumseh did an about-face, acknowledged the necessity of withdrawal, and in his last act of statecraft convinced his native allies to join in common cause.[41]

Perry, meanwhile, was aided by many advantages—the blessings of victory, the freedom of resupply, the ability of movement, the advantage of initiative. Even so, he had to bide his time and allow the Army to gather its forces for the strike upon Upper Canada's western spearhead. In addition, the Navy had to gather its vessels. By 27 September, when General Harrison's army was embarked, the fleet consisted of nine men-of-war and some eighty boats. The staging ground was Middle Sister Island, a small island four miles from Fort Malden. During these operations, observed Perry, utmost harmony existed between the Army and the Navy.[42]

At 3:00 P.M. on 27 September U.S. forces under Harrison landed on the Canadian shore. They did so at a place recommended by Perry, who had spied out the terrain in the schooner *Ariel*. This was three miles below or south of

Malden. Once landed, the troops marched up to the smoldering ruins of Fort Malden without opposition. With Harrison were forty-five hundred men. Harrison now detached seven hundred men under Gen. Duncan McArthur to repossess Detroit, and this was accomplished with the capture of British troops and the defeat of native allies. Other Indians took evasive action. "No opportunity was offered to the officers under my command to shew their Gallantry," said Perry in his report to the secretary of the navy, "but Sir, they evinced throughout, the greatest disposition to be serviceable in transporting the Army and rendering it, every assistance in their power."

On the thirtieth Perry sent the *Niagara, Lady Prevost, Scorpion,* and *Tigress* into Lake St. Clair in pursuit of British vessels said to be loaded with baggage and artillery. They did not find them. He personally took the *Ariel,* accompanied by the *Caledonia,* into the River Thames, there to cooperate with the Army. The *Porcupine* was also engaged in this service. Meanwhile, other vessels were employed transporting troops and provisions for the land forces. American naval dominance flowed upstream on the Thames, and Perry said the gunboats *Scorpion* and *Tigress,* joined by the *Porcupine,* were the only vessels able to cross the bar, with six feet six inches clear of the ground. They were effective upriver until such time as the river banks became too high or too thickly forested for their guns to be of use. They got as far upriver as a place called McCrea's, all the while keeping company with the Army. There they waited the course of the pending battle under guard of 150 infantry. After the defeat of the British, they took back a large quantity of captured ammunition and stores.

Meanwhile, Harrison lost no time in carrying his plans into effect. On the twenty-seventh his army (embarked at Portage) landed at Sandwich and Malden. Three days later, that is, on the thirtieth, the Kentucky mounted infantry, numbering a thousand men, arrived on Upper Canada's soil. The "mounted infantry" were, for the most part, Kentucky trappers and hunters, inured to the wilderness. They were fighters for whom the Indians had a chronic hatred. They had no polish as cavalry, only masterful abilities in harassing a retreating foe, dismounting when the time came, and pursuing the enemy with the fatal rifle. When followed by a foot soldier, the mounted Kentucky pioneer had deadly effect in a skirmish in wooded or parkland territory.[43] They had come north to assist at Fort Meigs, to recapture Detroit, and to carry the war into British territory. At their head was Col. Richard M. Johnson, a congressman who had trumpeted the conquest of Canada and who was now being given his opportunity. For days on end Johnson's mounted infantry gave chase to the British and their fifteen hundred native allies—up the River Thames.

Procter decided to make a stand at Moraviantown. But was equally determined not to be trapped there, conscious as he was of the size and resources of American forces flowing across the Detroit River. The ground was covered by beech, intermixed with maple and oak, but free from undergrowth. The field of battle was cut up by swamp and marsh. The British had drawn up between a swamp and the Thames River, therefore forming the left wing; the Indians formed the right wing. The British were spread too thin to keep close order. Harrison, acting on intelligence brought to him about the "opening of their files," determined to exploit this weakness by a stroke later understood as *concentration*, that is, refusing one wing to the enemy and reinforcing the other. Harrison decided to send in his power. "It is a blunder," said Harrison on receiving this news, "that they shall repent: we must alter our disposition; instead of sending Johnson to the swamp, he shall charge the British lines. Although without sabres, and armed with muskets and rifles, he will break through them." That he did, with the infantry following on to "take advantage of their confusion and complete their discomfiture." The 41st Regiment fired only one volley, and then with cavalry thundering through them, their loose ranks collapsed and they either retreated hastily or were captured on the spot.

The Americans took a great number of prisoners: 601. American losses were 7 killed and 22 wounded; British losses, 12 killed and 22 wounded. Eight pieces of artillery came into American hands, and among the trophies were three pieces from the Revolutionary War taken at Saratoga and York and surrendered by General Hull. A great number of small arms, estimated at upward of five thousand, were captured or destroyed. The 41st Regiment had not made its appearance; had it done so, claimed Harrison, it would have been taken on the field of battle. Thus ended the Battle of the Thames of 5 October.[44]

A few additional details, important in the larger story, may here be stated. The great Tecumseh fell in battle. Procter narrowly escaped, leaving his horse, chaise, sword, and papers on the road. Commodore Perry was there, as an aide-de-camp to General Harrison. Gen. Lewis Cass, later to feature in this account as governor of Michigan Territory, was there too, in a similar capacity.

No Indians were captured, but many were slain. "The only real resistance was put up by the Indians on the British right," concluded historian Reginald Horsman, who examined British and American records. "They fought with all the bravery and desperation induced by their long sufferings."[45] No ordinary battle to these Indians, this constituted their last stand, or more correctly, an episode in a much longer struggle to protect lands and rights. "Since our great chief Tecumtha has been killed," moaned the Ottawa chief Newash, "we do not listen to one another, we do not rise together. We hurt ourselves by it."[46]

Eventually Procter reached the head of Lake Ontario with his remaining troops. In December in Montreal he was court-martialed for his conduct, was found guilty on four counts, received a public reprimand, was sentenced to loss of rank and pay for six months, and remained on the Army's unattached list.[47] Procter tried to blame his troops, and Prevost issued an order of blanket reprobation on all concerned. The historian of his regiment has the most damaging retrospective on Procter: "The truth is that he was a bad and incompetent officer, who had been saved many times from the consequences of his own incapacity by the 41st, and in return for their good service had so mishandled the Regiment that they would work for him no longer."[48]

In retrospect, Perry's crushing victory placed Procter in disadvantageous circumstances. No commander could have stood the ground against such overwhelming force as the enemy then possessed. Procter's intentions differed from Tecumseh's requirements. But Procter's withdrawal was ineffective and muddled. He took too much time. The Indians had pressed upon him their urgent demands. Procter erred in waiting too long to take evasive action, and in the end he lost his army, his reputation, and, above all, his stout ally Tecumseh and his friends. It would take some considerable diplomacy, gift giving, and energetic commitment for the British to keep the devotion, self-interested or not, of their native allies.

While the southwestern frontier of British interests lay in chaos in late 1813, urgent preparations had to be taken to keep what little authority the Imperial forces had, and the only future lay farther north, on Lake Huron. Detroit had returned to American hands. Lake Erie had become an American lake.

The struggle for control of the inland seas now shifted northward to waters that never before had seen an American man-of-war. Washington gave Perry discretionary powers as to whether to stay or go. "Although there is much of importance yet to be done upon the Upper Lakes, which I should like you to bring to maturity," advised the secretary of the navy, "yet, if you think the service will not suffer by your absence, you are at liberty, as soon as the public interest shall admit of your departure, to proceed to Rhode Island and resume your command there." Perry was promoted to the coveted rank of captain and resigned his command, leaving it to Commo. Arthur Sinclair and another warring season.

In London the cold hand of responsibility had been placed upon the duke of Wellington's shoulders. Want of sufficient naval forces on the Great Lakes was being heavily felt. The Put-in-Bay disaster even blunted Wellington's enthusiasm for fighting a North American campaign. "I believe that the defence of Canada and the co-operation of the Indians depends upon the navigation of the lakes," he advised Earl Bathurst on 22 February 1814, "and I see that both Sir G. Prevost and Commodore Barclay complain of the want of the crews of two sloops of war. Any offensive operation founded upon Canada must be preceded by the establishment of a naval superiority on the lakes." And with a specific reference to the strategic geography of North America, he concluded, "In such countries as America, very extensive, thinly peopled, and producing but little food in proportion to their extent, military operations by large bodies are impracticable, unless the party carrying them on has the uninterrupted use of a navigable river or very extensive means of land transport, which such a country can rarely supply."[49]

III

~

The Nancy and Her Escape

SEASON'S CLOSE

he struggle for the Great Lakes, it has been often said, was a shipbuilders' war, but inasmuch as men-of-war could not be constructed in sufficient numbers for the annual summer campaigns,
many of the vessels that fought these campaigns were brought up from trade.
One such was the *Nancy*. She was an ordinary vessel for her period, much like
the American topsail schooners *Hamilton* (built in Oswego, New York, in 1809)
and *Scourge* (the former Canadian merchant vessel *Lord Nelson* built at what is
now Niagara-on-the-Lake in 1810–1811), which went down in a squall in 1813
and lay undisturbed until found in southwestern Lake Ontario 160 years later.
What has been written of the *Hamilton* and *Scourge* could be said of the *Nancy*:
"They were the transport trucks of their time, and as such are extraordinarily
important as representatives of traditional shipbuilding techniques of the early
nineteenth century."[1] Each had been pressed into military service. So it was
with the *Nancy*.

In late summer 1790 Messrs. Forsyth, Richardson and Company, a Montreal
firm prominent in the Old Northwest fur business, ordered a stout schooner to
be built at the shipyard at Detroit. "The schooner," boasted John Richardson, one
of the partners who went to Detroit to oversee the contract, "will be a perfect
masterpiece of workmanship and beauty." He confessed that "the expense to us
will be great," but with optimism he added, "There will be the satisfaction of her

being strong and very durable. Her floor timbers, keel, keelson, stem, and lower futtock are oak. The transom, stern-post, upper futtocks, top timbers, beams, and knees are all red cedar." The vessel, very commodious, could carry 350 barrels. A figurehead of a lady dressed in the present-day fashion, with a hat and feather, was ordered from the carver Skelling of New York. On 24 September the *Nancy*— "a most beautiful and substantial vessel"—met the waters of Detroit.

As for many a vessel launched from this yard, the inland seas offered a vast field for mercantile enterprise. In Great Lakes history the epic doings of the schooner *Nancy* play out a haunting scene in the tragic drama being exhibited on Lakes Erie and Huron. This heroic little sailing vessel's daring-do became in time the "stuff of legend," and the *Nancy* arose to the exalted status of one of the most famous vessels in Canadian and Great Lakes history. She plied Lakes Erie, St. Clair, and Huron for an unprecedented twenty-four years, led a harrowing existence in the War of 1812, and met a fiery end in the last year of the conflict.

Her beginning was a work-a-day affair, and she even bore a common name for ships of the era. She may have been named for Richardson's wife or daughter. She is not to be found listed among the dozen or so of the very same name, of the same era, in *Lloyd's List*. Why, in fact, she was called *Nancy* we have no clue. In any event she was a handsome craft. "She is spoken of here," attested Richardson proudly from Niagara, "in such a high strain of encomium as to beauty, stowage, and sailing, that she almost exceeds my expectations."[2] She measured sixty-seven tons burden. It is believed that her length was approximately eighty feet, her beam twenty-two, and her depth of hold eight.[3] She would have had, in addition to her master, a nominal crew of eight. In 1813, before she was taken over by the Navy, she had a mate, cook, carpenter, carpenter's mate, and four seamen.

In her early years the *Nancy* passed, as did all such fur-trading vessels on the upper Great Lakes, a humble and prosaic existence. Her task was to shift various supplies from Fort Erie, Lake Erie's portage near the Niagara River entrance, destined for the interior country, even for far-off Athabasca (in present-day northern Alberta), where Nor'Westers Peter Pond and Sir Alexander Mackenzie had opened bountiful commerce with the Cree and Chipewyan. Springtime in the year 1790 (and for many thereafter) found the schooner at the east end of Lake Erie, there to take on premier cargo for Sault Ste. Marie for transhipment to Grand Portage, at the westernmost rim of Lake Superior, almost a thousand miles away. The *Nancy* carried on this occasion as on others pots, axe heads, nails, blades, and arms and ammunition. She also took liquor and tobacco, woolen goods, and trinkets—

all precious goods with which to facilitate trade and engender native alliances upon which fortunes of the Nor'Westers depended so mightily.

The *Nancy* was an enabler of empire. At the close of every season, she freighted the fabulous wealth of the northern forest outward bound from Sault Ste. Marie and Michilimackinac for transhipment to Montreal and thence to auction in London. Beaver, marten, fisher, and other pelts all made fine skins for market. The *Nancy,* for a dozen years, kept up this profitable, necessary life-line of the Canadian economy. One of many such schooners of the North West Company's constituent firms, she was seen in many major ports of call— Michilimackinac, St. Joseph Island, Detroit, Amherstburg, Malden, and Fort Erie. Down the years she passed from one owner to another, as merchant vessels often do, and at one time the noted trader and traveler Sir Alexander Mackenzie had at least a share in her.

The *Nancy* became caught up in the fortunes of war. No sooner had news of the outbreak of hostilities in 1812 reached the British commandant of the garrison at Amherstburg, Lieutenant Colonel St. George, than he ordered the *Nancy* brought from McIntosh's wharf at nearby Moy, on the east side of present-day Windsor, to lie under the guns of the fort. His intention was twofold: first, to keep her out of American hands; second, to use her for future action. Some light brass guns, with which she had been armed, were taken as armament for rowboats on river patrol. She was described as capable of mounting six 4-pounder carriage guns besides six swivel guns, but what main armament she had is not known. Presumably she was regummed and made ready as a transport. From this point on she could be styled officially as His Majesty's Schooner *Nancy.*

In her first war service, on 30 June 1812, she steered for Fort Erie with the Provincial Marine's schooner *Lady Prevost*. On her return she sailed in company with the armed brig *General Hunter* and carried military stores and sixty men of the 41st Regiment of Foot, which participated in the British capture of Detroit. That particular summer, and the early autumn, the *Nancy* shifted back and forth between Detroit and Fort Erie. Thus did she continue her labors— a workhorse for British military needs on this besieged western frontier. Her skipper, the feisty and independent Capt. Alexander Mackintosh, knew hers was a life of evasion, her every requirement to stay out of the hands of American foes. One of her most celebrated duties came in late April 1813, when she sailed in the company of a few vessels carrying General Procter's division from Amherstburg to Maumee River and Bay (adjacent to present-day Toledo, Ohio), destined for the siege of Fort Meigs.[4]

How long she could survive in the face of rising U.S. dominance on these lakes remained in doubt. It is said that Mackintosh kept a barrel of gunpowder on deck at the ready so that he could blow up the vessel rather than have her fall into enemy hands. All along the Detroit frontier the British Army was waging a wilderness war against rising American forces. Beginning 31 July the *Nancy* worked in partnership with the fifty-nine-ton *Ellen,* also taken into the public service. Throughout August these vessels and others, including the *Chippewa,* worked the shallow, uncharted waters of the Ohio shore, moving thirty-five miles away from the Maumee River (as circumstances dictated) into the Sandusky River below Fort Stephenson, an American post then under siege by the British.

Sooner or later the ring of fire would lick at the British Army and its transport vessels, all of them hard-pressed on this borderland. The *Chippewa* would be lost at Put-in-Bay. The *Ellen* was burned by orders on 3 October, as the British force made its retreat up the Thames River.

Meanwhile, on 31 August, the *Nancy* sailed from Moy. She shaped a course for Michilimackinac, 280 miles distant, heavily laden (her draft being measured at an alarming seven feet two inches) with stores and provisions, mainly flour. She also carried from Moy a few passengers, most notably Capt. Richard Bullock of the 41st Regiment and his family, plus some agents and civilians.[5] Bullock was to relieve Captain Roberts, the commandant at Michilimackinac. The voyage consumed ten days, seven of which were spent struggling against currents of the St. Clair River leading to Lake Huron.

During this mission and its return Mackintosh of the *Nancy* could only learn, by bits and pieces, what was transpiring ashore: imperial fortunes were daily decaying. For instance, on 3 September, during the passage to Michilimackinac, the *Nancy* was at the mouth of the St. Clair River. "We were this day," notes the ship log, "informed by an Indian Chief called Black Bird that on the 1st Gen'l Procter with all his Troops had gone to Amherstburg, on the Am'n Fleet appearing off that place to the number of 5 sail." Mackintosh made inquiries ashore, but all informants, native and French Canadian, advised that the situation was desperate on the western frontier: Detroit and Amherstburg had passed to American hands. American cavalry were reported coming up along the riverside toward the *Nancy.* The schooner had lost her largest anchor, the "best bower," in Lake Huron. Accordingly, the *Nancy* had come down into the St. Clair, taken up a waiting position on the lee shore, hoping to put passengers from Michilimackinac ashore at a safe and convenient spot.

On the sixth an Indian brought Mackintosh news that American horse, or cavalry, were on their way upriver toward the schooner. Mackintosh had been on the lookout for American gunboats working north on the British side. He sent a scout downriver; meanwhile, he made preparations to blow up the *Nancy* at the first sign of a skirmish with the Americans. The *Nancy* sported two guns, and Mackintosh had shifted them to one side of the vessel in order to deal with any attackers thought to come from that side. In any event, at this juncture Captain Maxwell, a British Army officer, and his family were hurriedly placed ashore. They were immediately captured by the Americans.

"Soon after, which was about 1 P.M.," wrote Mackintosh, "some person sung out from the woods to surrender the vessel, that my property & that of the men's should not be touched." In his report to Captain Bullock, Mackintosh reported the action more thoroughly: "About noon a white flag was seen coming towards us in a canoe. About half an hour afterwards I was hailed from the shore by a Canadian, ordering me to give up the vessel, and [saying] that my property, as also that of the crew, should be respected. I went ashore to see who this man was. It was Lieutenant Colonel Beaubien, of the militia, who wished me to surrender the vessel to him, repeating what he had already said."[6]

One authority says Beaubien and the alleged fifty militia he commanded were either armed enemies or armed traitors. "He then said if I attempted to go out of the river he would fire on me the moment I should heave up, to which I replied I would return the fire." In fact, this is what happened. Mackintosh was making ready to leave, and was "fishing the anchor" when "they gave us a volley."[7] This the *Nancy* returned, and kept up for a quarter of an hour until clear of Beaubien and company.

Having fought off American militia demanding her surrender, then fought the current in order to regain Lake Huron, she recovered her "best bower anchor," which had been previously left there buoyed. The *Nancy* returned to Lake Huron unharmed.

The doughty master of the *Nancy* again shaped a course for Michilimackinac. Having escaped this difficulty the *Nancy* now faced another: a great storm. Here it may be noted that in 1679 LaSalle and his crew of forty in the barque *Griffon*, built at Cayuga Creek above the Niagara Falls and equipped at Black Rock, had shaped an intended course for much the same destination, St. Ignace of Michilimackinac. "For a time they bore on prosperously," wrote Francis Parkman of this first time that sail was seen on Lake Huron. The wide expanse of the lake spread before them like a sea. "Then," he continued, "the wind died

to a calm, then freshened to a gale, then rose to a furious tempest; and the vessel tossed wildly among the short, steep, perilous waves of the raging lake." Even
LaSalle urged his followers to commend themselves to heaven. They were on
storm-tossed Lake Huron for two weeks or so. They survived, boasted the soldier and empire builder Henri de Tonty, LaSalle's associate, the worst storm that
could be experienced on the most stormy seas.[8]

On 7 October 1813 the *Nancy* repeated the Lake Huron career of LaSalle's
flagship. After an unwelcome time, the sails of the *Nancy* filled at last, and she
soon chased away to the north, away from any American pursuers. Lake Huron's
calm gave way, as it customarily does, to a raging storm.[9] Before daybreak on
the eighth the *Nancy* was scudding under only her foretopsail. A tremendous
sea ran for five days. The *Nancy*'s log reports mountainous seas, dismal nights,
and frequent squalls heavy with snow and sleet.

For several days she sailed fearful waters choked with shoals and islands.
"What now must the reader think of our situation," runs the frank log entry
for 12 October, "on a lee shore, riding out a most violent gale of wind in the
month of October, with 2 very indifferent cables, & them of only 60 fathoms
each in length, with a scanty stock of provisions, consisting of one ps. of pork
& 1/2 a quarter of mutton? Tis true we had enough Biscuit, but what nour-
ishment was it for men constantly wet & wore out?"[10] The morning brought
no relief from relentless wind and weather: "At daylight our situation was
indeed a most critical one,—shoals in every direction leeward of us, with
some Islands which would have given us some shelter were we under their
lee, but we dare not attempt to weigh [anchor to proceed there] lest we be cast
upon the shoals."

The master would have preferred the Michigan shore of Lake Huron, which
was protected from southwesterlies. Instead, the *Nancy* was on the eastern, or
Canadian, shore in cold and severe weather about eighty miles north of the
rapids of River St. Clair, perhaps Clark Point, or Pine Point, as it was then called
(where the first navigational light consisted of a lighted lamp hung in a pine
tree). On the fourteenth an Indian canoe came alongside and the *Nancy* hoisted
British colors, the signal of alliance. The natives told the men of the *Nancy* that
they were in the neighborhood of La Cloche, with its white hills, that is, the
North Channel. La Cloche means the steeple, visible at a distance. Here lay a
new set of navigational dangers. The master soon altered course for Thunder
Bay, on the west side of Lake Huron, not a great distance from her position
before the storm. Within a few days, on the eighteenth, they were able to cast

anchor off the garrison and fort at Michilimackinac. There they discharged a few supplies and all the carefully guarded cargo of gunpowder.

The *Nancy*'s condition at this time may be described as disheveled. However, the British military department, desperate for transport, demanded yet another passage of the schooner—to Matchedash Bay, at the mouth of the Severn River in Georgian Bay, there to take on additional supplies for Michilimackinac. The month was now November, Huron's most treacherous season. Mackintosh did not want to chance it, the vessel being weak in sails and rigging. He accordingly demanded a survey, as was his right. Captain Bullock was obliged to grant one. The examining committee, under order dated 25 October, found that the schooner was not safe to be sent to Matchedash Bay on account of the insufficiency of her sails and cables. There was talk of cutting her down to the dimensions of a gunboat and arming her with four field guns (brought from Nottawasaga River) that would stand beside her own carronades. She escaped this fate, for such modification was pointless given the circumstances. Instead, she was sent to Sault Ste. Marie for repairs and reequipping. The officers and crew went into winter quarters. It seems to have been a cold but pleasant winter, for both the North West Company officers and the British military department were well fixed for rum and provisions. The season of hibernation was short, and with ice breakup another fighting campaign would begin.

Nancy led a furtive life in 1814. First she sailed for the Nottawasaga River entrance on 26 May to take on supplies delivered to the depot, Schooner Town, near the mouth of the river. Back she went to Michilimackinac carrying provisions for the garrison, presents for the natives, and supplies for the North West Company. By 17 July she had completed another return voyage bearing supplies that the commissariat had brought downstream to the Nottawasaga's mouth. She managed a third passage to and from Nottawasaga before McDouall decided to take her out of service, a subject to which we will return.

At this time a change of plans was thrust upon the British. Many more ships like the *Nancy* were required. In consequence of the American victory at Put-in-Bay, British commanders such as Captain Bulloch received notice from Major General Procter that supplies needed to be centered on Machedash Bay, in the southeastern corner of Georgian Bay, for forwarding to Michilimackinac. Under such disadvantageous circumstances—thrown back on the Niagara frontier, the head of Lake Ontario and York—the British made plans to build gunboats at Matchedash Bay. Their task would be to keep open the lifeline to Michilimackinac and into the interior.

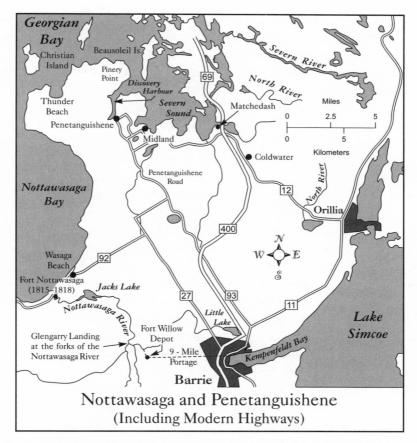

Nottawasaga and Penetanguishene
(Including Modern Highways)

The first British naval base and depot was at the mouth of the Nottawasaga River. It was here that U.S. naval vessels under Commodore Sinclair took such action as ended the career of the famous British schooner HMS *Nancy*. Penetanguishene, in the inner reaches of Georgian Bay and linked to supply sources by road, became a superb if small naval base and garrison.

Indian agent Robert Dickson, upon whom much rested for keeping the Old Northwest in imperial interests, called for troops and artillery. He needed to support his personal command, the Michigan Fencibles, who had established a post at Green Bay. At Michilimackinac he needed reinforcements of twenty gunners, two hundred infantry, and four field guns. He also required tremendous quantities of flour and other foodstuffs besides presents for the Indians. Guns and powder were in short supply. All these had to come from Lake Ontario, especially from York and before that Kingston and Montreal. Dickson was not to be disappointed, and the measures taken to resupply him and to bring effective force into Lake Huron and beyond, so little known to history, ought to be the stuff of record and of legend.

In the campaign of 1814, which would start as soon as navigation would open on Lake Huron, the British intended to fight on this frontier with renewed vigor. Hardships lay ahead of them in the type of forest or backwoods warfare that expediency now necessitated. True, they held Mackinac Island as their northern anchor of empire, the key to the straits, to northern trade, and to their Indian alliance. Even so, the place lay exposed to an attack in force, and even a fitful raid at night might cause havoc. Food supplies, always carefully parceled out, could not last indefinitely. The three lifelines of Mackinac Island—to French River on the east, Fort William on the west, and Nottawasaga River and Matchedash Bay on the south— remained tenuous and uncertain. Of these, Nottawasaga River, which flows into Georgian Bay near its southern end, had gained recent prominence as a resupply base and nascent naval depot. *Nottawasaga* means "outburst of the Iroquois" and the river mouth had seen Iroquois outward bound for the northwest frontier.

The urgent need for seamen on Canada's lakes continued, and Commodore Yeo at Kingston worried about inadequate numbers for the various vessels in commission and those being constructed. From HMS *Indian* and other British warships calling at Quebec, 220 seamen were transferred to the lake service. They reached Kingston before the freeze-up of 1813. Yeo, still desperate, requested another 200 to 250 for manning the ships building on Lake Ontario. Inasmuch as there was not hope of bringing such reinforcements in by sea to Quebec, the sole alternative was to march them across from Saint John, New Brunswick, to Quebec, a snowshoe passage of 190 miles, completed 21 January to 22 March 1814.[11]

While the British advanced such arrangements as were necessary for the following spring's campaign, when navigation could resume, they lived in dread of U.S. ships-of-war opening up a spirited campaign against British shipping on the upper lakes. Landings by American amphibious forces were anticipated. British and Indian scouts scanned the horizons at Mackinac Island for enemy sail. Thus, while resourceful forces in the heartland of the Upper Canada peninsula constructed bateaux and hacked pathways through forest over which desperately needed supplies might come north from York to Georgian Bay and Lake Huron, thinking officers such as Lt. Col. Robert McDouall of the Glengarry Light Infantry perfected their plans for the relief of Michilimackinac and the recapture of Prairie du Chien. In so doing they were putting in place one of the most amazing feats of North American military history.

IV

~

The Water Rats

FORT WILLOW AND NOTTAWASAGA, MICHILIMACKINAC, PRAIRIE DU CHIEN

"When Barclay and Procter were defeated in the autumn of 1813 it seemed that there could be no hope for the British at Michilimackinac." So wrote Col. William Wood, prominent early Canadian military historian of the war. To this he added the following curt analysis of British disadvantages: "The regular line by Lake Erie and the Detroit was closed and the other two lines were so roundabout that supplies and reinforcements sent by them could never match those sent by the Americans, who held the easy southern lines. All that was left was one by the Ottawa and Lake Nippising, and another overland to Nottawasaga, which could be reached from York, and which, when reached, offered a line into Georgian Bay and thence across Lake Huron."[1] In these circumstances so much depended on supplies, on depots for supply, and, above all, on communications kept up between Nottawasaga and Michilimackinac.

After the close of the 1813 warring season, when the northern lakes and forests lay under ice and snow—and when winter means of communication came into existence, with snowshoes, skis, and sledges—planners for the next year's campaign busied themselves. Getting men, supplies, and ammunition to the continental heartland constituted the duty of the Quartermaster's Department of the British Army based in Montreal. Similarly, the U.S. Army was resupplied from Philadelphia, Pittsburgh, and elsewhere. Shipbuilders on both sides of Lake Ontario continued their feverish work of readying their fleets for the decisive year on the Lakes campaign. In distant Lake Huron the only indication of anything resembling a unit of naval power was the *Nancy*. Following necessary repairs, required because of October last's tempest, she had come out of the yard at Sault Ste. Marie and sailed to Michilimackinac. There her commander, Captain Mackintosh, was relieved, and a young lieutenant in the Royal Navy was given command.

In the upper lakes the course of the war was shaped now by external forces. While the American warships on the Lakes might have enjoyed local authority, the force of British ascendancy was beginning to throttle American power at its source and heartland. By 1814 Britain was able to shift its great military weight against the United States. Hitherto British statesmen had taken a defensive position, largely content to hold ground against American assaults, or to fight defensive actions to maintain pressure on the enemy. Likewise preoccupied with Napoleon and the French Navy, the Royal Navy had other major duties than effecting a blockade of American ports. But in 1814 that changed greatly, and now the commander in chief on the North America Station had sufficient forces at his disposal to seal up all American ports. Britain proclaimed the whole coastline under blockade. He ordered the raids in the Chesapeake, including the White House, and authorized the taking out of that obnoxious privateering base, Baltimore. The Admiralty likewise made plans for two great operations—an invasion of American territory via Lake Champlain and the assault on what was thought to be the soft underbelly of the enemy, New Orleans and the lower reaches of the Mississippi River. These two enterprises were less than effective, in fact, disastrous to British arms. Yet it speaks to the turn of the tide which gave Britain such advantage that such expeditions could be mounted in the first place. In summarizing the U.S. military response to this sea change it may be noted that the U.S. government "mismanaged its limited opportunities against Canada," says Russell Weigley, the authority on the American way of war, and in doing so squandered its credit with the public for the continued prosecution of the conflict. "Against the ominous prospects of 1814," he continued, "it could do little more than trust in the regional military commanders of the threatened districts to muster enough local manpower and equipment under peril of invasion and to improvise tactics which could turn the threats back."[2] The national military strategy became uncoordinated in consequence: no concentration of American muscle could be made given domestic weakness. Meanwhile, British preponderant power could apply pressure on all frontiers. Thus, when Captain Bullock commanding at Michilimackinac requested reinforcements of two hundred infantry and twenty artillerists, suggesting that a stockaded blockhouse be built on the heights overlooking Fort Mackinac, thereby preventing an American repetition of the British action of 1812, Prevost approved the plan to reinforce Michilimackinac.[3]

At this stage of the interior war, Lt. Col. Robert McDouall of the Glengarry Light Infantry Fencibles makes his appearance.[4] McDouall, born in Stanraer, Scotland, was a veteran of British campaigns in Egypt and at Copenhagen and Martinique. Thus he was no stranger to amphibious operations such as were being entrusted to him in the upper Great Lakes. He also was known to the commanding officer of British forces in Canada, Sir George Prevost, and served under him in the attacks on Sackets Harbor, Niagara, and Stoney Creek. The North West Company's prominent director William McGillivray had carefully briefed him on military requirements for the interior war. Prevost decided to send McDouall to Michilimackinac, there to report on the state of imperial affairs. McDouall had a touch of the messianic about him, and with him, in war, violence had no limit. His hard-hitting actions left the Americans a little breathless, and his superb tactical sense coupled with this great experience in the field was to prove of great value.

McDouall had an immense practicality about himself, and had it in mind that in the absence of a British fleet or other means of transport on Lake Huron gunboats must be built to convey troops and supplies to Michilimackinac. In fact, given the absence of a stout schooner to carry arms, ammunition, and provisions to the isolated Michilimackinac, an armada of small boats would be needed. The choice design was the bateau. Long the favorite of waterways campaigning (Benedict Arnold employed them on the Kennebec River during the 1775 invasion of Quebec, and the French used these watercraft on many a river and lake campaign), they were nominally thirty feet in length, made of pine three-quarter's of an inch in thickness, were shaped like a shallow dory, and could be rowed by four oarsmen on either side. They could hold some forty men and could move through the water under canvas like an ell. Having no keel or dagger board, they were at the mercy of most winds, except a following wind. Their most reliable means of power was oars.

The location chosen for building these necessary craft was hidden in the heart of the Upper Canada bush, at the forks of the Nottawasaga River, a place that came to be known as Glengarry Landing. Here good wood was available, and a dry location to make the craft. The forks of the Nottawasaga lay, in turn, downstream from a place called Willow Creek Depot, or Fort Willow as it is called nowadays, on the upper rivulets of the Nottawasaga River. Here the British kept their supplies and bivouacked for the long winter.

McDouall's approach to the forks of the Nottawasaga River began in severe wintry weather. In February 1814 he quit the comfortable confines of the garrison and naval depot Kingston on Lake Ontario. With McDouall trudged 10 officers, 30 shipwrights, 21 seamen, 11 gunners in charge of four field pieces, and two companies of the Royal Newfoundland Regiment— about 250 men in all. First they had to cross Lake Simcoe, which they did over ice and snow. Once ashore at Kempenfelt Bay, and keeping on a westward course, McDouall and party followed the old Indian trail commonly called Nine Mile Portage. Eventually, after hard slogging, McDouall and company reached the Minesing Swamp.

Here, on a dry promontory, he selected a site suitable for a palisaded fort with assorted storage buildings within. This was called Willow Creek Depot, or Fort Willow. From adjacent heights of land could be seen in the distance the Blue Mountains of the Bruce Peninsula, dividing Georgian Bay from Lake Huron beyond. At Willow Creek Depot they put up, or completed, a cluster of log structures, eight in number, also a blockhouse and a sawpit. They enclosed the depot with a palisade measuring about 190 by 280 feet.

Meanwhile, downstream at the forks of the Nottawasaga, the shipwrights worked steadily to build the new fleet. The work was arduous in midwinter conditions. By mid-April, when spring made its appearance, twenty-nine bateaux were ready for launching upon Willow Creek. Supplies and gear were loaded once the craft were afloat and tested. The war materiel included long cases of guns, lead for making bullets, kegs of ball and powder, boxes of knives and hatchets, and the four field guns. But still the water was too shallow and the river course too dangerous to admit the transport of the soldiers. Accordingly, a march downriver was commenced. The date was 22 April.

So early were the British in their 1814 preparations that ice on the upper parts of the Nottawasaga River was still firm and the men had to open a channel through it. The bateaux slipped downstream in the spring currents. The soldiers trudged through bush and water as required. After two days' travel (and forty miles of progress) on the Nottawasaga River, to which Willow Creek had joined, McDouall's armada arrived at the lower reaches of the Nottawasaga. A landing was made on the west bank of the river near its mouth. And on the night of the twenty-fourth of April, "in a dismal spot upon the northeastern shore of Lake Huron," they encamped.[5] North and west across fields of ice and open water as far as the eye could see, lay Mackinac Island, distant 360 miles. The prospect of crossing the lake was daunting and not for the faint-of-heart.

McDouall, with unimaginable toughness and the memory of Brock under whom he had served as aide-de-camp still fresh, now hastened his plans and prepared for the grand northern voyage. Any bateau that needed repair received attention. Guns, supplies, and foodstuffs were rearranged as required and carefully stowed. Everything stood in readiness, and on 25 April the first campaign of the row-boat war began—from the Nottawasaga destined for Michilimackinac.

The party of Lake Huron argonauts consisted of the Royal Newfoundland Regiment, gunners for two or three 6-pounders and 3-pounders, some Canadian volunteers, and a naval lieutenant and twenty-two subordinate officers and men of the Lake Ontario squadron. Altogether they numbered ninety. They embarked for Michilimackinac in twenty-four bateaux, all deeply laden with military stores and provisions. As adjutant to Lieutenant Colonel McDouall went Lt. Andrew H. Bulger of the Royal Newfoundlanders, a man hungry for promotion and one feeling victimized that others had overlooked his abilities. Like many who accompanied him to Nottawasaga from Kingston that winter of 1813–14, he was a seasoned soldier. Present at the capture of Detroit, he had been in a naval force that harassed the Americans on the Upper St. Lawrence. Besides, the battles at Fort George near Niagara-on-the-Lake, Stoney Creek, and Crysler's Farm were all part of his experience. No Newfoundland son saw more action in this war than Bulger. He was to play a conspicuous role in the wilderness west of Michilimackinac, in the Prairie du Chien campaign. And when in 1847 a campaign medal was struck, finally, for the Great Lakes service during this war, Bulger was the only survivor and thus the only recipient.

"There was no covering for the men," remarked an early historian of Canada in admiration, "suffering from the severity of the season, for 19 days they struggled on the northern waters of Lake Huron, through immense fields of ice, continually exposed to extremely snowy weather, and to intense cold, which would have daunted men less bold and resolute.... These men fulfilled their trust with the greatest intrepidity."[6] Boisterous weather occurred during most of the passage, and for days on end the men battled the elements. Only one bateau was lost, and the little expedition arrived on 18 May without human loss or injury. In this hazardous expedition the officers and men behaved remarkably well.

The garrison at Michilimackinac gave the newcomers a rousing welcome. Immediately, Colonel McDouall set about strengthening the defenses against an attack that he knew would come sooner or later from the American fleet.

Shortly thereafter, many natives arrived to bolster the strength of imperial forces. The energetic, determined Robert Dickson (known as "Red Head" to the natives) brought about two hundred western Indians, mainly Sioux and Winnebagoes, to Michilimackinac. This, in turn, encouraged other natives to join the cause. Others rallied to the flag and acted in self-interest. By the end of June, in fact, enough soldiers and native warriors were there to take the offensive, confident as McDouall was that the fort could be held with a cadre. In the circumstances, his resources were undeniably thin. So while the Americans were making plans to regain Michilimackinac the British in the person of McDouall were doing likewise to regain an ancient Canadian fur-trading post known as Prairie du Chien, about 450 miles distant from Michilimackinac.

One month after arriving at Michilimackinac, in late June, McDouall learned that the Americans had taken Prairie du Chien. He realized that if the enemy was not ousted from that post, "there was an end to our connection with the Indians. . . . Tribe after tribe would be gained over or subdued, & thus would be destroyed the barrier which protects the great trading establishments of the North West & Hudsons Bay Companies."[7]

Prairie du Chien, a handsome field fronting on the east bank of the Mississippi River, measured about six miles long and three wide. It lay immediately upriver of the Mississippi's confluence with the Wisconsin River. As a post it was, said Jonathan Carver, there in 1766, one of the most delightful settlements visited during his wilderness travels, containing in all about forty buildings and upwards of two hundred Indian warriors. About a decade after Carver's visit French Canadian traders arrived and settled. They camped on territory claimed by Spain, and from time to time Spanish river galleys mounting cannon and blunderbusses made voyages of reconnaissance and patrol upriver to it from St. Louis.[8] But new empires were replacing old in rapid succession. Spain's dominion here gave way to France's and in turn to that of the United States (which by the Louisiana Purchase acquired sovereignty). Thus before the War of 1812 it constituted a stout Canadian fur-trading and agricultural post on the Upper Mississippi River. Long after the sovereignty of this territory passed to the United States it remained, in effect, a Canadian fiefdom. This key to the trade of the upper watershed of the great river was similarly invaluable to British Indian agents engendering the military alliance of the natives. Then followed the Battle of Tippecanoe and the burning of the Prophet's town, which so energized Tecumseh to mount his long campaign against the Americans. The Indian patriot cause swept through Wisconsin, Illinois, and Missouri, especially along the Mississippi, as far north as Prairie du Chien.

This Canadian post was a thorn in the side of American commercial and political interests. Western territorial governors, who prepared for an Indian war, grew wary of the Winnebago and the swift revenge that might come in due course from native cries for freedom from encroachment. "Indian hostilities are no longer a matter of conjecture," warned Governor Ninian Edwards of newly erected Illinois Territory in February 1812. Winnebago and Sauk made reprisals early in the war. American officials seem to have done nothing to curb the disaffection. In these circumstances, Dickson's work as British Indian agent was easy: following Brock's message, he began enrolling Indians as auxiliary troops. From frontier requirements derived the Indian alliance with the British against the Americans. Historian Louise Kellogg put it this way: "Thus was the war, which threatened between the Indians and the American frontiersmen, merged in the greater conflict between the two nations."[9]

Dickson knew that British sympathizers at Prairie du Chien would welcome British military support from Michilimackinac. He also knew that many tribes would eagerly enter into a war against the Americans. Dickson decided to lead the Indians, and he took a leading role in the operations on the Detroit frontier. He established a base at Lake Winnebago and there worked up the alliance against the Americans. And he developed a grand strategy for this area, including a defense of Prairie du Chien by Capt. Francis Dease, in command of a small militia force. In consultation with Colonel McDouall at Michilimackinac in June 1814, Dickson received full and unequivocal support for all actions in the interior. Indeed, McDouall commended the Indians to the care of Dickson.

In any combat with the Indians of this region, brutality would become ever apparent: native victors would capture native women and children, kill mothers, and send the children to Quebec as slaves or *panis*. At least one nation, Menominees (or Fallavoines, as the Canadian traders called them), were reputed to kill their own wives and children before they went into battle, so that in case of defeat the enemy could not take any prisoners of the nation. As early as 1780, some Fox near the forks of the Mississippi told some visiting Indians, as the trader and agent John Long recounted, "Brothers, we are happy to see you; we have no bad heart against you; although we are not the same nation by language, our hearts are all the same: we are all Indians, and are happy to hear our great Father has pity on us, and sends us wherewithal to cover us, and enable us to hunt." To this, the visiting chief, Warbishar, an Ottawa, replied,

"It is true, my children, our great Father has sent me this way to take the skins and furs that are in the Dog's Field . . . lest the Great Knives (meaning the Americans) should plunder them."[10]

Native peoples attached to Prairie du Chien held the British alliance in high esteem. The great and first war chief of the Sioux Nation, La Feuille, or the Leaf, put forth this entreaty to Captain Roberts at Michilimackinac on 5 February 1813, at the midpoint of the war: "My Father: As a Cloud is appearing over the heads of thy Children whom thou has put under my care, and that the Americans mean to take possession of this piece of land, I would wish to clear it, but I want your help." He pointed out that whites had sent news to him about the state of affairs at Prairie du Chien. "Come and assist me as soon as possible," he said. To this he added, "I have talked with the Saques [Sauk], Outagamies [Fox], Ouinebagoes, and we have all but one heart." He signed it with his mark, "Thy Friend, La Feuille."[11]

The Indians and mixed-bloods, or Métis, clung faithfully and expectantly but with a growing sense of desperation to their British patron. This is demonstrated in an appeal from the traders of Prairie du Chien to Roberts at Michilimackinac, dated 10 February 1813. "There is no necessity of pointing out to you their intentions," J. Rolette, their representative, wrote of the Americans. "The public talk of all these [Indian] nations was for the purpose of joining themselves to oppose the Americans and prevent their coming up to this place, being convinced that their and their children's lives depend upon it— They do not want good will, but powder and Arms are what they are in need of, and a person to represent the British Government."[12]

In 1814 Prairie du Chien had become an object for U.S. military planners. Indeed, when Dickson was visiting McDouall in Michilimackinac in June, the Americans had already launched their campaign to secure Prairie du Chien and fortify it against the British. On 1 May the Americans, under well-known transcontinental traveler Governor William Clark of Missouri Territory, had left St. Louis in five barges, or keelboats, carrying 61 regulars and 140 volunteers all under his command. Two of the barges were fitted out as gunboats, the larger bearing the name *General Clark*. En route to Prairie du Chien the Americans dealt the Sauk a crippling blow at Rock Island, forcing the native surrender on condition that the Sauk would now take up arms against the Potawatomi and Winnebago. Elsewhere the Fox agreed to similar terms. On 2 June the party reached Prairie du Chien. The Americans took it that day without difficulty, for Captain Dease and his small militia guard retreated to the woods.

Miles

| 0 | 50 | 100 |

| 0 | 50 | 100 | 150 |

Kilometers

← Route of Governor William Clark from St. Louis to Prairie du Chien.

◄--- Route of British expedition to retake Prairie du Chien.

Expeditions to Prairie du Chien, 1814
(State Boundaries Shown)

From Fort Mackinac, a force of Michigan Fencibles under British command went by the old fur-trading route through Green Bay and the Fox-Wisconsin passage to recapture Prairie du Chien, a North West Company post taken by U.S. forces that had traveled upriver on the Mississippi.

At Prairie du Chien the Americans erected a fort 70 feet wide by 130 feet long, in the triangular shape of a ravelin with two bastions in the rear and one toward the river, with earthworks thrown up around.[13] The Americans called the place Fort Shelby, in honor of the governor of Kentucky. Lt. Joseph Perkins, in command, made preparations to hold the post, where the Stars and Stripes first flew over what later became the state of Wisconsin. For his part, a contented Governor Clark moved downstream for St. Louis, leaving behind the two gunboats to protect the post from the riverside. Fort Shelby grew as an American military post, with two blockhouses, each with a cannon, and a ten-foot-high picket enclosure with various log huts to house troops. The detachment under Perkins consisted of 55 privates, 1 fifer, 3 corporals, and 2 sergeants. In the gunboats, together, were 135 volunteers, "dauntless young fellows from this country," said Clark. But on the last day of June one of the gunboats slipped its moorings and moved downriver: the sixty-day term of the volunteers had expired. It was time for them to go home. On board the *General Clark,* the remaining gunboat, all was in readiness for an enemy attack thought likely to come soon. This gunboat, moved opposite the fort, mounted a 6-pounder on her main deck and a 3-pounder.

At Michilimackinac, McDouall learned that an American force had ascended the Mississippi from St. Louis to Prairie du Chien and was busily completing a new fort. This news reached him 22 June. At the risk of weakening his own position, he completed plans to send a force of 150 Michigan Fencibles under command of Lt. Col. William McKay, a Nor'Wester.[14] The Michigan Fencibles, like all voyageur units of the imperial cause in this war, were zealous partisans, and from their superior knowledge of the country and native ways, they rendered material service to the success of British arms.[15] The object of McKay's forces was "to dislodge the American General from his new conquest." McDouall also dispatched a number of officers, including Lieutenant Bulger, some North West Company men who had entered the service of the king, and various agents attached to the Indian Department, accompanied by their native associates. Dickson remained at Michilimackinac. Some indication of tribal sentiments is given in McDouall's observations: "A greater part of my Indian Force was from the countries adjoining La prairie des Chiens, they felt themselves not a little uneasy at the proximity of the enemy to their defenceless families, but on the arrival next day of the Sussell or tête de Chien, a distinguished Chief of the Winebago Nation (who came to supplicate assistance) & on his mentioning the circumstances of its Capture, particularly the deliberate & barbarous murder of seven Men of his own Nation, the sentiment of indignation & desire for revenge was universal amongst them."[16]

McKay, with 75 volunteers and 136 Indians, left Michilimackinac in a canoe on 28 June and reached Green Bay six days later. At this settlement they rested and completed their preparations to advance against the American outpost that stood at the other end of the Fox-Wisconsin waterway. They took in another company of militia, about 30 men, and added some 100 Indians, both Menominee and Chippewa. Six large barges were used in the expedition up the Fox River, and they were flanked by numerous native canoes. At the Wisconsin portage some Winnebago joined them for the passage down the Wisconsin River. McKay sent scouts ahead and from them learned of the state of American defenses and preparations.

On 17 July, a Sunday, the British force, about 650 in all, assembled on the outskirts of Fort Shelby. The imperial forces made, in the words of Lt. Augustin Grignon, "a very formidable display for that quiet place."[17] The Americans were astonished by the sudden arrival of these unwelcome guests. The British with their flags flying and their officers in red coats were a spectacle to behold. McKay sent Lieutenant Perkins a demand to surrender. Perkins replied, sharply, that he was "determined to defend to the last man."[18]

The British opened a steady artillery barrage on the Americans, aided by great marksmanship of a gunner, Bombardier Joseph Keating, and those that served the only British field piece. First they peppered the *General Clark,* which was fixed in such a position off shore so as to train her guns as a defense against any attack from land. Two-thirds of the sixty-eight rounds that Keating's gun fired at the gunboat hit the mark.[19] Under this press of fire, the Americans cut the hawser, allowing the *General Clark* to drift down the river. Then the gun crew turned their attention to the fort. The siege continued. Lieutenant Perkins balked at surrendering; he kept up the defense of Fort Shelby. On second thought—considering his dwindling supplies of ammunition, medical stuffs, the absence of a boat (for escape or communications), lack of water, and the superior numbers of enemy—he decided to capitulate. Thus, after two days' defense against the sole British artillery piece, which had been used to great effect against the gunboat and fort, the Americans, sixty-six in number, put up the white flag. They did so late on the nineteenth.

When McKay received Perkins's appeal to the mercy of British officers, McKay, who happily accepted the flag of truce, warned the Americans not to come out of the fort until the following morning. As he told Perkins, he could not guarantee the safe passage of the Americans in the face of possible Indian reprisal. The American commander readily consented to this, and the next morning, the twentieth, the American forces marched out with the honors of war. "It was a precarious moment. Although a plot was formed by the Winnebago to murder the unarmed soldiers," concluded Kellogg, "McKay and his aids guarded the Americans with assiduous care, and after a day or two placed them and provisions on board one of his own boats, when after giving their parole they were allowed to return to St. Louis." As the same author states, "McKay's conduct at the capture of Fort Shelby greatly redounds to his credit, as a soldier and a Briton."[20]

McKay noted, reviewing the success of the forces under his command, that the Michigan Fencibles, who manned the gun, behaved with great courage, coolness, and regularity. This is an important observation from the commander, for the Michigan Fencibles, a sort of local territorial or home guard, had been raised mainly at Michilimackinac from among fur traders and employees of the Indian Department. Inured to the frontier, they proved themselves to be quintessential bush fighters and, when trained, good gunners.

McKay had a less high regard for his Indian allies, who angered him. "They despise the idea of receiving orders from an officer that does not hold a blanket in one hand and a piece of pork in the other to pay them to listen to what he may have to say," he wrote acidly in his report to McDouall.[21] The Indians could not be restrained—as McKay knew so well. In a way, the Indians as allies were following McKay's plan: once the British commander knew that the one American gunboat, which had left the *General Clark* at Fort Shelby, had drifted downstream, he sent off native runners with kegs of gunpowder and instructions to get the Sauk at the Rock River rapids into action against this boat, which McKay reasoned would likely ground there. Two days after the surrender of Fort Shelby, on 21 July, at the rapids, the Indians discovered six American keelboats—"barges," according to the British document. Three of them (under Maj. John Campbell) were armed, and they lay at anchor for the night during the course of ascending the Mississippi with the intent of relieving Perkins at Fort Shelby. That night, the party of Indians, having in their possession four kegs of gunpowder, fell upon the lowermost barge. The results of this savage vengeance can only be imagined.

At Rock River rapids the Indians were complete in their stroke. McKay, who learned of the event from a few Sauk and two Canadians, described the abject fury of the Indians. The Sauk, Fox, and Kickapoos who engaged in this action lost two men and one woman, he noted. Then he got to the details of native martial technique: "To give an idea how desperate the Indians were, the women even jumped on board with their Hoes &ca, some breaking heads, others breaking casks, some trying to cut Holes in her bottom to sink her, and others setting fire to her Decks—as one of the Barges was making from shore the Ioway that came from McKinac with me, jumped on her deck and with his Hatchet cut a hole, and fired his gun among the Americans in the boat—they plunged into the River and made his escape ashore."[22] "This," reported McKay to his superior, McDouall, on 27 July from Prairie du Chien, "is perhaps one of the most brilliant actions fought by Indians only, since the commencement of the war."[23]

Loss and casualty totals vary widely. The Americans lost at least eight privates and two sergeants, but the British report said that the natives killed about one hundred Americans. They took five pieces of U.S. ordnance—two 3-pounders and three mortars. They burnt the barge. The Americans attached to the other barges, seeing this disaster, and knowing there were British troops at Fort McKay, made their escape. The remaining American boats reached St. Louis on 6 August.

The Americans could not allow their lost Fort Shelby to remain in enemy hands and soon made plans to oust the British from American territory. They also wished to check the Indian threat. A man of ability and future preeminence was detailed for the task. Maj. Zachary Taylor, twenty-nine, a Virginian brought up in Kentucky, already a distinguished commander, was instructed to move upstream from St. Louis to take the post. He led an expedition of three hundred soldiers in eight barges supplied with several cannon. At the Rock River rapids on 4 September Taylor's fleet anchored and faced heavy gunfire from British militia (headed by Capt. Duncan Graham, fur trader turned soldier) and Indians. Little water was left in the river at that late season. Taylor had no room to maneuver, confined as his boats were to the narrow river channel. Troops could not easily be got ashore. No protective gunfire could be given in support of a landing. In the event, discretion seemed the better part of valor, and Taylor ordered a return downstream.

Thus ended the expedition to regain Fort Shelby, the last attempt by U.S. forces to gain control of this key post on the Upper Mississippi and Wisconsin area. This was an early campaign by Taylor against Indians, and later, in 1832, he took part in the Black Hawk War, and still later, in 1837, he prosecuted war against the Seminoles. Commander of the Army of the Rio Grande against Mexico in 1845–46, he became a national hero. This famed frontier warrior became twelfth president of the United States in 1848 but died in 1850 of illness.

Prominent in British countermeasures against Taylor's force had been Capt. Thomas Anderson, McKay's successor in command at Fort McKay (or Shelby as the Americans had called it), the celebrated Sauk chief Black Hawk, and, to repeat, Duncan Graham. "We are determined to dispute the road with them inch by inch," Graham had boasted, and, indeed, they had.[24]

Episodes such as those at Prairie du Chien and the rapids of Rock River, coming as they did in the third year of the war, did wonders to maintain the Indian alliance and keep up imperial influence in the Old Northwest. These military actions in Wisconsin, unknown in Canadian history, hardly ever mentioned in U.S. history textbooks, represented in decisive and clear miniature the character of frontier warfare.

In the interim, and while the Prairie du Chien campaign was in progress, the British planned as best they could for the defense of Michilimackinac. What had been acquired by surprise at the outset of the war had now to be held by resolution, discipline, and heroism. Sooner or later the abundant power of the U.S. Navy's Lake Erie fleet would sail down upon the island fortress and command its surrender by force or starvation.

Holed up at the fort at Michilimackinac, Colonel McDouall worried about diminishing supplies and of the gargantuan appetites of his native allies. In late May he sent General Drummond an urgent appeal. The commissariat under Mr. Crookshank ought, he requested, to deposit immediately at the Nottawasaga River's mouth another three or four hundred barrels of pork and flour. Otherwise, McDouall warned, Michilimackinac would soon be in danger. Already rations to the Indians had been cut back, even at the risk of offending the Indians. Daily he was distributing sixteen hundred pounds of rations. Flour and pork were desperately needed. Also in short supply were twenty stands of arms, left at Lake Simcoe, various stocks and clasps for guns, two hundred more pairs of shoes and four hundred more American socks, leather for shoe repairs, and ten sixteen-gallon casks of rum. The flour and pork, McDouall continued, should be in bags so that it could be stored in canoes, "as I may have no other means of getting them."[25] His lifeline was tenuous, his future bleak.

So excessively powerful were the Americans on the Lakes in naval force that McDouall saw no point in keeping the *Nancy* in service. He "silently acquiesced" to Lieutenant Poyntz's opinion that even if the *Nancy* were fitted out "she could not show herself before the force which the enemy could bring against her, because I derive more advantage from her guns on shore than I have hope of her doing from her being equipped with them."[26]

Lt. Newdigate Poyntz, RN, was McDouall's least favorite ally. McDouall considered Poyntz to be possessed with an overinflated ego. Poyntz showed no appreciation for the nuances, political or otherwise, of joint operations. "Lieutenant Poyntz told me," reported a peeved McDouall, "that he conceived he commanded *all afloat,* and of course the whole expedition, when we were in Batteaux." We do not know what Poyntz thought of McDouall. But McDouall wished "most heartily" that his naval counterpart, Sir James Lucas Yeo, still had under his control on Lake Ontario this "pertinacious Lieutenant . . . who, full of his own consequence, as Commanding on Lake Huron (Comm[anding] what? not a vessel) and a great stickler for naval etiquette, is constantly disposed to cavil, and on the watch for opportunities in his naval capacity, to oppose what I wish."[27] McDouall found Poyntz uncooperative, and the transport of supplies to Michilimackinac was stalled because of the latter's high-handed behavior.

McDouall's advice to Yeo was enough to fix Poyntz's return to Kingston. It was for this reason that the command thus fell to Miller Worsley, whose predominant role in the 1814 British naval operations on Lake Huron are subjects that run through the next two chapters. If Poyntz's behavior had been found so offensive as to justify McDouall's complaint, Worsley's was to prove just the opposite, and the joint measures undertaken in the coming year, against long odds, justified the change of naval command.

V

~

Eagle against the Beaver

COMMODORE SINCLAIR'S
LAKE HURON CAMPAIGN

or the 1814 campaign season in the upper Great Lakes, Secretary of War John Armstrong knew that the British would seek to reestablish their power on the Thames River, in keeping with Governor Simcoe's old heartland-defense concept, and renew their dealings with western tribes. Therefore, Armstrong reasoned, American plans should call for such measures as "to give to our naval means a direction which would best obstruct or defeat such movements or designs." With that in mind, Armstrong wrote, "an order has been accordingly given by the navy department, to employ the flotilla, in scouring the shores of the more western lakes, in destroying the enemy's trading establishment at St. Joseph's, and in recapturing Fort Michilimackinac." For the projected campaign, measures were taken to use Detroit and Malden as garrisons and to assemble five thousand regular troops and three thousand volunteers and militia by 10 June. The tasks would necessarily be as follows: protect Malden and Detroit, make hazardous any British communication with the western Indians, reduce Michilimackinac to a perfectly useless enemy possession, force the abandonment of Fort Niagara, and take from the British their motive for continuing the naval conflict on Lake Ontario.[1] So much depended on the U.S. Navy based at Presque Isle. "Without, however, the aid of naval means this force will be comparatively inoperative, and necessarily dispersed, but with such aid, competent to great objects."

Armstrong knew that every success to American arms hinged on operations on the Niagara Peninsula, the anvil of this war. Armstrong had no love of Lake Erie as a battle zone, for it was a poor way to approach the heart of Upper Canada and was as inconvenient in that regard as Lake Ontario. He contended that the best way would be to strike at Burlington and York, that is, around the left and right flanks of the Niagara Peninsula, and thus establish a barrier. He had even less fondness for Lake Huron as a place to campaign. He was reluctant to commit forces to this theater, for this was likely to be a waste of men and ships that might, in any event, be better employed elsewhere, particularly on Lake Ontario, thus easing Maj. Gen. Jacob Brown's intended entry into Upper Canada. The Cabinet was divided on the Lake Huron adventure. Even Secretary of the Navy William Jones was reluctant.[2] Such resistance and dissension could not overcome the necessity of dealing with British forces in the continental interior. The U.S. Navy and U.S. Army were of necessity drawn to Lake Huron, there, with expectation, to destroy this back door of Upper Canada so dangerously open to trade and infiltration by the enemy and his native allies.

Armstrong knew that as the secretary of war he could not direct the forthcoming war effort on Lake Huron without complete support and cooperation from his counterpart, the secretary of the navy. The respective departments began willingly enough. War planning in Washington proved easier than that in the field.

On 1 April, in conformity with directions from the secretary of the navy, Commodore Chauncey instructed the master commandant at Erie, Jesse Elliott, to prepare the brigs *Niagara* and *Lawrence* and other such vessels as required for proceeding into Lake Huron as soon as the ice would permit. The objective was to reduce the posts of the enemy in that lake. The directive called for Elliott to go to Put-in-Bay, take command of two ships waiting there, and sail for Detroit, mooring his vessels under protection of that garrison.

Chauncey further advised Elliott:

I have applied to the Secretary of War for a detachment of 6 or 700 men under the command of a judicious officer to accompany you into Lake Huron. I presume that the Secretary will instruct the Commanding General at Detroit to furnish the men which you will receive on board and proceed with all possible expedition to Michilimackinac, make your arrangements, land and take the Fort if it can be done without too great a Sacrifice. If you leave a Garrison and proceed with the Fleet and remainder of the troops and reduce St. Josephs and any other posts or places that you hear of—If Machedash (the place where the Enemy is building two vessels) could be destroyed it would be of very great importance but it ought to be approached with great caution as I understand that it is some distance up a River and no doubt well guarded. You will therefore inform yourself well upon every point [before] you put too much at hazard. After accomplishing these objects upon Lake Huron you will cooperate with the Army upon any enterprize where the Enemy can be annoyed.[3]

All was well intentioned. Yet delays, both political and military, ensued. The Navy Department worried that, the St. Clair River being so narrow, enemy forces might mount batteries on its banks that could command these waters, putting any American warships that might venture this way at great risk. An additional anxiety was lack of trained sailors, and, in consequence, the need to bring up militia to serve in the ships. The War Department did not share the Navy's worries, and thought that the British were not likely to reinstate themselves on the eastern banks of the Detroit River and on Lake Huron. Indeed, Army intelligence advised, no British forces were known to be within one hundred miles of the intended passageway.

Elliott's responsibilities for carrying out the Lake Huron campaign fell to Capt. Arthur Sinclair. Washington had decided to establish a separate command for Lake Erie. "The enemy, it is understood, is making efforts to create a force on Lake Huron, and the moment is at hand when our Squadron on Lake Erie must be actively employed, not only in keeping secure possession of that Lake, but a part of the Squadron must immediately proceed into Lake Huron, in order to rout the enemy, retake Michilimackinac, take St. Joseph, and thus secure the entire command of the Upper Lakes." These instructions from the Navy Department, dated 15 April, invested Sinclair with the command on Lake Erie and called for him, with his stout fleet of seventeen vessels, to prosecute the war against the enemy with energy. In particular, Sinclair's instructions called for him to (1) prevent the enemy from gaining any ascendancy, (2) attain the complete command of all the waters between Erie and Lake Superior, and (3) reduce the posts of Michilimackinac and St. Joseph as well as that at the mouth of the French River. The seventeen vessels were considered to be more than sufficient for these tasks. Sinclair was to hide away the *Detroit* and *Queen Charlotte* in Erie Harbor, the former Presque Isle, in such a secure place so that the enemy could not recover them. For the Lake Huron campaign Sinclair's first task at Presque Isle was to enter into correspondence with his counterpart, Lt.

Col. George Croghan, commanding at Detroit, "asking of him all the information he may possess relative to the passage into, and navigation of Lake Huron; and of all the circumstances connected with your expedition, the nature and extent of which you will explain to him."[4]

And what of the force of the enemy? Sinclair was told that two small detachments of British seamen and mechanics had been sent to Lake Huron:

> They are constructing some sort of Naval Force. Rumour says two Brigs, but if the fact is so, they must be of small force. They are also said to be building a number of Boats on Lake Simcoe, and have recently transported considerable quantities of Naval and Ordnance Stores to York. . . . The Boats are doubtless intended to convey these stores, through the waters emptying from Lake Simcoe into Lake Huron at Gloucester Bay, on the E.S.E. extremity of Lake Huron. It is on the shore of this Bay they are constructing their Naval Force. For this place you will make a prompt and vigorous push; destroy, or capture, whatever they may have prepared; and, before the alarm can be extended to St. Joseph's, at the Mouth of French River, which place it is expected you may readily reduce, and get possession of all the property and stores deposited there, and leaving a force to protect that port, if tenable, or not liable to be attacked with a superior force, thence proceed to Michilimackinac, which, with the communication of the enemy being entirely cut off, and the place destitute of provisions, will doubtless prove an easy conquest.[5]

In the right hands, these long-winded if precise instructions could have been followed to speedy and successful conclusions. Commodore Sinclair, however, lacked the royal jelly of a good fleet commander. Hypersensitivity, ambition, and anxiety plagued him. Though an able commander of small vessels, he was, writes Christopher McKee, "self-serving, arrogant, and insensitive to the feelings of others, and he had a history of less than excellent relations with his subordinate officers."[6]

His Army counterpart, the young Croghan, age twenty-three, a Kentuckian and an officer of the 17th U.S. Infantry, had stoutly defended Fort Stephenson against General Procter the previous year. Caution was his hallmark. He liked strength in numbers. He organized a force for the Lake Huron campaign, which he classified in complaining tones as "diminutive." Croghan had learned "from the latest Indian account" of the strengths of the enemy's several garrisons of Michilimackinac, St. Marys and St. Joseph. All were stated to be weak, and that of Michilimackinac it was estimated could not exceed forty regulars and Canadians. Even so, Croghan was reticent. To Sinclair he wrote, "I fear, Sir, that

85

in the present reduced state of my force, I shall not be able to afford you any valuable assistance, indeed I cannot (unless previously reinforced) pledge myself to cooperate with you in any way, which would be likely to drain my troops from the *immediate* defence of this place [Detroit] and its dependencies."[7]

Croghan had learned that at Matchedash the British had built twenty-five boats, each carrying two guns, and he concluded that they were probably bateaux used more for provisioning those posts than for acting offensively. He was correct in this assumption. Croghan planned to help the Navy by building a fort (eventually called Fort Gratiot). He explained to Sinclair his reasoning: "I am well aware of the annoyance that your Fleet would meet with in passing up the strait, should the Enemy by batteries, gunboats or otherwise, command to block up the entrance into Lake Huron and shall therefore make immediate preparations for establishing a strong post at the point on which Fort St. Clair formerly stood." On 14 May elements of the 2d Infantry commanded by Capt. Charles Gratiot established Fort Gratiot on the west bank of the St. Clair River, half a mile from the outlet of Lake Huron (now in the town of Port Huron, St. Clair County).[8] Some 150 men were stationed there.

Two weeks later, on 22 or 23 May, a pair of U.S. men-of-war plus six gunboats, containing about three hundred men, passed up the River St. Clair bound for Lake Huron. For a time three schooners—USS *Caledonia, Scorpion,* and *Ohio*—cruised in company on the lake, all under Lt. Samuel Woodhouse. Indian allies told British commanders of these developments, and this intelligence caused further worry that McDouall's "last brigade of boats for Michilimackinac," which had cleared Nottawasaga River mouth on the twentieth of the same month, might not have reached its destination safely. As it was, the two forces missed each other.

Meanwhile, at Detroit (where news often came concerning the state of affairs at Michilimackinac) Croghan feared the worst and contended that the North West Company would do all in its power to reinforce Michilimackinac. The matter settled heavily on his mind, for he now took the ominous view that it would be hard to oust the British from the island fortress. He worried constantly. He dug in his heels, refused to supply the troops required, and even imagined that the British had one thousand men defending Michilimackinac. "The position of Mackinack is a strong one, & should the enemy have determined on holding it, he has had time to throw in reinforcements."[9] Thus Croghan declined to cooperate with the Navy in operations in Lake Huron until ordered to do so by the War Department.

By 1 June the Navy Department had issued revised orders to Sinclair, calling for a more select naval force than previously imagined. These instructions called for examining the several ports of Lake Huron in order to ascertain the real force and designs of the enemy in that quarter, and there to frustrate every enemy project. The recovery of Michilimackinac besides the capture of St. Joseph would be important for bringing the Indians to the side of the United States. The president had expressly informed the secretary of the navy that in this operation private property was to be respected. "It will be of importance to return to Lake Erie, as soon as may be," Jones wrote, "in order to guard against any unusual or unfavorable change of circumstances, which may possibly take place during your absence. You will leave the Squadron on Lake Erie as strong as possible, for in the event of disaster, it will not be practicable to send reinforcements of seamen from the Atlantic Ports in due time." Thus he was to take no more seamen on his northern cruise than absolutely necessary to work the guns, with a few for the rigging. The secretary was reluctant to send both brigs, the *Niagara* and the *Lawrence,* into Lake Huron, for the duties of the squadron on Lake Erie remained heavy, consisting chiefly of ferrying troops hither and yon. But he gave Sinclair discretionary powers to decide if one or both were needed.[10] The nervous Sinclair decided, in the circumstances, that he needed as much force as he could muster for the northern cruise. He took both and wore his flag in the *Niagara.*

On 19 June the U.S. squadron sailed from Presque Isle for Michilimackinac "with a full breeze," said Usher Parsons. By the twenty-first the warships were off Malden, where the destruction of the public buildings was clearly evident. On 3 July these naval units sailed unopposed from Detroit. Seven of the largest vessels of the Navy's Lake Erie squadron, mounting sixty guns in all and manned by five hundred seamen and marines, were deployed on this service. When the ships gathered off Fort Gratiot, near the exit of Lake Huron, Perry's old flagship *Lawrence* and Elliott's *Niagara* were the largest vessels then seen in those waters. These champions of Put-in-Bay now had new commanders. The brigs *Caledonia* and the *General Hunter* and two schooners, likewise veterans of the Battle of Lake Erie, the *Scorpion* and *Tigress,* and also the schooner *Ohio* completed the fleet—a sum tonnage of 1,170. The *Scorpion,* incidentally, had been in Lake Huron gathering intelligence of the enemy. To Sinclair she had brought news that the British were preparing a large naval force.

The secretary of war could not abide Croghan's reluctance and caution. Orders were sent him to cooperate with the naval commander. A detachment of U.S. artillery, with guns and howitzers, a battalion of regular infantry, and another battalion of Ohio Volunteers, in all one thousand men, were detailed for the operation.

Although Croghan and his seniors continued to worry that Detroit would now be defenseless, with British forces preoccupied at Niagara and Fort Erie in American hands the only real danger with regard to Detroit, under the circumstances, was an Indian force. "What under these circumstances have we to fear at Detroit—An Indian Attack!" wrote the secretary of war to Gen. Duncan McArthur, the western commander, in frustration and anger. "Is it not more probable that the Savages will be called and concentrated for the defence of Mackinaw?" He added: "There are a set of alarmists, who, from different motives, labor to keep the public in a state of fever. These fellows deserve to be scalped."[11] Croghan was instructed to leave behind a competent garrison, but drafts of militia from Kentucky and Ohio were called upon to provide added defense at Detroit until the return of the fleet. The alarm for Detroit was unnecessary, thought the secretary of war, and reports of great detachments having arrived from England were much exaggerated. Even so, the detaching of American men-of-war for the campaign in Lakes Huron, Michigan, and Superior[12] caused great anxiety for Army and Navy commanders at the senior level. The desire on the part of certain American officials to check the Potawatomi menace on the east and west shores of Lake Michigan underscored the expedition to attack British trade, fur posts, shipping, and garrisons.

Heavy winds and unexpected difficulties caused delays in getting the large sailing vessels through the flats of Lake St. Clair. "It has been a perfect monsoon here," complained Sinclair on 3 July in explaining his delay: getting into Lake Huron against a nor'easter was impossible. Then there was the shallowness of the straits, for instead of finding ten feet of water, as Sinclair expected, he found only eight. The rapids of the St. Clair had to be negotiated. The ships were proceeding into uncharted waters. No previous survey of a systematic nature had been made of this great freshwater sea, and this placed American commanders at a woeful disadvantage. For all these reasons, Sinclair's squadron did not arrive in Lake Huron until 12 July. The vessels wearing the Stars and Stripes shaped a course north by east, following the eastern shoreline (which is regular there) of Lake Huron. Surgeon Parsons marveled at how clear the water was: he could see large boulders looking like eggs deep down below the ship's waterline. The water temperature, he noted, was ten degrees Fahrenheit lower than on Lake Erie. By the fifteenth they had worked their way carefully through various channels and were abreast of Cabot Head with its appearance of slumbering lions. The mariners now steered south and east, possibly past Cape Chin and Cape Croker. There was talk abroad that perhaps the land lying now to the west (Bruce Peninsula) was in fact an island. Speculation mounted that perhaps an alternate way could be found back to the rapids of St. Clair. There was chatter, too, that the force had not gone far enough north before entering the waters leading to Matchedash Bay.[13]

The first order of business was to break up any British shipbuilding. Thus Sinclair planned to look in at Matchedash Bay, southeast Georgian Bay, where he might find a British storehouse and shipbuilding yard. He was correctly advised on these counts, and he suspected, too, that he might find there any transport vessels the British still could boast of, such as the *Nancy*, or vessels of the North West Company. He intended to find them, whether they were under weigh, at anchor, or in hiding.

Sinclair was searching for a channel, one past Hope and Christian Island, or Giant's Tomb, that would lead him into Matchedash Bay. From Lake Huron to Matchedash Bay Sinclair would face two barriers of islands. He had got through the first by sailing around Cape Hurd, abreast of where Tobermory now is, via the main channel, then east beyond Cabot Head and the extremity of Bruce Peninsula. Given the time devoted to the search it seems likely that he was trying to pick his way through the second barrier, beyond Hope Island. If, in fact, he was north of Hope Island, and into the rock-infested approach to Muskoka Landing Channel he would indeed have been beyond hope. But logic would suggest that he had not found the access to Midland Bay south of Beausoleil Island and thence via Severn Sound and Waubaushene Channel to Matchedash Bay. Without chart or sailing directions Sinclair could not find his way through this maze of rock and water, and sympathy alone dictates our understanding as to why he could not find the British shipbuilding establishment, so nicely squirreled away in the Upper Canada bush.

The secrets of Georgian Bay kept Sinclair from reaching Matchedash Bay. As he explained in his report of proceedings to the secretary of the navy, he "used every possible effort to gain it." Unable to procure a pilot for that unfrequented part of the lake, and finding it filled with islands and sunken rocks which would inevitably prove to be the destruction of the fleet, he had to give up the attempt. Croghan, who had a history of independent thinking bordering on rebelliousness,[14] put a slightly different slant on this matter. The joint commanders, by which he meant Sinclair and himself, imagined a safe arrival at Matchedash Bay in a few days. At the end of a week, Sinclair, for want of pilots, "despaired of being able to find a passage through the islands into the bay."

It was more complicated than that. Once again weather had played its strange hand in the course of the lake's affairs. Dense fog lay over Georgian Bay and enveloped the shoreline for days upon end. Sinclair, bereft of charts and sailing directions, without local knowledge or a pilot, had no intention of losing ships in those rock-infested and shoaling waters. Nor did he intend to become separated from any man-of-war boats he might send on reconnaissance duties. The Army's provisions were growing short. Secretary of War Armstrong later said that the idea of attacking Matchedash was abandoned in consequence of sundry impediments "arising from shoals, rocks, dangerous islands, perpetual fogs, and bad pilotage."[15]

At this juncture, on 16 July, Sinclair consulted with Croghan. They agreed to shape a course for St. Joseph. There they might procure such information as would determine their future operations. Underlying his intentions was the necessity to intercept any remaining North West Company trade and thereby knock off balance the Indian alliance. Any Nor'Wester vessels, therefore, offered tempting prizes for Sinclair's flotilla, and this prize hunt drew U.S. ships northward in advance of the military requirements for a successful campaign on Lake Huron.

St. Joseph Island was reached on 19 July with good winds. Sinclair expected to find a British garrison holed up there and, when once a little pressure were applied from ships' guns or from landing parties, ready to surrender. There was no one home. Again Sinclair faced disappointment. "The enemy had abandoned his work, consisting of a fort and a large block-house etc.; those we destroyed but left untouched the town and Northwest Company's storehouses," he reported to Washington.[16] He sent spies ashore, hoping to gain intelligence about Michilimackinac. They came back empty-handed. He sent in two launches and a total of two hundred men to destroy the fort buildings. The Americans left Fort St. Joseph a smoldering ruin. Once again they had been thwarted by an enemy they could not find. To that point in time no news had been gained of the enemy's whereabouts.

Good fortune now befell the Americans: they spied "a strange sail." This proved to be a trading vessel of the North West Company, the *Mink* of forty-five tons, heavily laden with 230 barrels of flour, making her way in light winds from Michilimackinac to St. Marys River via St. Joseph. She was fair game. The Americans, windbound, lowered boats from the *Niagara* and gave hot pursuit. They captured the *Mink* without difficulty.[17]

Besides her valuable cargo—for next to guns and ammunition, flour was the greatest need for warriors in this region—the prize yielded up that which the American commodore so desperately needed: information concerning the whereabouts of other enemy shipping. By an "intelligent prisoner" captured in the *Mink* Sinclair learned that transport for the American campaign on Lake Erie needed reinforcement. Sinclair concluded that certain naval forces deemed unnecessary for the intended assault on Michilimackinac should be sent to Detroit. Sinclair did not, indeed perhaps chose not to, name this "intelligent prisoner." Did the informant sing freely? Was he tortured? Was he bribed? History cries out for particulars of this well-placed tattletale. How Sinclair got him to tell all is not known and can only be imagined.

This informant did not quit with the recounting of precious details about the Lake Erie campaign. He told that various artificers (Sinclair terms them "mechanics") had been sent north from York for the purpose of building a flotilla to transport supplies and reinforcements to Michilimackinac. Heretofore imperial forces had kept secret all particulars of their stealthily waged campaign to Michilimackinac and Prairie du Chien. By this time it was too late to stop the British, for imperial forces had already slipped past, landed supplies and men at Michilimackinac, arrived in the Upper Mississippi watershed, and recaptured Prairie du Chien.

On 22 July, says Surgeon Parsons in his diary for that date, "Duel fought between Captain Desher of the Infantry and Lieutenant Burns of the Navy— the latter wounded in the chests." The location was St. Joseph Island, and presumably Parsons knew all about the particulars, though he did not recount them in his diary. This was an age of duels, and the mind wanders a little magically to thoughts of two Americans resolving their differences at pistol point on Canadian soil during the War of 1812.

We return to our narrative. Sinclair remained in the dark about British shipbuilding. His Matchedash excursion had been abandoned. Now, from the informant, he learned vital details of how the British were projecting their military power north of York and on to Georgian Bay. "An attempt was made," wrote Sinclair, "to transport them [artificers and supplies] by way of Matchedash, but it was found impracticable from all the portages being a moras." And so, he added, "they resorted to a small river called Nottawasaga, situated to the south of Matchedash, from which there is a good portage of three leagues over which to transport reinforcements and supplies from Lake Simcoe. This place is very narrow and has six or eight feet of water in it, and is then a muddy rapid shallow for forty-five miles to the portage where their armada was built and their storehouses are now situated. The navigation is dangerous and difficult, and so obscured by rocks and bushes that no stranger could ever find it. I have, however, availed myself of this means of discovering it."[18]

Sinclair had good reason to be pleased with himself. He had got the details correct, for this bush and swamp, then less drained than nowadays, offered just the opposite of an easy access across the Upper Canada peninsula. In particular, he had learned of the Nottawasaga River route, of Schooner Town depot, and of Fort Willow.

Prior to shaping his course southward for these targets, Sinclair had one final duty to effect in Lake Huron's northern reaches. When the *Mink* had been captured he had received intelligence that the North West Company's schooner *Perseverance* was lying above the falls at the lower end of Lake Superior, in wait to transport inbound cargo to Fort William. Accordingly, on 22 July, Sinclair dispatched two launches under Lt. Daniel Turner of the *Scorpion*—"an active enterprising officer"—to capture her and, if possible, ease her down the falls. His next target was therefore the North West Company's post on St. Marys River, Sault Ste. Marie. To get to the Sault from St. Joseph Island any American forces would have to proceed on St. Marys River against prevailing current and adverse winds. Out of the question was the use of men-of-war for this duty. Accordingly they were kept at anchor at De Tour Passage, guarding the western entrance to the main body of water on Lake Huron from the North Channel.

For his part, Croghan selected a detachment of regular infantry and artillery, about 280 in all, under a young Virginian, Maj. Andrew Hunter Holmes. Holmes had distinguished himself in the battle of Long Woods, or Battle Hill, the previous February in what was a hard-fought, partially successful encounter with imperial forces deep in the forested wilderness of the Thames Valley of Upper Canada. Holmes was a friend of Thomas Jefferson and younger brother of David Holmes, first governor and a senator from Mississippi. He served in the 24th U.S. (Tennessee) Infantry and was, as experience had shown, skilled in frontier expeditions. At Sault Ste. Marie he intended to add further success to his enviable record.[19]

Using ships' boats, the expedition made its way to its destination unopposed. Lieutenant Turner now takes up the story: "I proceeded on the expedition to Lake Superior with the launches. I rowed night and day, but having a distance of 60 miles against a strong current information had reached the Enemy at St. Maries of our approach about two hours before I arrived . . . carried by Indians in their light canoes, several of which I chased and by firing on them and killing some, prevented their purpose."[20]

The force had come to the Sault, a place of remarkable geographical features and unique historical characteristics, a legendary crossroads of the continent.

Sault Ste. Marie, a rock-strewn rapid through which the waters of Lake Superior flows abundantly, or empties violently, is about a third of a mile wide. Its length is estimated at three-quarters of a mile, and the descent of the water then about twenty-two feet. Below the falls lies an expanse of white foam. The lower end of the rapid forms two bays on which, in those days, several trading houses stood. The south or American side had the residence of John Johnston, U.S. customs agent, whose duty it was to stop illicit commerce on American territory. Next to Johnston's residence stood that of the old trader Jean-Baptiste Nolin, who with his large Métis family lived in opulent comfort. On the north, or Canadian, side could be seen the property of Charles Oakes Ermatinger, North West Company partner and agent, whose stone house, then being built, was intended to match Nolin's in elegance. Ermatinger had a windmill-powered grist mill, erected "to encourage agriculture," observed traveler Gabriel Franchère, "for the inhabitants of Sault Ste. Marie are not much addicted to work, and provided that they have enough potatoes, they are sure to catch enough fish to feed them for part of the year." Soil was fertile, and wheat and other grains were grown. In all, it was a promising little place, and a good way station for the Nor'Westers, and certainly for the prosperous Nolin and Ermatinger. The business of Sault Ste. Marie was shipping and forwarding. To ease the transfer of inbound and outbound cargo, the fur traders had completed a canal on the north side in 1798, with a lock measuring forty feet long and eight feet nine inches in width—large enough to hold the largest canoes of the fur business.[21]

Major Holmes's force landed on the Canadian shore without opposition. The date was 23 July. Only a few company employees and dependents met them, solemnly, and wisely took no action to defend themselves in the face of such overwhelming odds. From the Americans they might have hoped for some measure of humanity, some leniency given their defenseless circumstances. They were mistaken. U.S. soldiers destroyed all North West Company property, including sawmills, stores, houses, and vessels. The assailants were not satisfied with this. In the subsequent rampage they killed cattle, burnt horses in stables, took various *engagés* prisoner, and tore down whatever defenses they found. They ruined the gardens, which were rare in such northern climates. Nothing of the Nor'Westers remained intact. The Americans considered the fur post to be a prize of war. The U.S. naval officer present, Lt. Daniel Turner, maintained that private property had been respected. When Holmes's men attacked, and sacked and pillaged everything that seemed to belong to the Canadian company, Johnston, like a jack-in-the-box on the American side of the passage, seems to have popped up in his own patriotic way and put the torch to property of the North West Company and then retired without doing any other damage to any other individual.[22]

The Americans had accomplished their mission—to ruin the fur traders' post and to cut the links of the northern fur trade. And, by this savage stroke at this choke point of commerce and forest diplomacy they intended to interrupt Indian military power flowing down from northern forests. In later years the American action would be labeled shameful. At that time and place such episodes of frontier warfare, with all such measures of brutality, were customary and commonplace. And it speaks to the characteristic nature of frontier warfare in North America.

At this juncture, Lieutenant Turner sought out the Nor'Wester schooner *Perseverance,* of eighty-five tons, which like the *Mink* had been recently built on Lake Superior. Leaving matters ashore to Holmes, Turner proceeded to the Lake Superior end without a moment's delay. There he spied the schooner.

The enemy, he says, "finding they could not get off with the vessel I was in quest of, set fire to her in several places, scuttled and left her. I succeeded in boarding her and by considerable exertion extinguished the flames and secured her from sinking." Turner then "stript her," that is, lowered the rigging, and prepared for getting her down the falls. On board the *Perseverance* he placed a man in charge and told him that he would get a reward (this had been offered by Sinclair) if he succeeded or would face death in case of treachery. Adverse winds prevented early action, until the 26th, "when every possible effort was used." It was heaven or hell. She could not be got over safely. The channel was rough and the current ran at an alarming twenty to thirty knots. She bilged (was stoved in or sprung a leak), filled with water, and became a wreck. "She was a fine new schooner," noted Turner, with regret, but he added, as consolation, that her loss would be severely felt by the North West Company. "Had I succeeded in getting her safe, I could have loaded her to advantage from the Enemys Store houses. I however brought down four captured boats loaded with Indian goods to a considerable amount." "The capture of the *Perseverance,*" said Sinclair, "gave us the complete command of Lake Superior."[23] What happened to the man in charge of this last fateful voyage of the *Perseverance* is not known.

Once Lieutenant Turner's boats carrying Major Holmes's soldiers left Sault Ste. Marie, the Nor'Westers scurried to prepare a defense in case the enemy should pay a return visit. Indians camped at nearby Pine Point agreed to help in case of need. The Nor'Westers, short of provisions, went on half rations. They sent a canoe to Michilimackinac with news of the event. It returned without accomplishing its mission—the island was blockaded by American warships. To get news to the garrison would have meant running great risk of being taken prisoner. For some time the situation of the Canadian fur traders at Sault Ste. Marie, and on Lake Superior, was grave. The Americans had come close to throttling all the trade flowing through the Sault.

With this North West Company's key northern post of Sault Ste. Marie knocked on the head, much of the enemy shipping destroyed, and the flow of bounty to the Indians threatened, the Americans focused their energies and attention on that which they had lost, in 1812, to their total surprise and anger— Michilimackinac. At this precise moment, it may be remembered, Colonel McKay and his frontier guard were campaigning in faraway Wisconsin—at Prairie du Chien. If this were not enough to weaken Michilimackinac, Lieutenant Worsley and his sailors were away at the southern end of Georgian Bay, at Nottawasaga, there hurriedly loading as many supplies for Michilimackinac as they could store in the *Nancy*. At Michilimackinac, therefore, Colonel McDouall had for defensive purposes a reduced force of regulars, militia, and Indians. As for guns it is said that the defenders had but two—a 6-pounder and a 3-pounder. No artillery officer was among them to instruct and discipline those who served the guns.

On 26 July Sinclair's fleet appeared off Mackinac Island. They anchored off the southeast end of Round Island and south of Mackinac Island, adjacent to Bois Blanc Island. Sinclair, who had not deployed any vessels in advance to collect information on the enemy's strength and disposition, now sent the brig *Lawrence* and schooner *Scorpion* to patrol the passage leading to Lake Michigan lying between Bois Blanc, the mainland and Point St. Ignace. A tedious spell of bad weather, said Sinclair, prevented a reconnaissance of Michilimackinac and delayed procuring intelligence about the enemy's much-dreaded Indian force. The time drew on relentlessly for a landing to seize the island and oust the imperial forces.

By 31 July the Americans understood that, according to rough estimate, there were about three hundred regulars, one hundred militia and four hundred Indians defending Michilimackinac—a considerable number. Sinclair grew cautious. Croghan, who had made his own inquiries on the mainland and

95

among the islands, returned to the fleet, says Parsons in his entry for that date, "with the determination to fight." Croghan's numbers, as given above, had been gleaned from two captives taken at Point St. Ignace.

From their ships the Americans spied out the British movements, looking for all possible weaknesses in their defenses. From friendly intelligence they learned about the best landing places. They pondered the various possibilities for the impending assault. For nearly a week the American men-of-war kept up a blockade, which characteristically grew tedious and became a source of nagging regret. The commanders dithered and could take no decision, and thereby lost all advantage of surprise. Here the oft-quoted maxims of James Wolfe, who had survived the horrors of a combined operations shambles against the French at Rochefort in 1757, are worth quotation:

> I have found out that an Admiral should endeavour to run into an enemy's port immediately after he appears before it; that he should anchor the transport ships and frigates as close as he can to the land; that he should reconnoitre and observe it as quickly as possible, and lose no time in getting the troops on shore.... On the other hand, experience shows me that, in an affair depending on vigour and despatch, the General should settle their plan of operations so that no time may be lost in idle debate and consultations when the sword should be drawn; that pushing on smartly is the road to success, and more particularly so in an affair of this nature; ... that in war something must be allowed to chance and fortune, seeing it is in its nature hazardous and an option of difficulties.[24]

On 3 August Croghan announced his determination to land. The artillery pieces, carried in the *Mink,* were now available. A delay had occurred because she had been lost in fog and out of touch with the commanders. Final preparations were made for the landing and assault.

On the morning of 4 August troops were in a situation to land on Mackinac Island. For some days previous the joint commanders, Sinclair and Croghan, had assessed all prospective landing places. Bombarding Fort George at the outset would have been a valuable commencement of the battle. However, the U.S. vessels lacked howitzers or guns that could train at high elevation. Thus direct fire on the British post was out of the question. What could be effected, given the fact that the ships could anchor within three hundred yards of the beach, was a landing of troops under cover of the guns, the testing of the enemy's strength, and a retreat to the ships when necessary.[25] This seems to have been their limited objective, but it was not in conformity with their superiors' expectations and orders.

The commanders looked for a good beach on which to land infantry and haul guns ashore. This was precisely where the British had landed when they took the place from us, Parsons noted. They chose the shoreline at Dowsman's Farm, situated at the opposite side of the island from the fort, on the northwest side of the island. Here the vessels anchored. The U.S. vessels were ranged in line of battle. They trained their ordnance on the open, gently rising ground that led from water's edge toward the woods beyond. The ships' guns, mainly carronades, could fire grape and canister to cover the landing of troops. All was intended to be completed without opposition or difficulty.

In the face of an anticipated, robust assault, the British commander had been obliged to act with decision and flexibility. "My situation was embarrassing," confessed Colonel McDouall, who fully comprehended that he stood at a numerical disadvantage. "I knew that they [the Americans] would land upwards of 1000 men; and, after manning the guns at the fort, I had only a disposable force of 140 to meet them."[26] McDouall had a keen eye for defensive advantage. On the summit of the cliff overlooking the open ground he had his men throw up a strong redoubt. There McDouall took up his position, though one a bit exposed to enemy fire as well as removed from the fort. Roads lay upon his flanks, and these he expected would be well known to the enemy on account of information provided by former residents. McDouall left 25 men guarding the fort, and so slim were the forces at his disposal that he could not spare a single man to guard these approaches. In sum, McDouall's forces consisted of a lieutenant and an ensign and a small detachment of the 10th Royal Veteran Battalion; 2 noncommissioned officers and 11 gunners of the Royal Regiment of Artillery; a lieutenant colonel of the Glengarry Light Infantry Fencibles (McDouall himself); 2 captains, 4 subalterns, 6 sergeants, 4 corporals, and 120 privates of the Royal Newfoundland Fencible Infantry; a lieutenant and 36 rank-and-file of the Michigan Fencibles; and two companies (totaling about 100 men) from the North West Company militia units raised at St. Joseph and Sault Ste. Marie; and, not least, 350 warriors of various Indian nations. In all, the imperial force numbered about 650.[27]

If comparatively weak in numbers, he was strong in position. Behind and on the rear flanks lay woods. Before lay clear ground and an open field of fire down a gradual slope. McDouall had reason to conclude that imperial forces were in a fine state of defense. McDouall counted on Indians to prevent the Americans from gaining the woods, where they might run free and unopposed. He gave strictest orders that his men, lying within the protection of the natural breastwork, the redoubt, were to hold their fire until such time as they could

97

pour in a murderous fire. In these circumstances, the garrison and the Indians, all in high spirits, awaited the enemy.

McDouall's nagging concern was want of provisions in the event of an extended American blockade. Twice that spring of 1814 the *Nancy* had brought supplies and reinforcements from southern Georgian Bay. Now she was in imminent danger of capture, for the U.S. squadron commanded all approaches to Michilimackinac. McDouall could not risk such a loss of equipment, men, and supplies. In consequence, at this eleventh hour he sent a courier, Lt. Robert Livingstone of the Indian Department, on an important mission. This young fur trader, recently resident at St. Joseph Island, had served at one time in the Royal Navy and subsequently in the Royal Canadian Volunteers. In a swift canoe he slipped by the U.S. ships. He was bound for Georgian Bay to deliver McDouall's urgent instructions to the commander of the *Nancy* to take her as high up the Nottawasaga River as possible and there to dig in to face the American naval forces which, given their strength in these waters, surely would soon arrive.[28]

McDouall got early warning of American intentions when, on the eve of the landing, 3 August, the American fleet anchored off Dowsman's Farm. Fort George rose before them on the spine-like ridge, and presumably the British had at least some of their guns placed there with a commanding view of all approaches. Croghan, we know now, had decided to land in open ground and there occupy some advantageous position from which they could "annoy the enemy" by slow, steady approach under cover of artillery. Croghan believed that once the Americans had taken up their favorable position McDouall would, of necessity, be obliged to attack or risk the desertion of the Indians. The Indians, he said, "would be very unwilling to remain in my neighbourhood after a permanent footing had been taken."[29]

Surgeon Parsons's account takes up the story as seen from the *Lawrence*:

> August 4th. Off Mackinac. Pleasant. At about 9 o'clock signal was made for armed vessels to get under way. At about half past 11 came to anchor in line of battle abreast the N.W. side of Mackinac Island, where there is a spot partly cleared on which the British landed when they took the fort from us [12 July 1812]. The land is low. At one [P.M.] the troops began to disembark. At two a firing commenced from the vessels which cleared the shore. At three o'clock the troops were formed at a short distance from the shore and at quarter past three firing commenced with field pieces, and shortly after musketry.[30]

The naval fire support had been of little effect and did no effectual damage to the defenders. To counter the landing and enemy guns McDouall had ordered the two British field pieces to do what they could. Their gun crews put up an indifferent fire, for no artillery officer was there to provide direction. The Americans declined to meet the British on the open ground. Instead, the Americans eased along the forested perimeter and did so despite some initial Indian resistance. McDouall, seeing the rising tide of American advance, sent a party of Michigan Fencibles to counter it.[31]

Now, however, the Americans complicated their arrangements. The men-of-war shifted anchor so as to get behind McDouall's left flank. Troops landed from those vessels advanced by road toward the British emplacements. Accordingly, McDouall, so as to maintain communications, shifted to an intermediary position. There he gathered his force and in an act critical to the success of the whole operation gave support to the Fallavoines and their chief, Thomas, who opened a spirited fire upon the enemy. Americans were taking casualties at an appalling rate: many officers and men lay dead or wounded upon the field of battle. By 4:30 P.M. the American force was in retreat. Boats were ready at the shore to receive them. The retreat was well conducted under cover of the guns of their ships anchored within a few yards of the shore.

The reembarkation was effected that evening; immediately thereafter the vessels hauled off. In the words of Surgeon Parsons:

> At half after five the direction of the firing indicated that our army was on the retreat. At 5 o'clock firing ceased, and most of the troops were on the shore from which they had marched. Boats were on shore ready to receive them. Maj. Holmes was killed early in the action, and Capt. Desha wounded. Capt. Vanhorn was mortally wounded and [also] Lieut. Jackson. The report of killed and wounded of the regulars stands thus: [12 killed, 40 wounded, 3 missing] . . .
>
> Lieut. Jackson was wounded through the bowels a little below and to the left of the navel; the ball passed out a little above the [os] innominatum (part of the pelvic bone) on the left of the spine; a small portion of omentum passed through the front (abdominal) wound. Capt. Vanhorn was also wounded in the same manner. A sergeant was wounded through the stomach and died in the night. A private [wounded] through the left lung bids fair to recover. The other wounds were slight, that occurred to the men on board the *Lawrence*. Weighed anchor and stood off about one mile. The retreat was well conducted.[32]

Casualty figures for this encounter bear testimony to the size of American losses: sixty-six killed, wounded, or missing is the American list. Heading the list of American officers dead was the bonny Maj. Andrew Hunter Holmes, the conqueror of Sault Ste. Marie, whose loss was much lamented by his comrades. On the fifth U.S. forces requested the body of Holmes, and this was granted. Of the wounded, seven died aboard the ships.[33] As to imperial losses, one Indian killed is the tally.

The American attack, repulse, and retreat at Michilimackinac necessitated some explanation to higher command. It fell to Commodore Sinclair to give an explanation. He pointed to the geographical problems of a successful landing and assault: "Mackinac is by nature a perfect Gibraltar, being a high, inaccessible rock on every side except from the west, from which to the heights you have nearly two miles to pass through a wood so thick that our men were shot in every direction, and within a few yards of them, without being able to see the Indians who did it, and a height was scarcely gained before there was another within fifty or one hundred yards, commanding it where breastworks were erected and cannon opened on them." In other words, the farther the Americans had advanced, the stronger they had found the imperial forces and, in consequence, "the weaker and more bewildered our force were." Sinclair says that the U.S. officers were picked out, killed or wounded, by the Indians without seeing any of them. American soldiers became lost and bewildered. They feared a massacre and, accordingly, demanded an immediate retreat. Colonel Croghan, in consequence, effected a general withdrawal. In the process, the left flank suffered heavy losses from the enemy's galling fire. The Americans then found safety under their ships' guns.[34]

The annals of amphibious operations are filled with illuminating examples of technique and of "lessons learned." In this case, the imperial forces were blessed with superior position. This, combined with tenacious fighting on the flanks plus the rapid deployment of reinforcements sufficed to keep the advantage for the defenders. Had the guns of the U.S. men-of-war been more effective the defenders might have been put at a disadvantage. Even so, the Americans used no degree of surprise, no stealth, no élan. Their frontal landing was anticipated. Their occupation of an open ground covered from forested flanks by defenders experienced in forest warfare showed no extraordinary military genius. The only diversion mounted—the shifting of the men-of-war—had been countered by the British. Indeed, the episode may be taken as an instance of how not to undertake a military occupation against open, rising, and forest-fringed ground in an insular setting. Here was no fort to conquer or force into submission, only a patch of ground that would prove to be a graveyard of those who sought to gain it.

Thus did the great prize—the fort and island of Mackinac—elude the Americans. As to the question of whether or not its possession in U.S. hands would have made any difference, it must be stressed that on control of Michilimackinac depended the strength, even pacification, of the native tribes. What was a sword in British hands might soon become a swift weapon of revenge and dominance in the hands of the Americans: the great majority of Indians knew this. Michilimackinac proved a distraction, for it had become the primary focus of American operations at the expense of other military goals. As Lieutenant Turner reported to Commodore Sinclair, had they not been preoccupied with Mackinac Island, forces could have been sent into Lake Superior to break up all the important Nor'Wester establishments. "The capture of Fort William alone," he wrote with regret, "would have destroyed the enemy's trade, as that is his general rendezvous, from which his extensive trade branches in all directions, and at which place there is never less than a million in property, and at this season of the year it is said to be twice that amount."[35] The same informant bemoaned the fact that such a grand opportunity would never recur.

Although the capture of the *Mink* and *Perseverance,* with their precious provisions, proved of serious consequence to the Nor'Westers, in fact, just before the arrival of American forces at Sault Ste. Marie, a parade of richly laden trading canoes, heavily escorted by a specially outfitted armed *voyageur* militia, had passed through the lock with only two days to spare. Once among the islands of Lake Huron's North Channel, it effectively eluded the Americans and entered French River in safety. In the flotilla was a cargo of peltry valued at one million dollars. The war had not checked the flow of wealth of the Canadian northwest and the interior trade that fed Montreal.

And what of Colonel McDouall, defender of Michilimackinac? He was awarded the highly touted honor Commander of the Bath in February 1817, and he rose to become a major general. "Solid, dedicated and astute," says his biographer Robbie Allen, McDouall was representative of many British military and naval personnel "serving with courage and quiet distinction in British North America during the War of 1812 while their confrères were enjoying the limelight cast by the Napoleonic battles of Salamanca and Vitoria."[36] That wry statement speaks volumes about the comparative perceptions of the importance of campaigning in the wilds of North America as opposed to those in the Iberian Peninsula. Both campaigns were of signal importance in British policy. It is only the bias of history that has rendered the North American interior campaign such a neglected topic of study. Fair to report, however, in terms of scale, the battles at Michilimackinac and Prairie du Chien were of diminutive stature. Even so they were turning points in this continental war. McDouall's campaigning, and the logistical arrangements that sustained them, kept control of the interior posts. And on these, in turn, rested the ever-prominent native alliance upon which the fortunes of British America depended.

Detail of a *View of Amherstburg, 1813*, showing HMS *Detroit* on the stocks and nearing completion. *Watercolor by Margaret Reynolds, Parks Canada, Fort Malden National Historic Site*

Amherstburg Navy Yard, Upper Canada, early September 1813. HMS *Detroit*, HMS *Queen Charlotte*, and the other vessels of the British fleet make ready to meet the Americans to see who would command Lake Erie and all waters above. Blockaded, or watched by U.S. naval forces, the squadron under Commo. Robert Heriot Barclay sailed to "engage the enemy more closely." *Painting by Peter Rindlisbacher*

Robert Heriot Barclay, RN, heroically but unsuccessfully fought to keep open British sea lanes on Lake Erie upon which the fortunes of the British campaign in the Old Northwest depended heavily. The defeat of British men-of-war under his command on 12 September 1813 forced a British defensive posture in northern waters, one not overcome by U.S. superiority in arms. Barclay was tried by court-martial for the loss of his flotilla. He was fully and honorably acquitted. *Artist unknown, J. Ross Robertson Collection (T15259), Metropolitan Toronto Reference Library*

Sir James Lucas Yeo, RN, commodore and commander in chief on the Lakes of Canada, 1813–1815, shown here in 1810. To maintain the Royal Navy's strength on Lake Ontario, he starved the Lake Erie squadron of guns, ammunition, and seamen. He blamed Barclay for the disaster at Put-in-Bay. *Painting by Adam Buck, J. Ross Robertson Collection (T15241), Metropolitan Toronto Reference Library*

Oliver Hazard Perry, USN, commander of the victorious fleet at Put-in-Bay, the Battle of Lake Erie, 12 September 1813. A gallant and brilliant tactician, he shifted his flag from the badly mauled brig *Lawrence* to the *Niagara. Oil painting by Gilbert Stuart and Jane Stuart, the Toledo Museum of Art*

Badly wounded, Robert Barclay is assisted on the deck of HMS *Detroit*. All British officers were killed or wounded in the Battle of Lake Erie with material effect on the ability to serve the guns. *Watercolor by J. C. H. Foster (1976), Parks Canada, Fort Malden Historic Site*

Tecumseh in a 1902 engraving. He realized the consequences of the British naval defeat on Lake Erie on 10 September 1813. He died in battle at Moraviantown, Upper Canada, 5 October 1813. *National Archives of Canada (C-003809)*

The U.S. fleet under Commo. Arthur Sinclair enters Detroit River in passage to Lake Huron in July 1814. Sinclair, on orders from the secretary of the navy, sailed from Lake Erie through Detroit River and Lake St. Clair in the U.S. brig *Niagara* (*left foreground*). At far right is the U.S. brig *Lawrence.* In the distance are various U.S. schooners. This little-known cruise involved the destruction of the British transport *Nancy,* the unsuccessful assault on British-held Mackinac Island, the destruction of the North West Company's establishment at Sault Ste. Marie and the abandoned British post Fort St. Joseph, and the loss of the schooners *Scorpion* and *Tigress* to the British. Plagued by lack of navigational data, U.S. warships did not find the British shipbuilding locale Matchedash Bay, southeastern Georgian Bay. *Painting by Peter Rindlisbacher*

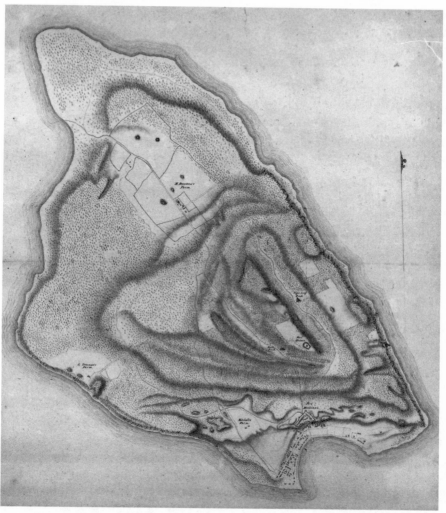

Map of the Island of Michilimackinac, by Eveleth, 1817. This shows (*top left*) the field of battle in 1814, the approach to the British fort, and (*lower right*) the crescent-shaped bay of the village. *William L. Clements Library, University of Michigan*

U.S. brig *Niagara*, flagship of Commodore Sinclair, positioned by anchors fore and aft, bombards the shore in preparation for the landing of U.S. Army personnel at the attack on British-held Fort Mackinac, Michilimackinac Island, on 4 August 1814. The force never reached its destination. This badly mauled assault party withdrew to the *Niagara* under cover of the ship's guns, thus closing a disastrous amphibious campaign from which many lessons were learned (and many subsequently forgotten). *Painting by Peter Rindlisbacher*

Fort St. Joseph, a British military post and trading station, head of Lake Huron, as portrayed by Edward Walsh in 1804. From this post British military forces proceeded to take Fort Mackinac in 1812. A joint military and naval force under U.S. command destroyed the post in 1814. *William L. Clements Library, University of Michigan*

Fort Mackinac, in the distance, showing in the foreground the bay and village, 1813. The British transport schooner *Nancy* is shown delivering men, material, and supplies and taking off dispatches and other messages. *Illustration by Richard Dillon, William L. Clements Library, University of Michigan*

Sault Ste. Marie, showing how the rapids led to Lake Huron from Lake Superior, 1804. Fur-trading establishments lay on both sides of the waterway, the larger, owned by the North West Company, can been seen with the trading vessel (*right*) on the north side at the head of St. Marys River. To this post came a joint U.S. Navy–U.S. Army expedition in 1814 that wasted the North West Company establishments. A British merchant schooner, the *Perseverance,* was captured above the falls but did not survive the ordeal of bringing her down the rapids. *View by Edward Walsh, William L. Clements Library, University of Michigan*

The *Nancy*, fabled British supply schooner, formerly of the North West Company, ended her remarkable career on 14 August 1814 inside the mouth of the Nottawasaga River, where her commander, Miller Worsley, RN, had placed her to prevent her from falling into American hands. Her "bones" were later discovered and preserved. *Artist unknown, Columbia River Maritime Museum*

Left to right: U.S. warships, the schooners *Tigress* and *Scorpion* and the brig *Niagara* (flagship of Commodore Sinclair), fire at HMS *Nancy* and the blockhouse at the entrance of the Nottawasaga River, 14 August 1814. *Watercolor by Irwin John Bevan, The Mariners' Museum, The Bailey Collection, Newport News, Va.*

Old trading post at the entrance of the Nottawasaga River, 23 April 1815. Up this river the *Nancy* was secreted away, but she was fired at by various vessels of the U.S. Navy, including the *Niagara* on 14 August 1814. For many years a gap could be seen in the trees where gunfire had cleared the horizon. *National Archives of Canada (C-002475)*

U.S. schooner *Scorpion* (*left*) is attacked and captured at dawn on 6 September 1814 by the former U.S. schooner *Tigress* (*right*) under command of Lt. Miller Worsley, RN. Three days previous, on the evening of 3 September, Worsley had led a boarding party from canoes to seize the *Tigress* in Detour Passage, Lake Huron. Worsley renamed the *Scorpion* HMS *Confiance* and the *Tigress* HMS *Surprize*. *Watercolor by Irwin John Bevan, The Mariners' Museum, The Bailey Collection, Newport News, Va.*

British commandant's house and barracks, Collier's Harbour, Drummond Island, head of Lake Huron. Occupied by British forces in 1815 on the occasion of peace being proclaimed, it was abandoned in 1828 upon the decision of the International Boundary Commission declaring it U.S. territory. *Wood engraving (1850), based on a drawing by J. J. Bigsby, National Archives of Canada (C-011665)*

Capt. W. Andrew Bulger, commandant, saying farewell at Fort McKay, Prairie du Chien, Wisconsin, Upper Mississippi River, 1815. On this occasion the British flag ceased to fly over this post, which reverted to American control, and Indians fired a salute. *Pen and watercolor by Peter Rindisbacher (c. 1823), Amon Carter Museum, Fort Worth, Texas*

Barracks and military and naval establishment at Penetanguishene, Ontario, as seen from the Outer Harbour, 1837. *Watercolor by R. Dartnell, Royal Ontario Museum*

Ice boat at Penetanguishene, recreation for naval and military officers, c. 1845. *Watercolor by Philip J. Bainbrigge, National Archives of Canada (C-11914)*

A replica of HMS *Tecumseth* (so spelled on the Navy List) plies the waters of Lake Huron and Georgian Bay. *Discovery Harbour, Penetanguishene, and the Marine Heritage Association (2000)*

Grand River Naval Depot, winter 1817. On the north shore of Lake Erie, the British naval establishment at the mouth of the Grand River gained importance when the British lost control of Lake Erie late in the War of 1812. Shown wintered are two of four schooners kept there by the Royal Navy. *Painting by Peter Rindlisbacher*

Naval and military establishments, Penetanguishene, showing sawpit (*foreground*) and assorted buildings, including artificers' huts, surgery, hydrographer's house, and bakery. *Photo by M. J. Mulloy (2000)*

Officers' quarters, naval and military establishments, at Discovery Harbour, Penetanguishene, built to War Office specifications. *Photo by M. J. Mulloy (2000)*

U.S. brig *Lawrence* live fire exhibit, showing reconstruction of midship section, Erie Maritime Museum, Erie, Pennsylvania. *Photo by Art Becker, Erie Maritime Museum*

HMS *Tecumseth* (*left*) and HMS *Bee*, a Durham or gunboat, at Discovery Harbour,
Penetanguishene. *Photo by M. J. Mulloy (2000)*

U.S. brig *Niagara* replica seen under full sail. This reconstruction was commissioned 1990 and is known as the "flagship of Pennsylvania." Headquartered in Erie, she makes summer cruises with professional and volunteer crews and is a living reminder of the age of fighting sail on the Great Lakes and elsewhere. *Photo by Bob Lowry, Erie Maritime Museum*

The crew of the U.S. brig *Niagara* at work. Manning the yards, living proof of historic naval heritage. *Photo by Bob Lowry, Erie Maritime Museum*

VI

~

Lieutenant Worsley's Little War

TAKING THE SCORPION AND TIGRESS

"*T*he destruction of Barclay's squadron," wrote Theodore Roosevelt with accuracy, "left the Americans undisputed masters of the upper lakes; and exactly as they had begun their career by a cutting-out expedition [against the *Detroit* and the *Caledonia*], which enabled them to acquire the nucleus of their squadron, so now they, in their turn, suffered by a couple of cutting-out expeditions, in which the British performed, at their expense, two really brilliant feats, though on a small scale."[1]

These British cutting-out expeditions failed to turn the tide that would have allowed imperial forces to mount an offensive. Even so, they were highly advantageous to the British strategy of the last year of campaigning—establishing a defensive. Bringing a pair of schooners, *Scorpion* and *Tigress*, into eager British hands allowed the imperial forces to hold key positions, one of which was Michilimackinac. This episode also enabled the British to keep up the traffic with native allies upon which, once again, the profit, power, and political fortunes of the British Empire in the northwest frontier of North America depended.

We left Commodore Sinclair and his naval force fresh from having destroyed the North West Company post at Sault Ste. Marie. In his hunt for all Nor'Wester and British War Department vessels in Lake Huron, Sinclair knew that HM schooner *Nancy* remained at large. He had obtained intelligence that her commander, Lt. Miller Worsley, RN, was at Nottawasaga River entrance,

Georgian Bay, taking on supplies with intention to sail to Michilimackinac and there to unload them.

Having more than enough naval force at his disposal, Sinclair decided to deploy only a portion of his fleet in the quest. Accordingly, he detached the brigs *Lawrence* and *Caledonia,* with some of Croghan's troops, to Fort Erie, where American forces were laying siege to this beleaguered British bastion of the Niagara Peninsula. Any such reinforcements could be useful there. The remaining vessels-of-war, including the *Niagara,* and a total of 450 men were to attack a post at Nottawasaga River considered far less powerful than the fortified watchtower at Michilimackinac. Therefore Sinclair's next job was to cruise to the south, to the bottom of Georgian Bay, not his favorite sailing ground.

The commanding officer of the *Nancy,* Lt. Miller Worsley, though only twenty-three at the time, had a good deal of war experience. This son of a well-heeled Isle of Wight clergy family had, like Barclay, fought at Trafalgar, in fact, in the very same vessel, HMS *Swiftsure.* Sent from Bermuda with Barclay and seven other officers to the Lakes in July 1813, Worsley had done well in the attack on the American base at Oswego, 6 May 1814. Then he had been ordered north and west to take up the naval command on Lake Huron previously held by that impossible-to-contain ego Lt. Newdigate Poyntz, who, as we have seen, had invited the disdain of Colonel McDouall.[2] Worsley lists his rank as lieutenant and commander. Unlike his predecessor, Worsley had no pretensions. Nor did he sport any grand visions of a floating empire in which he was supreme maritime commander. Rather, he exhibited the sort of hard-headed realism that made him the perfect partner to his army opposite, McDouall. And if McDouall could reach Michilimackinac by bateaux, then, if necessary, surely a naval officer could do likewise.

In July 1814 Worsley crossed overland to Nottawasaga River with twenty seamen, and he took command of the *Nancy.* On 1 August he sailed from Nottawasaga for Michilimackinac. He was intercepted by the messenger Lt. Robert Livingstone, already mentioned, and from him received McDouall's orders, dated 28 July, to take the *Nancy* into hiding at Nottawasaga.

McDouall's instructions suggested that Worsley place the *Nancy* as high as possible up the Nottawasaga River and there put up a blockhouse. This structure, McDouall advised (giving his naval counterpart some suggestions as to shore fortifications), should be loopholed for musketry and have embrasures for his 6-pounders. These measures would allow for the defense of the *Nancy* should the Americans attack, which McDouall considered as highly probable.[3]

Pursuant to orders, Worsley steered back for Nottawasaga River. He took the *Nancy* safely over the bar of the Nottawasaga. He placed her so she was hidden from the enemy's view, or so he hoped. Here the stream runs parallel to the Lake Huron shore, and thus forms a narrow peninsula, or rather what might be called an immense sandbar. The whole is now known generally as Wasaga Beach. Upstream, at Schooner Town, lay the landing where military and naval supplies were kept and marine repairs undertaken. Even before the war, this hideaway had existed. As noted, at this place McDouall's "water rats" had made their last minute preparations before setting out across Georgian Bay and Lake Huron bound for Michilimackinac and distant Prairie du Chien. To this place over the course of the previous year had come supplies, arms and ammunition from Willow Creek Depot and before that from Fort York, Kingston, and Montreal.

Commodore Sinclair in the *Niagara,* with the schooners *Scorpion* and *Tigress* in company, arrived off the entrance of Nottawasaga River. The American warships anchored. Sinclair says he was fortunate to find the *Nancy* loaded with provisions, clothing and supplies for the troops at Michilimackinac. The next day, pursuant to Sinclair's instructions, the U.S. ships took up positions anchoring opposite to the *Nancy* and "within good battering distance [of the blockhouse]." Sinclair takes up the story: "The sand hills and trees frequently interrupting my shot, I borrowed one of the 8 1/2 inch howitzers of Captain Croghan, mounted it on one of my carriages and sent it on the peninsula under command of Lieutenant Holdup. A situation was chosen by Captain Gratiot of the Engineers, from which it did great execution."[4] Mused the American sailor David Bunnell, "We . . . played upon them . . . warmly with our guns."[5]

For a time a spirited cannonade was kept up by the forces ashore. The imperial forces manned a 6-pounder from the blockhouse and two 24-pounder carronades, or "smashers," on the ground, all of which had been removed from the *Nancy.* But the British could serve the three guns with only twenty-three officers and seamen from the *Nancy* and nine French Canadians and twenty-three Indians under Robert Livingstone. "The Enemy defended himself very handsomely," said Sinclair.

Against such fire as the British could effect the Americans could answer with a powerful armament. The *Niagara* mounted eighteen 32-pounder carronades as well as two long 12-pounders. The *Scorpion* and *Tigress* each sported one long 12-pounder and two long 24-pounders.[6] In all, the Americans could boast of twenty-four pieces of ordnance and five hundred men.

Worsley recollected the odds in a letter to his father: "The enemy's force consisted of a 20 gun brig and three schooners mounting each a long 24 pounder with 450 marines. I however contended with them for my vessel from nine A.M. till four P.M. with my three guns, 24 seamen and 10 Indians." And so, Worsley continued, "Finding my little crew were falling all round me, I immediately formed a resolution to blow both up, which I did."[7]

Worsley had prepared a train of powder, running from the blockhouse to the *Nancy*. He had determined upon a plan to blow up the trusty schooner rather than let her fall into enemy hands. The young naval officer never had the chance. Lieutenant Holdup's gunners were finding the range. A shell from the American howitzer burst in the blockhouse, blowing up not only the blockhouse but also the *Nancy*. Frequent and heavy explosions below deck in the *Nancy* made impossible the task of saving her. "She was therefore, with her valuable Cargo, entirely consumed," recounted Sinclair. As close as can be calculated, this celebrated schooner of Canadian and Great Lakes history ended her career a few minutes after four o'clock in the afternoon of 14 August 1814. Lost with the *Nancy* were 303 barrels of flour and pork, hundreds of pairs of shoes, shoe leather, stocks and clasps, and candles. A British boat, "called a gunboat but unworthy the name," was captured.

In such desperate circumstances, Worsley had no option but to do the next best thing: take evasive action. He and his men took cover in the woods and escaped "to the great astonishment of the enemy," says Worsley. The imperial forces took away valuable arms and supplies. "We walked that night with our wounded and dying 36 miles before we came to any house," Worsley told his father. "We lost everything we had except what we stood upright in."

Sinclair's landing parties went ashore to reconnoitre and give chase, and some considerable distance away from the *Nancy* chanced upon the British commander's desk, containing various items of correspondence[8] which showed the value of the schooner to the intended resupply of Michilimackinac. "They have nothing afloat now on that Lake. The *Nancy* appeared to me to be a very fine vessel between the size of the *Queen Charlotte* and *Lady Prevost*." Sinclair, on Colonel Croghan's advice, decided not to fortify and garrison the Nottawasaga River entrance, concluding that it would be impossible to protect it from overland attack from York during winter. Sinclair therefore quit Lake Huron, bound for the easier climes of Lake Erie. And in his report to his superior, Secretary of the Navy Jones, he had some unflattering comments to make about "a rocky ironbound shore" unforgiving in its steepness and lack of anchorages, prone to thick fogs and thus a place of extremely dangerous navigation.[9]

Sinclair had clearly miscalculated. Keen to fall back to the safer Lake Erie, where admittedly military obligations were demanding his attention, he failed to grasp that two schooners would not do to command all the requisite needs of Lake Huron. Thus, while the squadron made for Lake Erie all that was left were the *Tigress* and *Scorpion* to deal with the canny fur traders and their military and Indian associates. "The English were not so simple as to let two small vessels rule this lake," noted the American sailor Bunnell who was a witness, "but took advantage of this blunder of our commander, to be revenged for the loss of their navy."[10]

Worsley's little war was not yet finished, only somewhat disadvantaged by the American barrage. At this time, too, some canoes of the North West Company, heavily laden with goods for the Indian trade, effected their escape from the mouth of the Nottawasaga to the north, destined for the mouth of French River, a nexus of canoe routes.

On 15 August, on the eve of his return to Lake Erie, Sinclair gave directions to Lt. Daniel Turner, commanding the *Scorpion* and the *Tigress,* to remain at Nottawasaga and keep up a rigorous blockade "until you shall be driven from the Lake by the inclemency of the Season, suffering not a boat or canoe to pass in or out of this River." The *Tigress* was retained in these waters in case either of the vessels should suffer accident and need assistance. Turner was given discretionary orders to send the *Tigress* to cruise for a week or two in waters about St. Joseph Island, in order to intercept the enemy's fur canoes moving between St. Marys River and French River. Sinclair contended that one vessel was sufficient to blockade the Nottawasaga.

Sinclair disliked the exposed nature of Nottawasaga Bay, for, as he pointed out to Turner, it had no anchorage to protect it from northwest gales. Sinclair, using the captured log book from the *Nancy,* learned of a small island in the southwest of the bay (Hen and Chicken Island, White's Bay, Collingwood) that might provide some security, and of islands to the north (Christian, Beckwith, and Hope) that would give good anchorage. Leaving nothing to chance, Sinclair suggested that Turner shift anchorages from time to time and always be on the lookout. He was to keep watch at night so as to avoid surprise attacks which the enemy "might be driven to by his desperate situation, as the Blockade must starve him into a surrender by the Spring." He also instructed Turner to make an accurate survey of Nottawasaga Bay and to extend his hydrographical inquiries as far east as the elusive Matchedash Bay, "observing all its Islands, Creeks, Bays, Shoals, Anchorages, Courses, Distances & Soundings, particularly attending to the kind of Bottom." If Michilimackinac could not yet be taken this season its trade should be strangled and its communications severed. These tasks fell to the commanders of the two American men-of-war. "It is all important," Sinclair wrote, "to cut the enemies line of communication . . . on which his very existence depends." As a final act before leaving, he felled trees to annoy enemy's navigation of the river.[11]

For a few days, the *Scorpion* and *Tigress* lingered off Nottawasaga River entrance. The pickings were nonexistent. A late-summer storm obliged Turner to lift the blockade and abandon any idea of a survey of Matchedash Bay. The schooners therefore quit their station and steered for St. Joseph Island. There their officers and men hoped to find a happier hunting ground, for this island stood, it should be remembered, adjacent to the narrow channels through which all North West Company vessels must pass on their regular routes between Sault Ste. Marie and French River.

At that moment the state of imperial fortunes on Lake Huron could be described as critical. It is worth recounting here the various successes of American arms on that inland sea to that date. Put-in-Bay (of September of the previous year) allowed U.S. naval power to flow northward into Lake Huron unopposed by British warships. North West Company ships all had fallen prey to the U.S. Navy, or were at risk. British naval units had been reduced to a few bateaux and several canoes. Such naval lieutenants and seamen who were at Lake Huron or Georgian Bay had no men-of-war. It may be added that just after Sinclair sailed from Nottawasaga the aforementioned storm occurred. The flagship *Niagara* lost all her boats and had sprung her mainmasts. She put into Detroit for repairs and then returned to Presque Isle. Nor had they anything in the way of a regular establishment ashore. No naval reinforcements were possible given the state of affairs on the Niagara frontier, where the two armies were locked in combat. British policy makers had never figured on this state of affairs. The only fulcrum of power was Michilimackinac, where the garrison was holed up awaiting resupply and the course of events.

In such circumstances it is no wonder Worsley took two days to consider what he ought to do. He could have made his way back to Fort York and there awaited further instructions. Instead, he determined upon his own little scheme of warfare.

We now return to 18 August. On that date Worsley, who had gathered his forces, slipped out of the mouth of the Nottawasaga River in two bateaux and one canoe. Accompanying him were eighteen seamen equipped only with small arms and muskets. We do not know the precise route of the bateaux's northern journey. Presumably it consisted of the route picked through channels of the island-infested granite shore of eastern Georgian Bay, that also taken earlier by McDouall—from Christian Island north to Pointe au Baril, thence to Byng Inlet and the Bustard Islands, and along the north shore of Georgian Bay, through the pass where Kilarney is today, and thence west along the splendid, almost vacant North Channel to its western limit and Michilimackinac, St. Joseph, and Drummond Island. Six days later, on the eve of the Indians spying the two American schooners, *Scorpion* and *Tigress,* Worsley was within 8 miles of St. Joseph Island. Worsley calculated his distance covered as 380 miles—or about 63 miles per day. His men had suffered greatly: they had been, he said, "exposed to great hardships and privations of every description having only what we could shoot or catch by fishing to subsist on."[12]

On 24 August Worsley, forewarned via native report, saw the enemy's schooners under sail between islands off St. Joseph. No nervousness is expressed in his report of proceedings to his superior. Yet the way Worsley tells of this aspect of the war, timing and patience counted for everything: "Seeing no probability of my being able to pass them in my Bateaux unobserved, owing to the narrowness of the channel, I determined on concealing them [the bateaux] in a secure place, in the choice of which I was greatly assisted by Lieutenant Livingstone of the Indian Department, who had accompanied me in his canoe from the Nottawasaga River and whose zeal and activity for the Service I beg to acknowledge."[13] As soon as the bateaux were hauled ashore and hidden from view, Worsley, with his aide, took to a canoe and under cover of night made for Michilimackinac. Worsley's intention was to parley with the commandant, Colonel McDouall. From McDouall he hoped for assistance in the cutting-out expedition he was then devising against the enemy.

Worsley's appeal to McDouall met with immediate assistance. McDouall held energetic views on forward measures of warfare: like Roberts before him, and Worsley now, he saw the advantages of taking the initiative. His support for Worsley came in two ways: first, a detachment of the Royal Newfoundland Regiment under Lieutenant Bulger was named to accompany Worsley, the seamen, and the armada of four bateaux. Second, two guns were given for the expedition—a 6-pounder for Worsley's bateau and a 3-pounder for Bulger's. It was a joint expedition of the Royal Newfoundlanders and the Royal Navy, under the supreme command of Worsley. Worsley, a stickler for protocol, correctly says he gave command of the second bateau to Bulger (and students of army history will be amused that the Navy granted to the Army such autonomy and responsibility). Gathering the force took a day and a half. On 1 September, all ready, Worsley quit Michilimackinac for the Detour, reached the next evening, 2 September, having covered thirty-six miles.

From McDouall, Worsley had learned that the American warships had several canoes of Indians with them. In consequence, "a select body of Indian warriors," that is, trustworthy, loyal natives, were detailed to accompany the expedition. These were headed by Indian Agent Dickson, to whom Worsley credits the "good order and regularity" during the course of the expedition.

On the third Worsley left his boats in hiding in a small bay, wisely choosing to press ahead in his canoe to spy out the spot where the American schooners were known to have been cruising five days previous. He found but one vessel, anchored some six miles from his force. The vessel, the *Tigress*, rode at easy anchor in midchannel of the Detour, her sentinel post.

Worsley deemed it prudent to conduct his attack under cover of night. He returned to where his bateaux and men were in hiding. Again gathering forces, he set off for the Detour, leaving at 6:00 P.M. for the anticipated action.

"The night being favourable," reported Worsley of the darkness that permitted such stealth, "we had approached within ten yards of the Enemy's schooner before they hailed us, but before we had time to get alongside, they fired their gun which providentially missed us at the same time opened a smart fire with their small arms with very little effect. We soon got alongside and gained the Deck where the contest was short, the Enemy being driven below from whence they however fired several muskets which unfortunately killed one of my seamen." At about 9:00 P.M., in the midst of a great thunderstorm, men aboard the *Scorpion* ten miles distant thought they could hear gunfire.

So came into Worsley's waiting, needy hands the fine U.S. schooner *Tigress* mounting one long 24-pounder. She had had a complement of thirty-one officers and men, commanded by Sailing Master Stephen Champlin, who with the rest of the officers was severely wounded. In the action the Americans lost one killed, four wounded, and three missing (reported killed and thrown overboard). By contrast the British lost two seamen killed and seven soldiers injured plus Lieutenant Bulger, who was also wounded. "Our loss in this affair was trifling," concluded Worsley.

The American prisoners were taken to Michilimackinac, and there they learned to their horror what had happened to the fate of some of the American soldiers who had fallen on that field. Six who had been mortally wounded had been scalped. A surgeon left for dead had been inhumanely butchered. The details were unimaginably wicked. From Michilimackinac the British took the prisoners across Lake Huron and then to Lake Simcoe, which they crossed. They were marched overland to Little York, as one sailor called it: "I entered Little York this time with far different feelings from what I did two years previous—then I marched in victorious to the tune of Yankee Doodle, but now I was a prisoner of war."[14] Sixty were marched to Kingston under military and Indian guard, and some made their escape to serve in the U.S. Navy at other times.

The order of business turned to preparing to attack the enemy's other vessel, which Worsley understood to be anchored some distance away among some islands. Worsley sent Lieutenant Livingstone in his canoe to investigate. Two hours later the young Indian Department man, the heroic scout of this entire campaign, returned with glowing news that the enemy's schooner (the *Scorpion*) was at that precise hour heading up to Worsley.

The British commander calculated that given the distance separating the two vessels, the second schooner could not have heard the fire of cannon and musket and, in consequence, must be ignorant of the fate of her consort. His logic was sound. Even had the gunfire been heard through the thunder, no precautions were taken aboard the *Scorpion*.

Worsley takes up the story: "I determined not to alter the position of the *Tigress*—but to keep the American Pendant still flying. This I did being aware that if she once had a suspicion of my being an enemy she would escape me from her superior sailing [qualities]. Everything succeeded to my wishes. Unsuspicious of what had taken place she anchored within two miles of me." The officers and men of the *Scorpion* were unaware that the *Tigress* lay in British hands.

That night passed without incident, "and as day dawned on the 6th Inst. [September] I slipped my cable and ran down under my jib and foresail." Worsley kept ten or twelve hands on deck, a nominal number for the watch, with the rest ready in the hold and cabin except a few soldiers. These he had covered with greatcoats and other items so as to prevent any cause for suspicion. The ruse was seemingly complete. But the American sailor Bunnell tells us that he thought that as the *Tigress* stood down on the *Scorpion*, "something told me that all was not right." He continues: "I communicated my suspicions to the rest of the crew, and they only laughed at me. They said, 'the English have no vessels on this lake, and what have we to fear?' While we were discussing the subject, the *Tigress* having got across our bow, fired a twenty-four pounder, and immediately boarded us with twenty soldiers, twelve sailors, and about one hundred Indians. We were all taken prisoner without firing a gun."[15]

Worsley has a slightly different perspective on this episode. "So little were they apprehensive of our design," he wrote, "that they were employed washing decks, when within about twelve yards of her I fired the long 24 pounder which was the signal for the soldiers in the hold to board. I immediately ran on board of her, when the soldiers fired a volley, and boarded with the whole of my crew." This vessel was "immediately carried" and the British flag hoisted above the American.

Thus did the second enemy schooner come into British possession. Worsley confirmed that the second prize was the U.S. schooner *Scorpion*, Lt. Daniel Turner commanding, mounting one long 24-pounder and a long 12-pounder stowed below, and having a complement of five officers and thirty-one seamen. In the action, the Americans suffered two killed and two wounded, the British, one wounded. "Thus you see," Worsley wrote proudly to his father, "after a series of hardships I have got two schooners both finer vessels than the *Nancy* and have providentially escaped unhurt."

The British were buoyed by their success. In reporting the capture of the U.S. schooners, Lieutenant Bulger, the joint commander, noted that the rowing expedition had been undertaken in perfect order and silence. The attack on the *Tigress* had been well planned and executed. The enemy had fought bravely. The second capture was equally daring. "Everything was so well managed by Lieutenant Worsley," wrote Bulger of the taking of the *Scorpion*, "that we went within ten yards of the enemy before they discovered us. It was then too late; for, in the course of five minutes, her deck was covered with our men, and the British flag hoisted over the American." Bulger added, "To the admirable good conduct and management of Lieutenant Worsley, of the Royal Navy, the success is to be in a great measure attributed; but I must assure you, that every officer and man did his duty."[16]

When news of the double success reached Commodore Yeo at Kingston, he had every reason to be delighted with the results on Lake Huron. "I have great satisfaction in transmitting to you, Sir, for Their Lordships information," he wrote the secretary of the Admiralty, John Wilson Croker, "the copy of a letter from Lieutenant Worsley commanding the Naval Establishment on Lake Huron detailing the Particulars of an admirable, planned, and gallantly executed enterprise." Their lordships expressed formal appreciation of the gallantry of those involved. Worsley's actions attracted attention and acclaim. His exploits were praised by McDouall and Lt. Gen. Gordon Drummond, who described Worsley as this "able, active and intelligent officer . . . of conciliatory manner." In other words, he was superb in making arrangements for joint operations. Drummond thought Worsley deserved more that the Admiralty gave him, "a pat on the back." "It would have afforded me still greater pleasure," he put it most gently, "had their gallant young leader Lieutenant Worsley been so fortunate as to have received a stronger mark, by promotion, of their Lordships good opinion; an honour of which, as far as I am aware I am capable of judging [he] appears to have been highly deserving."[17]

Poor health and increasing penury now dogged Worsley. He remained in his Lake Huron command but in October fell ill to the prevalent lake fever. He spent the winter in sick quarters on Lake Erie on half pay and was back commanding the *Scorpion* in April 1815, when he delivered news of the peace to Michilimackinac. For a time, he had command of HM brig *Star* on Lake Huron and was eventually sent home to England. The Canadian war proved costly to Worsley in other ways. His spare clothing, his chronometer or timekeeper, all his nautical instruments, and two hundred pounds were lost at Nottawasaga during the *Nancy* episode. His destitution at this state of affairs was later revealed in his appeal to King William IV in 1832 (see Appendix B). The fruits of victory brought him early promotion. On 13 July 1815, Worsley, who had completed his necessary two years' service as lieutenant, was promoted to the rank of commander.[18] He never was employed in the Navy after the war, though he had a compensatory stint in the Coast Guard. He died in 1835.

The North West Company claimed £2,200 compensation for the loss of the *Nancy* and a sum of £1,743 5s. 0d. for wartime services. The government reimbursed accordingly. A tally of allowances paid to the Nor'Westers indicates that they were further indemnified for various services for 1813 and 1814, bringing the grand total for her war services to £3,943 5s.[19]

Worsley's cutting-out expeditions provide models for tactics in small-boat warfare in which stealth, surprise, and, if necessary, violent engagement all play a part. The separation or division of enemy forces also aided the attackers as one by one they picked off the enemy. "This was," wrote Theodore Roosevelt with admiration, "an exceedingly creditable and plucky enterprise."[20] The American commanders had grown careless, and native informants had tipped off the British that the vessels lay apart from one another. For all of these reasons the Americans paid a heavy price.

News of the unusual and untimely loss of the two American schooners reached Washington at least one week before President Madison reported, ludicrously, "A part of the squadron of Lake Erie has been extended to Lake Huron, and has produced the advantage of displaying our command of that lake also."[21] The first casualty in war is truth. Perhaps, however, Madison had been misinformed. The loss of warships to the enemy in such a fashion was to have no parallel until a century and a half later, when in 1968, during an undeclared war, North Koreans captured the USS *Pueblo*.

Report of the loss of the *Scorpion* and *Tigress* cannot have been pleasing to the United States Navy, more especially because the vessels had been seized, in each instance, by means of surprise. In Boston Harbor, aboard USS *Independence*, a court of inquiry, presided over by Capt. John Shaw, gathered to investigate the cause of the capture of the two men-of-war. One wonders what sort of questions raced through the minds of board members. Did they ask, How was it that one warship had been shanghaied in the dead of night by a mixed or irregular force of the enemy? Had U.S. officers been inattentive to duty? And how was it that a second vessel had been caught by surprise, in daylight, with the crew scrubbing down the deck? Who was to blame for this calamitous series of events injurious to the honor of the service?

The court knew of Commodore Sinclair's attempt to blame Lieutenant Turner for this "mortifying loss." The *Scorpion*, said Sinclair, could have defended herself better, especially in view of the fact that Turner had selected his own crew. In fact, Sinclair had warned Turner that the British then holed up at Mackinac Island were likely to attempt to take the enemy's men-of-war so that they could break the blockade.[22]

The court received from Turner a narrative of proceedings. In this Turner detailed why he had gone north from Nottawasaga River so quickly: as soon as Sinclair had departed for Lake Erie, a furious gale from the northwest had come upon the two ships keeping up the blockade, a ship's boat was lost, a safer anchorage was sought but not found by either vessel, and soon a second gale occurred, and before long the two vessels were on the lee shore of Georgian Bay. "The sea having full sweep over us," Turner declared, "I feared both vessels must be lost unless we left the bay which we did on the 23rd [August]." Before departing Nottawasaga Bay Turner consulted with all officers, and they all agreed with his decision to quit that station and lift the blockade. Reaching St. Joseph, "a safer and equally advantageous station," on the next day, he took up his station cruising from the north end of St. Joseph Island to French River. (Turner intended to intercept any North West Company traffic and also to survey the entrance to French River. It is not likely that he got anywhere near hard-to-find

French River but rather confined his purposes to watching the approaches to St. Joseph Island.) And on the fifth of September he got under way from his most recent watching anchorage and approached the *Tigress*, anchoring about five miles from her. "I had no signals either for night or day on board and had no means of preparing any." And, his narrative explains, "previously to parting with the Commodore the want of signals had been made known to him—he informed me he had none but his own set."

Turner now takes up the details of the capture of his vessel: "The enemy under American colors & with almost the whole of his men secreted, and some of those that were to be seen dressed in the clothes of the American Officers, and men formerly on board being close on our larboard quarter fired and boarded at the same time. I sprang from my berth upon the alarm—but before I could gain the deck, tho' undressed, I had several cutlasses over my head and was threatened with instant death, if I offered to move. My deck was covered with the enemy. I knew that resistance would be entirely in vain, and surrendered."[23]

The facts of the matter, as the Board of Inquiry thought fit to print in its official report of decision,[24] were that Lieutenant Turner in the *Scorpion* had been cruising near the mouth of French River on the night of 3 September when the *Tigress*, Lieutenant Champlin, had been attacked by the enemy in five large boats and nineteen canoes carrying some three hundred sailors, soldiers, and Indians. The attack, it was noted, had been made in pitch darkness. The British had not been seen until close on board. Nor were they discovered by the sound of their oars. Every attempt was made by Champlin, his officers, and men to defend the *Tigress* with bravery and skill. But all of the officers were cut down. The overwhelming numbers of the enemy prevailed.

As to the loss of the *Scorpion*, this was attributed largely to "the want of signals," that is, poor communications. The gunner in charge of the watch did report to the sailing master that the *Tigress* was bearing down under American colors. No indication of suspicious intent was realized by Lieutenant Turner, and a few moments later the *Tigress* ran alongside of the *Scorpion*, "fired, boarded, and carried her." The British masquerading as Americans had done the trick: "It appears to the court, that the loss of the *Scorpion* is, in a great measure, to be attributed to the want of signals; and owing to this deficiency, no suspicions were excited as to the real character of the *Tigress*; and from some of the English officers and men on board of her being dressed in the clothes of her former officers and men, and the residue of the enemy's crew being concealed, a surprise was effected, which precluded the possibility of defence." The court in its wisdom, having the whole testimony before it, concluded that the conduct of Lieutenant Turner was "that of a discreet and vigilant officer."

Worsley renamed the *Scorpion* HMS *Confiance* and the *Tigress* HMS *Surprize*. The taking of the American schooners gave the British new leverage on the upper lakes. Not only did it bless them with two armed ships for which they had been so wanting. Michilimackinac could now be resupplied. The French River entrance could now be guarded, giving protection to Canadian fur-trade shipments. It also enabled them to distribute many goods and presents to the Indians. A large native alliance could bring a swarm of Indians down on the American-held posts.

The fear of this was not lost on one U.S. Indian agent, B. F. Stickney, at Sault Ste. Marie. "If our fleet does not go up very early in the Spring into Lake Michigan," he wrote in worrying tones, "we may expect a visit from the yellow gentry of the North."[25] The new worry became once again the protection of Detroit. Indian chiefs told American agents that soon the springtime would bring enemy attacks.

In planning for frontier warfare for the coming season, 1815, American authorities hoped to use Indian disaffection to their advantage. They knew from native reports that some Indians were destitute of both clothing and provisions. Prominent chiefs gave indication of switching sides, and of aiding the United States against the British.[26] The War Department planned an expedition of mounted infantry to secure American interests in southwest Michigan Territory. This was abandoned for logistical as well as fiscal reasons. In fact, frontier posts lay exposed. Gen. Duncan McArthur of the U.S. Army, who was instructed to undertake the expedition, described the defenseless state of Michigan Territory in spring of 1815, when he wrote to his superior in Washington: "Every house in the Territory of Michigan is a frontier, there are no back settlements, nor will the Country admit of any. In case of an Indian War, no part of it can be protected."[27]

McArthur did not stop there; he even charged Michigan residents with trading with the enemy and giving hostile Indians the means of subsistence. He went so far as to blame Detroit citizens for Colonel Croghan's failure at Michilimackinac the previous summer—"in the first place, by communicating with the enemy, every circumstance relative to the expedition, and secondly by discouraging the Officers and men by repeatedly stating the impracticality of taking Mackinac, and even addressing a written petition to Col. Croghan praying him to disobey his orders from the War Department and abandon the expedition."

Officers were resigning from the Army on account of poor pay or failure to be awarded prize money. Bounties in good land were not forthcoming as promised. Resentment and low morale seemed rife. Treachery and treason seemed rampant in Michigan Territory. McArthur imagined disloyalty in his midst; untrustworthy native informants and American inhabitants surrounded him. Some indication of his doubts about American loyalties is given in his letter of 6 February 1815 in which he planned the next year's campaign:

> Should the war continue, I am of opinion, that such of the inhabitants as are friendly and disposed towards the United States ought to be removed into the interior, and those who would prefer taking part with the enemy sent to him. And the Country laid waste. Should the enemy appear disposed to continue his burning on our Seaboard, would it not be well to send a force into Canada next summer which would lay it Waste. And in this way interpose between us and the enemy, a desert which he could not easily pass? For service of this kind Volunteers from Kentucky and Ohio can be had. But I am of opinion that no volunteer force can ever again be prevailed on, to go to Detroit for the protection of the inhabitants of the Territory. Their conduct convinced the late mounted volunteers, that they were the most dangerous of our enemies.[28]

Had they known the appallingly bad circumstances of the enemy the American war leaders might have been less willing to seek an early peace. In distant Prairie du Chien, for instance, misery reigned that last winter of the war. Disaffection was rampant. The place was destitute of provisions, sociability, harmony, and good understanding. At Michilimackinac, similarly, the nearly starved garrison had been placed on reduced rations. From Ancaster, Upper Canada, agents reported the destitute conditions of the natives and warned that without food supplies the former allies of the British were likely to die. Thus this great irony: that those who had been prepared to fight for the king were now surely to die because of the war.[29]

In those last days of the war on the upper Great Lakes the British clung by their fingernails to the interior trade. They propped up their Indian alliance by the promise of presents for the forthcoming season of military campaigning. They acted on faith. The senior naval officer planned as best he could for the springtime's exertions. "The two schooners that were captured by Lt. Worsley are the only vessels we have on Lake Huron," he reported anxiously to the secretary of the Admiralty. "It is my intention to order one of them, if she can be spared, into Lake Erie, whilst the other will remain to victual and attend the garrison at Michilimackinac."[30] In other words, at that stage, the British faced the next warring season with but two ships, one each for Lake Erie and Lake Huron. He imagined that the Americans would not repeat the mistakes of the past year; instead, they would pour all their growing military might into Lake Huron and Georgian Bay where such faltering and tragic consequences to American arms had been witnessed in 1814.

It is true that the material capabilities of British sea power, so long disadvantaged on Lake Huron, had been given a splendid reversal of fortune by Worsley's capture of the two American schooners. They yielded hard-to-acquire stores and supplies for Lake Huron.[31] Commodore Yeo was not far off the mark when, on 12 October 1814, he confidently wrote the secretary of the Admiralty, John Wilson Croker, that this "admirably planned and gallantly executed seizure" had three benefits of obvious merit. First, it saved the post and garrison at northwestern Lake Huron, then posted at Michilimackinac. Second, it allowed a friendly intercourse with the natives of that quarter. Third, it protected the trade of the North West Company. These ranked as the most obvious benefits of this superb coup. But there was another benefit to British arms. The action, concluded Yeo, "has proved a ground work for a naval Establishment on that Lake, which, in my opinion is more necessary than one on Lake Erie, and which I shall not fail to form this Winter."[32]

Worsley was not alone in his daring-do. A somewhat similar action had been effected by Cdr. Alexander Dobbs of HMS *Charwell* and Lt. Copleston Radcliffe of HMS *Netley* between the hours of 11:00 P.M. and midnight on 12 August 1814. Three American men-of-war, the schooners *Ohio, Somers,* and *Porcupine* (the last two veterans of the Battle of Put-in-Bay), each with thirty men, under command of Lt. A. H. M. Conklin, were moored snugly under the guns of Fort Erie. That post was then in American hands. The schooners had been placed in such position so as to flank British units in any approach made against it. Lacking any means on the lake to use against the American vessels the British resorted to other measures, those of improvisation.

The British naval officers with seventy-five seamen and marines, using a gig carried upon their shoulders fully twenty miles from Queenstown on the Niagara River to Frenchman's Creek, and then an additional eight miles through woods to Lake Erie, put their craft into the water and made for the enemy. They took the two former vessels by surprise, and then allowed the vessels to drift downriver, where they were secured. The action was marked by "heady and gallant conduct" against a greater force, said Dobbs.[33] This cutting-out expedition brought into British hands two more schooners, the *Ohio* and the *Somers*, each sporting three long 12-pounders. The *Porcupine* was not captured. In all, it was a great feat of arms and surprise, and was no discredit to the American forces. The British renamed the *Ohio* the *Huron* and the *Somers* the *Sauk* for their tribal allies. By this stroke, as if by magic, the British fleet on the upper Great Lakes had been doubled.

These reinforcements buttressed British naval power at the close of 1814, and as Commodore Yeo and others planned for the next season's campaign, the Admiralty had under consideration means of sending well-disciplined sailors to the Great Lakes theater. At this late date they were remedying one of the problems that had given them such difficulty throughout the conflict.[34] But Yeo had his own special plans for these "drafts" of seamen: they were to be destined for his own great flagship, then nearing completion, the 104-gun ship-of-the-line *St. Lawrence*. It was Yeo's habit always to keep the best for himself, as the unfortunate Barclay had learned to his cost at Put-in-Bay. The British naval commander in chief on the Great Lakes still thought in grandiose terms, all the while neglecting what was the obvious lesson of this war: that frigates and corvettes, brigs and schooners were the best means of conducting a naval war on these inland seas, and, more, that what could not be won in a fleet action could be acquired in those cutting-out expeditions which were the hallmark of naval warfare on these lakes.

British plans for the next year of the war, that is, 1815, called for a general increase in the numbers of the army, a strengthening of fortifications and armaments, and a naval buildup on the Great Lakes. In addition to the *St. Lawrence*, a seventy-four-gun ship was started at Kingston and the hope and expectation was that this act would discourage the Americans from doing likewise. Three frigates and two heavy brigs were being talked about for construction at Isle aux Noix near Montreal. For Lake Erie a decision was made to buttress the northern shore on its eastward extremity, with particular attention to the choke points of communication and control. Thus Turkey Point, which after the Battle of the Thames had lost for the British most of southwestern Upper Canada, acquired enhanced military status. Turkey Point, Point Ryerse and Port Dover had military posts. Turkey Point had some possibilities as a naval base, but Port Maitland at the mouth of the Grand River, to the northeast, was found preferable. Fort Norfolk at Turkey Point was intended to house three hundred soldiers, and a blockhouse there was commenced during the winter of 1814–15 under Lieutenant Wilson of the 37th Regiment of Foot. This establishment, and the small naval establishment at Port Maitland, had brief lives. It would take only ten years for the sites to revert to a wild state or be used for other purposes than defending Upper Canada.

For Lake Huron, meanwhile, the Admiralty made provision for the building of a frigate of twenty-four or twenty-six guns. Yeo was of the opinion that this vessel, plus the two American schooners recently captured and a few gunboats being built, would ensure naval ascendancy there. Lake Erie had been abandoned as impossible to establish a naval force there.[35] Of the "phantom frigate" of Penetanguishene not much is known except that Captain Collier, who had been detailed to develop the Penetanguishene Road, was superintending the building of the frigate in January 1815, and seamen were being requested for her. She must have been well advanced in construction when, on 25 February, news reached Yeo at Kingston that the peace treaty between Great Britain and the United States had been signed.

VII

~

The Uneasy Peace

BRITISH AND AMERICAN
QUESTS FOR SECURITY

In the making of the peace, the British seemed at a disadvantage. "Considering everything," the great commander the duke of Wellington told the prime minister, Lord Liverpool, "it is my opinion that the war has been a most successful one, and highly honourable to the British arms; but from particular circumstances, such as the want of the naval superiority on the Lakes, you have not been able to carry it into the enemy's territory, notwithstanding your military success, and now undoubtedly military superiority, and have not even cleared your own territory of the enemy on the point of attack." This advice was dated 9 November 1814. British ministers were then pondering American offers of peace, and Wellington was anxious to bring the conflict with the United States to a conclusion, and to effect an honorable peace. In his view Britain had no right to claim any territory, for despite its strong military position in North America it had not held any territory. No use, he said, to stipulate for the *uti possidetis*. "You can get no territory; indeed the state of your military operations, however creditable, does not entitle you to demand any."[1] He gave similar advice to Lord Castlereagh, the foreign secretary. Castlereagh proposed reconciliation and concord with the Americans. He wanted to put old scores aside and avoid controversy wherever possible. The Cabinet accepted this revised position, and the pace of negotiations, first begun 4 August, quickened.

An equally important British consideration was that over the strenuous negotiations on Indian affairs. At the peace table British plenipotentiaries had been unable to keep their promises to their native allies. Any thought of a quasi-independent Indian buffer state—the size of England, Scotland, Wales, and Ireland combined—which would have been carved exclusively out of U.S. territory, had to be abandoned. This idea died a long, slow death from August to December 1814 and was a sell-out on the grounds of political expediency for diplomatic results. Wellington was right: had British arms held territory then stipulation could have been made to force the creation of an Indian territory. As it was, that concept died on the anvil of Anglo-American accord. How could native treaty rights, so long accepted by British agents, be maintained south of the boundary? And what consequences would this have to the Crown's alliance with natives north of that same border? The answers were now clear. Britain would suffer great loss of credit with native peoples on both sides of the frontier. Article IX of the treaty specified that both countries would put an end to hostilities with all tribes and nations of Indians with whom they had been at war, and to return to these peoples such possessions, rights, and privileges, either enjoyed or entitled to, as of the year 1811; provided that these tribes or nations would agree to desist from all hostilities against the other power. In other words, this was a bilateral, mutual pacification treaty.[2]

As for American diplomatic positions in the negotiations, the return to peace without loss of national face was an overriding consideration. Matched with this was a desire not to abandon U.S. objectives for security in the North American continental interior. That meant having a free hand, unencumbered by British and Canadian interference, in the conduct of western expansion and Indian pacification. Tied to this was the urgent necessity of fiscal restraint on a scale hitherto unimagined in American governmental procedures.

The Peace of Christmas Eve, as it is called, contained fifteen articles. These may be briefly stated. Articles I and II called for a firm and universal peace plus the restoration "without delay ... [of] all territory, places and possessions" seized by either party during the war and still held by them. Articles III to VIII settled boundary questions from the Bay of Fundy to the Rocky Mountains, with international commissions to be established to decide ownership of Grand Manan Islands and islands in Passamaquoddy Bay, to find the "northwest corner of Nova Scotia" and the northwestern head of the Connecticut River—and to have a boundary surveyed—and likewise to determine the middle of the waterway through the St. Lawrence River and the Great Lakes (and to allocate every island to one power or the other), this to include Lake Superior to the northwest corner of the Lake of the Woods at which location the forty-ninth parallel became the boundary to the Rocky Mountains. Article IX called for the pacification of the Indians, and Article X obliged each power to restrain its natives from committing hostilities against the other; and it went further in stating that each power should refrain from using natives against the other in any future war. Other articles provided details of impressment, blockade, indemnities for losses, general amnesty, and ratification. Not included were particulars of fisheries rights.

The treaty specified that all territories were to be returned to their original owners as before the war. On this issue so much depended for the peace and prosperity on the borderlands between Canada and the United States—and equally important for the future relations with the native peoples and nations. John Quincy Adams, heading the U.S. delegation at Ghent, was not alone when he classified the Ghent arrangements as a truce rather than a peace.

In Montreal the partners of the North West Company had pondered the prospects of the treaty with acute anxiety. For they knew that Michilimackinac would have to be abandoned as all the western posts had been a generation before. This key to northwestern empire was bound to be sacrificed. William McGillivray, chief director of the firm, entreated with Prevost not to give up Michilimackinac. McGillivray poised the customary arguments of the fur traders: the security of Upper Canada rested on friendship with the western Indians; this rested, in turn, on the fur trade based upon Montreal. Britain ought to be able to continue trade to the Mississippi watershed, using waterways guarded by Michilimackinac. This post ought to remain open, if necessary in American hands, but not be closed. A reduction of American customs duties would ease tensions and promote cross-border trade. A new substitute for Michilimackinac would have to be found. McGillivray pronounced St. Joseph Island as most unfit for a military station. But within a week of this entreaty Prevost's command passed to Gen. Sir Gordon Drummond, and the Nor'Westers commenced their pressure upon him. Drummond was sympathetic to the viewpoint that Michilimackinac was one of the disputed islands through which the international boundary must pass, and this, to him, was reason enough to delay its transfer.[3] But this sly move could be countered by the Americans, and it was: they threatened a delay in withdrawing from Fort Malden, considered by the British and Canadians as key to the security of Upper Canada. Again, pressures on the southern frontier influenced the fortunes of the northern economy.

In December 1814, just as British and American diplomats were concluding their arrangements that would lead to the signing and ratification of the Treaty of Ghent, the two British armed schooners went into winter quarters on Lake Huron. The place selected was Nottawasaga River, scene of the fiery end of the *Nancy* and the depot for supplies destined for British forces in the northern field. HM schooners *Confiance* and *Surprize* gave to the place the name of Schooner Town. Confusion still existed in the official mind of British naval command as to whether Nottawasaga could remain a base of shipbuilding, supply, and refit. But already, as early as the spring of 1815, it was becoming clear that this was a most unsuitable location for a naval base, having no safe avenue of approach from seaward to such a tight river entrance, one so often plagued with a rising surf.

In the early months of 1815 four problems existed for authorities on the upper Great Lakes, both British and American:

1. How to bring news of the peace to all commanders
2. How to effect the peaceful withdrawal of respective forces without disrupting any arrangements that had been made, by either party, with Indian allies
3. How to enforce national laws along the waterland separating the two sovereignties when such a boundary was not clearly designated, especially in northwestern Lake Huron and Sault Ste. Marie
4. How to solve fiscal problems related to vast expenditures undertaken by both powers during the war, and thus how to demilitarize the Great Lakes in order to reduce expenditures without compromising respective national securities.

Meanwhile, nearly four and a half months had elapsed before Colonel McDouall, commandant at Michilimackinac, learned of the peace arrangements. On the evening of 24 April, the *Scorpion,* commanded by Worsley, brought him the news. McDouall was alarmed and annoyed at being literally out on a limb in such an exposed location, for there military intelligence was sparse and communications subject to falling into doubtful hands. He thus wrote his superior pointing out that "such a shameful & unprecedented delay might have occasioned, (& may have, for what I yet know) the loss of many lives."

McDouall, preoccupied with the pending military changes, discovered little to be pleased with in the treaty. He found perplexing the giving up of Fort McKay, the post at Prairie du Chien. To his way of thinking the treaty's Article IX afforded clear and circumstantial evidence that the Mississippi country— "so shamefully seized upon by the Americans in *June* last, & from which they were expelled in the ensuing month"—should again revert to the natives, "as it is expressly stipulated that they are restored to all the possessions, rights & privileges, which they enjoyed in 1811." Acting on instructions to withdraw the garrison from Fort McKay, McDouall directed Captain Bulger, who had command there, to act accordingly.

McDouall now turned to an equally disagreeable matter: fixing on a new site for a British post until such time as boundary commissioners, as set by the treaty, could determine which of the islands were in British and which in U.S. hands. "I have not the smallest doubt," he wrote angrily, "from the usual arrogance & unblushing impudence of the latter [U.S.] Govt. that *every effort* will be made by them to grasp what they can." He imagined that both St. Joseph and the large island close to the Detour, the most westerly of the Manitoulin Islands now known as Drummond, the latter of which possessed a good port, would be claimed by the Americans. He worried that these places would be abandoned. "*If so, it will retire us out of the reach of the Indians altogether, & give the finishing blow to whatever influence we yet possess amongst them.*" McDouall underlined this sentence for effect. Should Drummond Island, "the key to the whole Western Country," follow the expected fate of the first, St. Joseph, he added with prescience, this would be proof of "our disgrace" in the eyes of the Indians. It would be also "absolute submission to the American Government, that it would be most grossly deceiving ours, to hold forth the expectation of being joined by a single Indian, in the event of another war." In a future war the best that the British could hope for would be Indian neutrality.

American forces had left Fort St. Joseph in a shambles. Lt. David Wingfield, RN, there in May 1815, wrote, "The Americans had entirely destroyed the fort, if it was ever worthy of such a name, the barracks and several of the houses, and but two or three of those which were left were tenantable, as the Lake had risen three feet above its usual height, and the lower part was covered with water; at this time there were no inhabitants."[4]

To secure St. Joseph Island, McDouall sent parties to repair buildings and make them fit to receive the garrison and stores from Michilimackinac. He also sent provisions there. Knowing no guarantee existed that the British would keep St. Joseph Island he did all he could to increase its defensive capabilities. He kept to this policy until August 1815 when he did an about-face and shifted the garrison to what he regarded as the most useful island, Drummond. An Indian agency was kept up at St. Joseph Island but all military stores and some of the buildings were shipped to Drummond Island. In due time the handful of reconstructed buildings at St. Joseph Island fell into disrepair.[5] Unhappily, St. Joseph Island, a football in an international challenge cup, though at last on Canadian sovereign soil, passed into seeming irrelevance.

With reference to Tecumseh's brilliant campaigning against the United States, McDouall imagined such an Indian war directed upon Canada, once the native alliance turned from British adherence. "Of this be assured," he warned his superior, "that a more terrible enemy exists not, than a numerous body of Indians, *properly managed & led on*, in such a Country as Upper Canada." The natives remembered the destruction of their fathers by General Wayne in 1795. This had occurred "under the very guns of our Fort on the Miami River." Far from being assisted by the British on that occasion, the fugitives were even refused admittance to the British post and thus suffered at the hands of the Americans an indiscriminate slaughter.

To this McDouall added one final and telling paragraph on the nature of frontier warfare:

> I have taken every precaution to make known the news of Peace, and to put a stop to that predatory mode of warfare, which they [the Indians] are continually waging against the Americans. To effect this *entirely* among so many tribes, having such cause to hate that people, need not be expected. The Govt of the United States, therefore, will soon have a fair pretext to glut their vengeance against them, & gradually to root them out. They will probably stop all Powder from going to the Mississippi (when they get this place) without which, these nations must perish in the winter: the slow but sure poison of their Whiskey Stills will affect the rest, & in fifty years time, there perhaps will not be an Indian left, between this & the Rocky Mountains, to plague either party.[6]

McDouall reported his recent visit to the Ottawa nation, where he had proclaimed peace among them with the customary ceremonies. They had received him with strong statements of attachment. They begged him to represent them to their Great Father, at Quebec, their settlements, fields and comforts. "I believe they *wish* to be a greater distance from this American Garrison," he wrote of Michilimackinac, "& to be in the vicinity of our new post, & yet are naturally loath to quit the pleasant abodes of their ancestors, where they are now so happy, for worse lands yet uncleared, & in a colder climate." Still, such a move had much to recommend it. The Ottawa were prepared to shift with the British.

Some idea of the difficulties establishing peace in Indian territories is demonstrated in the experiences of that remarkably feisty Newfoundlander, Capt. Andrew Bulger. We now trace his steps of the previous year. In October 1814, fresh from the capture of those two American schooners, in which he played a conspicuous part, Bulger got McDouall's instructions to go to Fort

McKay. There he was to be commandant. Bulger was bold as well as dedicated, guided by duty and honor. At the same time he was pompous, easily affronted and intolerant of challenges to his authority. We can see him as the king's man of the Upper Mississippi empire, anxious to make his mark and willing to rub any opposition the wrong way on principles and practices of imperial rule. His opponent in such circumstances turned out to be Robert Dickson, that old hand in native relations and the British Indian Agent and Superintendent to the Western Indians. "The situation at Fort McKay was both dangerous and delicate," write Bulger's biographers, a little uncritically, "but through determined leadership Bulger preserved the security of the 200 French Canadian inhabitants of the area and maintained the Indians' allegiance to the British flag." He put down a mutiny among the Michigan Fencibles on New Year's Eve 1814, and, after a general court-martial had three offenders flogged. Bulger quarreled constantly with the interfering and devious Dickson about how the sagging Indian alliance could propped up. His instructions called for him to have control over the distribution of provisions and gifts to the Indian families. Bulger, puffed up with such authority, refused to let Dickson interfere. In early January 1815 Dickson was recalled to Michilimackinac. For his part, Bulger received an endorsement by the inhabitants of Prairie du Chien applauding his leadership and protection. From McDouall, his military superior, came glowing praise for his "judicious, manly, and energetic conduct."[7]

Bulger had no such skill as an Indian negotiator, a skill the ousted Dickson possessed by instinct and experience. News reached him in April 1815 that the Americans and not the British and Canadians would hold the wilderness empire south of the line. He had difficulties convincing the Indian allies, so accustomed to sweet British promises, that they must ratify the treaty acknowledging American sovereignty. Pursuant to orders from McDouall dated 1 May, Bulger planned to extricate himself from Fort McKay. This he did on 24 May. He abandoned the area to American occupation.[8] He did not do so, however, before distributing food, military supplies and gifts to the Indians. He made his way to Michilimackinac and then Quebec (reached 19 June), determined to get what he thought to be well-deserved recognition and promotion, the latter finally achieved in 1820. For a time he was civil governor in the Hudson's Bay Company's Assiniboia or Red River colony. But he had a falling out with his bosses. He made many enemies and eventually quit the post, spending latter years as military secretary in Montreal. He was later awarded the Naval General Service Medal, for his part in the capture of the American schooners *Tigress* and *Scorpion* by boats in the Detour Passage, Lake Huron; Bulger was then a lieutenant in the Royal Newfoundland Fencible Infantry (disbanded 24 June 1816). He also received the Military General Service Medal with bars for services at Fort Detroit and Crysler's Farm.

Meanwhile, in 1816, American workers and soldiers constructed the new post, Fort Crawford, on the spot occupied by Forts Shelby and McKay.[9] When Bulger had evacuated Prairie du Chien, he left behind as parting gifts various military supplies. These were his surplus of powder and ball, "a parting gift to his local Indian retainers," in the words of one scholar. Elsewhere the British attempted to shore up their allies. Colonel McDouall sent Captain Anderson of the Indian Department presents for the Mississippi tribes to the value of thirty-six hundred pounds. These guns, ammunition and general merchandise were "the last rewards of our power for their constancy, fidelity and courage."[10]

Sorting out where the British garrison at Michilimackinac was to be relocated bedeviled the British. St. Joseph Island would have seemed a logical place given the previous tenure of the place by the British Army. Imperial ministers looked on Drummond Island, nearer to Michilimackinac, as the better location. British military officers and Indian agents had disliked the location of their prewar post at St. Joseph Island. They regretted that there they could never be as snug and secure as once they had been at Mackinac Island, nature's own military bulwark. The British, accustomed to their strategic advantage at the great island fortress, remained reluctant to quit Mackinac Island. All details of the boundary issue were not resolved. The British accordingly stood in the way of letting U.S. customs officers do their duty. Indians had necessarily to pass Mackinac Island. British Indian Agents, similarly, worried that Indians would consider the British removal to Drummond Island as a clear sign of weakness and abandonment. The British held on to Mackinac Island as a bargaining point for keeping Bois Blanc (not to be confused with that near Michilimackinac), an island just offshore of Fort Malden. The worry here was that if the Americans retained Bois Blanc they would have a handy spot from which to mount ordinance that could be trained on Amherstburg or on the intervening ship channel. For all these reasons the British appeared dilatory and undecided.

The British could not delay indefinitely. In strict observance of the peace terms, these restitutions occurred: Fort Malden passed back into British hands on 1 July 1815, and Mackinac Island reverted to the United States on 18 July.

The British could not delay forever their removal of the Michilimackinac garrison. Meanwhile, the Admiralty sent instructions to the officer commanding naval forces on the Great Lakes, Commodore Sir Edward Owen, to make a reconnaissance of the islands on the Canadian side of the line with a view to recommending the best possible site for the intended garrison. Owen selected his best available officer to assist Colonel McDouall, the commandant at Michilimackinac, to fix on a site for the new post to which he might remove the garrison. He chose Capt. Edward Collier, RN, who in the previous winter had been employed opening the new road to Penetanguishene and transporting guns from York to Nottawasaga and Penetanguishene.

Collier examined all the lands and islands thought to be adjacent to the international boundary, circumnavigated St. Joseph Island, and had a look at western Manitoulin Island. He thought there was nothing more eligible than the western end of the latter island. In addition to specified military requirements—a good, defensible position and a commanding location for cannon to cover approaches and waterways—Collier noted that from a maritime point of view western Manitoulin had a fine place of shelter where a ship could also winter or undergo repairs. He agreed with McDouall that this place would do nicely, and was undeniably better than alternatives. The port, named Collier Harbour, was convenient to Lake Huron and the Detour, being the strategic waterway between Sault Ste. Marie and Lake Huron, but had some shoals that were particularly dangerous in bad weather. A pilot was needed to provide local knowledge.[11] Thus western Manitoulin, or more correctly, Drummond Island, was fixed upon.

But these remained largely unchartered waters, and until the International Boundary Commission could make its recommendation, the tenure of the British at Drummond Island was unsure. In December 1815 HM *Confiance* went into winter quarters at Collier Harbour, Drummond Island, where she was frozen in. Sailors built huts ashore. The officers hung their hammocks in the drawing room of Capt. Thomas Anderson of the Indian Department. As the captain of the *Confiance*, Lt. Adam Gordon (soon to be Lord Kenmuir), recorded, a "jolly and comfortable winter passed off and spring opened to the joy of all."[12] The *Confiance* was used as a survey vessel for the International Boundary Commission, and she carried the survey party of David Thompson, noted western mapmaker. "We were made as comfortable as possible in the gallant little *Confiance*," recollected the geologist and surgeon J. J. Bigsby. The vessel *Red Jacket* formed the American counterpart, and together the two parts of the commission had many friendly relations when they met in the western channels.[13] The survey arrangements were completed by 1821 but wrangling continued over two islands at the beginning of the boundary line at St. Marys River, one of these being Drummond Island. The British invested heavily in a new fort at Drummond, one which guarded the narrows leading to Sault Ste. Marie and Lake Superior.

The British out of dire necessity determined to set up their garrison at Drummond Island and, if diplomats at a later date determined that it was on American soil, a removal could always be effected. Satisfying the Indians and protecting British trade drove their policy which was always underwritten by a grudging reluctance to quit or withdraw from any port of the Indian trade. The Canadian fur traders, always willing to supply counsel to the British military which ran the Indian Department, continued to demand protection and there were old and trusty arrangements between government, military, and company which continued to drive British aspirations and actions.

Along this waterland border, natives and nonnatives alike had been accustomed to cross without hindrance before 1812. The British and their native associates, so long conditioned to unrestricted access across the boundary, did not conform easily to the new niceties of international law.

Lewis Cass, newly appointed governor of Michigan Territory, knew the difficulties of administering a jurisdiction where there was no centralized settlement, interminable forests, and a line of villages linked by the Detroit River and several tributaries, running from the Maumee River to the fort at Detroit. An Indian fighter himself, who had fought in the Old Northwest wars, Cass now had to call on all the resources at his disposal to maintain the republican fiat. "At Detroit my situation is at all times very unpleasant and sometimes very unsafe," he wrote. "Surrounded by drunken lawless Indians, doubtful friends and secret enemies, without any physical force at my disposal, and breaking in upon me at all hours of the day, their conduct and demands may easily be conceived."[14] British Indian agents continued to foster the grand alliance that had been so troublesome to the Americans.

To his numerous internal woes were joined those emanating from British practices and procedures. Cass was pestered by nagging problems with the British on rights of navigation. HM men-of-war continued to inspect U.S. shipping. The old and customary principle of search and seizure seemed to apply to the Great Lakes.

The infractions were petty but invariably troublesome to Cass and to others. Across from Detroit at Fort Malden, on British soil, the officer commanding, Col. Reginald William James, had instructions to follow as well as interests to protect and foster. Thus, when a Kickapoo named Akockis was shot dead on Grosse Isle, an American islet near Fort Malden, James took up the issue with Cass. He complained that Akockis was murdered by a shot fired from a boat carrying American soldiers. He warned Cass that the Indian law of vengeance would soon take effect. Under this, retaliation for past wrongs would be visited upon the Americans. Cass turned this matter aside and contended that American law would solve an American problem. In another case, an American merchant ship was stopped by a British man-of-war. The sharp diplomatic wrangle that derived from this case coincided with statements from the British minister in Washington that limits on naval armaments on the Great Lakes should be considered.

One particular incident brought the issue to the boil. On 3 September 1815, the young and zealous Lt. Alexander Vidal, RN, in command of HMS *Confiance*, landed at Grosse Point on the American shore. This was no courtesy visit under the White Ensign. Vidal had something novel in mind. His object was to recover some property and personal effects stolen by British sailors who had jumped ship when the *Confiance* had anchored in the St. Clair River. On American soil, Vidal recovered some articles and even apprehended a deserter, Thomas Rymer. However, Vidal in turn got caught, by U.S. officials, and was taken to Detroit where he was accused of unlawful actions, specifically of forcibly removing a man from U.S. territory.

Given such seemingly high-handed action by the overzealous naval commander, a brisk exchange of documents flowed between London and Washington. The diplomats worked long hours. The British argued that the deserter, once caught, had returned willingly to the service of the king. The Americans, by contrast, dug in their heels and insisted that force had been used. Vidal could not escape trial. Forcible confinement and kidnapping were set aside as grounds. Eventually, on an absurdly minor, unrelated charge of inciting a riot, he was found guilty before the Michigan Supreme Court. This resulted in a stiff fine, which was paid, curiously enough it now seems, by a draft upon the naval storekeeper at Kingston. Payment was delivered to the local sheriff and was passed along by him to the Michigan territorial treasurer. "The British were slowly awakening to the fact that in Cass they had caught at tartar," is the way a biographer of the scrappy Michigan governor described the results of Lieutenant Vidal's excursion ashore.[15] But the hungry Cass got only a slice of the loaf, so to speak.

It took some time before such nasty incidents ceased.[16] In 1816 the commander of HMS *Tecumseth* on Lake Erie boarded several American vessels, and the U.S. ambassador in London complained strenuously to the British government. That same year HMS *Huron* searched U.S. vessels near Malden. The British hunt continued for deserters and for smugglers. The British naval commanders acted on instructions from London to police the waterlands where traders, Indians, and settlers could see no boundary or otherwise wished that none such existed. Given the absence of customs patrol vessels and marine constabulary, cross-border raids and encroachments were a way of life. Thus until such time as the Admiralty issued a change of orders to officers commanding HM vessels, those young lieutenants and commanders who were responsible for policing the waters and enforcing the navigation acts were bound to follow their inclinations toward duty. Many, like the young Nelson in the Caribbean, were determined to "go by the book"—and hope their superiors would watch and judge their actions with approval.

In circumstances such as these, much depended on the personality and character of the naval commander. Cdr. William Bourchier, RN, having command on Lake Erie (and thus the Detroit River), seems to have been one of the most determined and conscientious of his kind.[17] With a sense of duty bordering on the obsessive, he exacted the right of search. He carried out his boarding function with clinical precision. This made his superiors nervous. The cautious attorney general of Upper Canada, realizing the difficulties that might ensue, ruled that the Great Lakes were not an extension of the high seas, and were thus "free to the navigation of vessels of the United States." Bourchier, having no instructions from his naval superiors to this effect, made it a rule that all American vessels passing Bois Blanc Island by its inside passage should be boarded and examined for British deserters. The Americans, for their part, regarded the said channel as an international waterway, and Bois Blanc to be still in dispute as to its sovereignty. Working in cooperation with the British garrison at Malden, Bourchier continued the role of enforcer and regulator.

The situation reached heated proportions in July of that same year, 1816, when an American brig was halted and boarded by a detachment of British troops. Two field pieces hauled from Fort Malden to the edge of the channel were trained ominously on the brig. American passengers, nervous and alarmed, filed urgent protests with Governor Cass and military authority. Of this episode, the ranking U.S. officer, Gen. Alexander Macomb, wrote at the time, "It goes to exhibit the determination of the British commanders, if not to make open war, at least to break the peace which has so happily been accomplished." And he feared the episode would inflame public sentiment and lead to bloodshed. Bourchier prepared for the worst, and even in an act indicating a certain degree of nervousness, sought advice from his superior as to what to do when faced with U.S. men-of-war. Bourchier's superior, Capt. J. Baumgart in Kingston, countermanded Bourchier's orders. He reprimanded him for adopting the rule of search and forbade him in the future to board vessels. Later, on advice of the British minister in Washington, the Foreign Office in London issued orders to stop the practice. Thus did the affair blow over, and the ticklish circumstances that were largely the doing of a zealous Bourchier, who was only following then existing orders, came to a happy ending. Bourchier was not the only commander in history trying to imagine what his superiors wanted in tight, unfamiliar circumstances. In this case, foreign policy finally caught up with circumstances on the spot. Bourchier deserves sympathy not condemnation for following orders.[18]

On the Great Lakes tensions eased, and they were effected because of the realization that freedom of navigation was essential to good commercial cross-border trading. Police actions, and boarding of vessels, only led to infernal entanglements that could not always result in convictions at court. The diplomats worked hard to lessen these tensions along this waterland.

But there was another compelling reason for deescalating this matter, and this was the financial. The United States was keen to reduce its Navy, and to lay up or sell as many vessels as possible, keeping only such vessels as were required to enforce the revenue laws. On 17 February 1815, that is the very next day after the Senate voted for ratification of the Ghent Treaty, a resolution for naval reduction was introduced in the House of Representatives. The U.S. secretary of state, James Monroe, suggested a mutual limitation of armed vessels on the Great Lakes. Before long this view was being taken up by British diplomats, principally the British minister in Washington, who knew all about Vidal and Bourchier and their problems.

In London, both in Whitehall and in Westminster, an energetic discussion was then going on about how to deal with the Americans and how to defend British North America. "If the British government should suppose that the United States are destitute of resources, the people reluctant to engage in a new war, on account of the events of the recent conflict, it is egregiously mistaken," warned a well-informed contributor to the prominent London journal *Naval Chronicle*. American resources, both material and human, seemed immense and widening, continued the same authority. American hearts and desires, it seemed, only awaited another war. U.S. ambitions to annex British North American colonies, the West Indies, and Spanish territories apparently knew no limits. The United States appeared resurgent in power and aggressive in intent. Looking at the past war, he lamented, "On the lakes, and on the ocean, the American stars were flying above the red-cross flag of England; the American ships were better built, better manned, and better fought than those of Britain; as is natural to suppose, when of two kindred nations equally brave, the one has an overgrown navy too large for its population and resources while the other has only a few select ships, the crews of which are all picked men and skilful seamen."[19]

Such well-informed commentators on Britain's naval prowess worried that in a subsequent conflict Britannia would lose its grasp and not be able to hold the scepter of Neptune. In future the United States would not again display such "nerveless impotence" as shown in the previous conflict. Quite the contrary. Means were being put in place for fulfilling the agenda of the powerful young republic. In looking at American naval preparations, another authority urged the British nation to "*look out to windward.*" With the United States making rapid strides as a naval power, it behooved the Admiralty to keep the Royal Navy in an efficient state. "If the dominion of the seas is once wrested from us," he warned, "the loss will be found irreparable, and the greatness of Britain soon brought low."[20]

On one occasion, in Parliament, a lord of the Admiralty hawkishly suggested a hefty naval increase for Canadian seas and waters and proposed a review of administrative practices of the late war that had rendered British capabilities so weak. In future, he said, as John Quincy Adams, the American envoy in London, reported to Secretary of State Monroe, "bumboat expeditions and pinchbeck administrations would no longer do for Canada. That Englishmen must lay their account for fighting battles in fleets of three deckers on the North American Lakes. All of this is upon the principle of preserving peace by being prepared for war." The Foreign Office worried about the possible growth of American military might and of renewed American designs on Canada. The prospect of a new war with the United States loomed large in the debates of Parliament.

Adams, never one to mince words, told Monroe, "We hear nothing now about the five frigates and the bits of striped bunting" for the British armament on the Great Lakes.[21] He had no hope that the American proposal for disarmament on the lakes would be accepted; in fact, he thought the reverse would happen, and that there would be a general naval buildup. He saw dark clouds on the horizon.

To the surprise of Adams and others, in April the British government willingly agreed to the American proposal, and stated that they wished to keep no ships in commission on the Great Lakes save what might be necessary for the occasional troop transport. Foreign Secretary Castlereagh agreed to the American proposal for universal disarmament on the lakes on grounds that "keeping a number of armed vessels parading about the Lakes in time of peace ... would be absurd."[22] Henceforth, Canadian defense would depend substantially on American goodwill and British diplomatic skill.

Such was the essence of what became known as the Rush-Bagot Agreement of April 1817, among the sequels to Ghent. Under the Agreement the British and the Americans agreed to limit their naval forces on inland waters to one vessel each on Lake Champlain and Lake Ontario and two vessels each on the upper Great Lakes, none to exceed one hundred tons or to have more than one 18-pounder gun. Implementation quickly followed. Orders dated 29 May came from the Admiralty to pay off the whole of HM vessels on the Great Lakes and put all vessels "in ordinary," that is, laid up, or placed in reserve.[23] The measure was so swift, so all encompassing that the British commodore at Kingston, Upper Canada, registered a protest to the Admiralty. "In place of leaving a small vessel of 100 tons on each lake," he wrote on 4 June 1817, "we are reduced to a boat's crew on the civil establishment."[24] Disarmament was in the air that summer. The Americans followed suit.

Orders were issued under which vessels were stripped or sold, hardware was stored, and military capacities of all vessels was reduced absolutely. The demilitarization was virtually complete by 1819. The specifications of Rush-Bagot were met by the Royal Navy. In that year the British force on Lakes Erie and Huron consisted of the following: for Lake Erie: schooner *Confiance,* 95 tons, 2 guns; schooner *Sauk,* 87 tons, 2 guns; schooner *Surprize,* 74 tons, 2 guns; and schooner *Huron,* 65 tons, 2 guns, plus four decked gunboats; and for Lake Huron: schooner *Newash,* 166 tons, 4 guns; and schooner *Tecumseth,* 166 tons, 4 guns.[25]

In later years there were revivals of military preparation. Violations to Rush-Bagot occurred from time to time to 1914, and Anglo-American naval rivalry on the Great Lakes continued. In the circumstances, as Commodore Barrie did in 1819, all commanding officers could do is to urge the Admiralty to maintain a force at least equal to the Americans on the Great Lakes.[26] That became a rule of thumb for many years. In the history of international relations this Agreement for the demilitarization of the Inland Seas and the supposed extension of the principle to the land frontier ranks as an outstanding example of mutual demilitarization. In fact, the gradual process did not produce mutual disarmament until after the Treaty of Washington in 1871.

Meanwhile, and as quietly as they could, British statesmen made plans for a renewed war on the upper Great Lakes. Leaving nothing to chance while the diplomats and plenipotentiaries in London, Washington, and Ghent were sorting out differences, British statesmen and boards of Admiralty were erecting a new means of sustaining the profit and power of the British Empire on the northern Great Lakes.

VIII

~

Penetanguishene

SHEET-ANCHOR OF THE NORTH

*T*he Ojibwa name *Penetanguishene* means "look, it is falling sand," or "the place of the white rolling sands," derived from a bank of sand formerly seen when entering the port. It was nature's naval secret, so to speak, hidden away as Commodore Sinclair had discovered, from the broad waters of Georgian Bay. Access to this port was tricky in the days of sail, for the Watchers, on a wide shallow bank, guard the north entrance approach leading to Giants Tomb Island, with its unmistakable profile. Similarly, on the south, Christian, Hope, and Beckwith Islands, likewise protected by rocks and shoals, make difficult the entrance to the outer roads of Penetanguishene Harbour, or Penetang Harbour, as it is now denoted on charts and sailing directions. Approaching from the northeast point of densely wooded Hope Island (where a lighthouse now signals advice), a course taken eastward toward Brébeuf Island would bring a mariner to Outer Harbour, that is, Penetang Outer Harbour, whence a southerly course steering clear of a dangerous shoal ledge off Pinery Point, would make possible safe access, by way of a dogleg channel, to a sheltered inlet. The mariner would have reached Penetang Harbour, a superb and commodious sheet of water, with high wooded shores and a mud bottom.[1]

At various points around Penetang Harbour small anchorages or bays exist (most nowadays occupied by yacht clubs and marinas). This prized basin, off the usual haunt of travelers, is a jewel of northern yachtsmen. In the days of fighting sail its intrinsic values were seen clearly by the Royal Navy officers who came to examine and report on its prospects.

Even as of that early date, Penetanguishene was blessed with many historical associations. Ruins of a French establishment could be seen as late as 1815. Etienne Brulé and Samuel de Champlain had come this way during their explorations. The cross had followed the sword. The Jesuits had promoted their mission to the Huron nearby, and at the next port to the east, Sainte-Marie among the Hurons, they kept up a mission from 1639 to its demise in 1649. These waterways and lands had seen all the viciousness, all the tragedy of the Huron-Iroquois wars.

Penetanguishene's strategic value had been recognized by the governor of Upper Canada, John Graves Simcoe. A road was planned from Lake Simcoe to this port on Georgian Bay, and the whole scheme was designed to give a military route north and west from York on Lake Ontario. In 1798 agents acting for the Crown had purchased from "the Chiefs of the Chippeway tribe or Nation of Indians" the aboriginal title to a goodly portion of the area, and the islands in the harbor.[2] This enabled the government to build a naval base and military fortifications there without native interference—if and when required.

It took the War of 1812 to make clear to those responsible for the defense of the Upper Canada frontier that a naval base, complete with good shipbuilding and repair facilities, ought to be established at Penetanguishene. In the circumstances, it was too little, too late and the British just about lost this war in these waters on this very point. By dint of hard-earned experience, Nottawasaga River, and the storage place at Schooner Town, proved unsuitable: the river mouth was treacherous and difficult of access. Nottawasaga River entrance had proven a dangerous place. When Lt. David Wingfield brought HM schooner *Surprize* back into the river after surveying southwest Nottawasaga Bay, the lower pintle was sheered off when the rudder failed to clear the bar; ironworks previously salvaged from the *Nancy* saved the day. What was needed, therefore, was adequate anchorage, defensive potential, and land links to York and Kingston. If a lake-going fleet were to operate just such a good base would be essential. The future of Upper Canada's frontier on Lake Huron and Georgian Bay would come to depend on this fact.

The war had revealed the acute dependence of the Royal Navy on the Army for its means, and this unhappy state of affairs made difficult the task of any naval officer commanding. On this score, Commo. Sir Edward Owen, Yeo's successor, pulled no punches in his reports to the Admiralty on the defense of the Lakes frontier. He found during his own examination (and these views were confirmed by others junior to him) that the north shore of Lake Erie had no secure anchor-

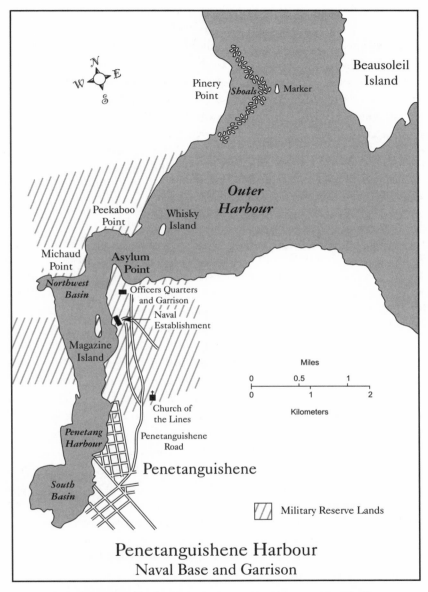

Beausoleil
Island

Pinery
Point   *Shoals* ◊ Marker

*Outer
Harbour*

Peekaboo
Point   Whisky
          Island

Michaud
Point   Asylum
Northwest   Point
Basin   ■ Officers Quarters
              and Garrison
              Naval
              Establishment

Magazine
Island

Miles

0   0.5   1

0   1   2

Kilometers

✝
Church of
the Lines

*Penetang
Harbour*   Penetanguishene
           Road

Penetanguishene

*South
Basin*

▨ Military Reserve Lands

Penetanguishene Harbour
Naval Base and Garrison

In the inner reaches of Georgian Bay, an annex of Lake Huron, Penetanguishene Harbour became a naval base and garrison after the close of the War of 1812. One of the great harbors of the world for mariners, it was in the age of fighting sail an active shipbuilding locale and a British and Canadian "anchor of empire" in the continental heartland.

ages, and that the best way to defend the Upper Canada peninsula was to be strong on Lake Huron. This called for the establishment of a naval headquarters there as well as a shipbuilding yard. The best that could be done for Lake Erie was to have a gunboat or two stationed at the Grand River's mouth. Policy makers had no intention of waging a war on 1812 principles. Amherstburg was written off as a liability, though the Thames River (similarly defended by a gunboat or two) seemed vital for control. Here Commodore Owen recalled to mind the strategic thinking of Governor Simcoe. Owen, a man of enormous ego, was independent as well as outspoken in his views. But in regard to the defense of Upper Canada his advice was largely accepted by a grateful Admiralty.

The war also had revealed how little surveyed were these treacherous waters. "Peace renders not the less important the duty of examining and reporting upon the defences of the Water Frontier," wrote the secretary of the Admiralty in his instructions.[3] Follow-on instructions called for an exploration of "such parts of the lake Frontier as may be necessary . . . to report . . . upon the Naval defence thereof."[4] Such views coincided nicely with those of the head of the Hydrographic Department of the Admiralty, Capt. Thomas Hurd, who in 1814 bemoaned "the great deficiency of our Nautical knowledge in almost every part of the World, but more particularly on the coast line of our own Dominions."[5]

Methodically and slowly (for such projects were always underfunded in those days) the survey proceeded. Back and forth the crews ran their lines and made their calculations accordingly. On Lake Erie every hope turned to disappointment. The north shore of Lake Erie offered no suitable refuge. Inshore waters proved too shallow for men-of-war or transports. Breakwaters would need to be constructed so as to give the requisite fourteen feet of water for the intended warships. The shoreline was thickly wooded, a promising thing in itself given the need for ship timbers, but no fit place existed to build a ship. Coastal defense was similarly problematic. As of 1815, given the inaccessibility to military transport, not one sentinel, and not one gun, stood on Lake Erie's north coast between Fort Erie and Amherstburg. The latter, too, had detractions to postwar thinkers, who readily imagined the place might again become hostage to fortune and more likely than not captured and torched by Americans landing unopposed from the Detroit River.

What about Lake Huron? It was less well known and certainly less surveyed than Lake Erie. "Of the navigation of Lake Huron, scarcely anything is known," commented the senior naval officer in Canada.[6] The entry to Lake Huron, that vulnerable and politically sensitive frontier, made up of the Detroit River, Lake

St. Clair and the St. Clair River, demanded close surveying. A survey in search of an appropriate site for a naval base for Lake Erie at the mouth of the Grand River and near Turkey Point by the *Confiance* in the summer of 1815 had yielded only disappointment. Later that season the *Confiance* shifted westward again, this time to examine the Detroit River (where, as noted, the commander, Vidal, got into time-consuming difficulties with U.S. authorities and courts).

It was late summer before the hydrographers found themselves free to concentrate on northern waters. For this duty, Commodore Owen left the detailed work to his half-brother, William Fitz William Owen, whom we shall call Surveyor Owen. Surveyor Owen commenced a running survey of the east shore of Lake Huron. He made a "particular survey" of the main channel leading to Georgian Bay, then known as the "open gatt" or Manitoulin gap. He likewise initiated a running survey of the Bruce Peninsula. He examined Iroquois Bay (renamed Nottawasaga Bay), Penetanguishene Bay, and adjacent waters. He found previous charts distorted and wanting in detail—and thus of no practical value to either seaman or landsman. Surveyor Owen, incidentally, left place names to commemorate important naval personages of the day: Capes Hurd and Croker, Colpoys Bay, and Griffith Island, named in turn for the head of the Hydrographic Department, the secretary of the Admiralty, and the last name of the admiral commanding the North America Station.

Eventually, Surveyor Owen was able to send to the Admiralty a prodigious gift: eighteen plans that he and his assistants had completed.[7] These valuable drawings, which predate Henry Bayfield's magnificent work, provided the first comprehensive indication of the shores of Lake Erie, Lake Huron, and Georgian Bay. Owen's findings pointed toward prospects of the overland route from York to Georgian Bay, as difficult as it was. But of all his examinations that of Penetanguishene was of utmost importance. He had heard about its advantages and great potential as a base.

In early October 1815, when the leaves would just be turning in that glorious north country, Surveyor Owen sailed from Nottawasaga River entrance bound for Penetanguishene. His object was to investigate thoroughly its suitability for a naval base, shipyard and military arsenal. It should be noted that he was not the first to examine Penetanguishene: that was undertaken by Lieutenant Poyntz, on Yeo's instructions, in mid-November of the previous year, 1814. November is always a dangerous season in which to sail Lake Huron.

"The Harbour," Poyntz had advised his superior in glowingly terms, "is one of the finest I ever saw, having plenty of water for the largest ship to go in, and good anchorage, both within and without, with soft bottom." He found that the shore fell away nicely, giving good anchorages. As for prospects of shipbuilding the place was blessed with much black oak, ash, elm, cedar and other species. He identified three good shipbuilding places but was partial to the eastern shore, for it was healthiest. Poyntz also remarked on the possibilities of defense, noting the harbor entrance and the little island within it. Any vessel approaching would have to pass batteries erected at the entrance. The new road, the Penetanguishene Road from Lake Simcoe, was soon to come out near the eastern point of the harbor. Everything seemed suitable, except a long shoal lying on the west side of the outer harbor. If this hazard were marked with a buoy, mariners could steer clear of the only known navigational danger of an otherwise perfect harbor.[8] In February of the next year, 1815, Capt. W. R. Payne, Royal Engineers, made a plan of Penetang Harbour showing what works he thought necessary for defense of the intended dockyard. These defenses and the yard were to be placed north of the town plot, which had been surveyed and marked out in 1811–12.[9]

Surveyor Owen's duty was to reconfirm the details of Poyntz's reconnaissance and to put a new face on these discoveries, for Poyntz had been yanked from his sea command because of Colonel McDouall's objections to his highhanded attitude. Surveyor Owen, in addition, was a hydrographer, and this task, to examine Penetanguishene and surrounding waters, was only one of many duties undertaken in the course of a distinguished career in hydrography.

Owen sailed from Nottawasaga River in HMS *Huron* (ex–USS *Ohio*), the Cleveland-built schooner that he found a choice vessel in high seas. He passed through the shallow cut between Christian Island and the mainland, leaving the rock-infested Watchers on his left and observed Giant's Tomb likewise to port. He than entered the outer roads of Penetanguishene, with Beausoleil Island and the passage to what is now Midland Harbour also on his port side. After completing this large loop, he came to Penetanguishene Harbour.

Surveyor Owen found Penetanguishene entirely to his liking and drew a plan of the harbor. "At Penetanguishene," he wrote, "I made a particular examination of the spot chosen for an Establishment: it is on the side of a steep hill, and immediately behind a small Island called Dobson's Island [named after Midshipman Dobson, but now known as Magazine Island], and not above a cable's length [six hundred feet] from its shore." Not attracted to the narrowness of the shoreline, where the shipyard and ways were intended to be, he nonetheless was able to make a glowing recommendation to his superior. "Possessing all the advantages of shelter and easy navigation to its immediate neighbourhood," he advised, "the Harbour of Penetanguishene appears to me decidedly the most appropriate place on this Lake for a naval arsenal; and, when to this is added the vicinity of our Establishments on Lake Ontario, whence its supplies may always be certain, even if the carriage be difficult, I do not imagine it possible to find a spot better suited to such a purpose." He recommended a commissariat depot be placed on Christian Island. Some storage and shipbuilding facility had to be near the Nottawasaga's mouth, and the place was kept up for several years. To Owen's thinking Penetanguishene had every merit, particularly if it were intended that a frigate or other large vessels were to be constructed, as was the possibility in 1815 and 1816.[10]

Surveyor Owen's recommendation passed to Commodore Owen, who in turn forwarded it with his own favorable advice to the lords commissioners of the Admiralty. The commodore's recommendation bore the date 25 November 1815, and it is an indication of the remoteness of Kingston from the seats of power in Whitehall (and the necessity to consult with the War Office) that it was not until 6 July 1816 that the recommendation was acted upon. On that date Penetanguishene was named naval arsenal for Lake Huron, and the Admiralty ordered that the establishment at Nottawasaga be moved to Penetanguishene. At the same time the vessels *Tecumseth* and *Newash* were removed from Lake Erie to Huron, and the more shallow-draft *Confiance* and *Surprize* were shifted from Huron to Erie.[11] For the establishment at Penetanguishene Commodore Owen called for a purser to superintend expenses (do local audits because of remoteness from Kingston), a gunner (to look after the guns stored ashore that needed to be kept in good condition so that they could be put aboard men-of-war "at a moment's notice"), a quartermaster of shipwrights, six shipwrights, two sawyers, two blacksmiths, and various persons to be hired and kept on the purser's list as required.[12]

Commodore Owen's successor on the Great Lakes was Capt. Sir Robert Hall. In judging his policies and actions it may best be remembered that in those days the Navy was run on patronage. Hall was a loyal follower of Rear Adm. Sir Thomas Byam Martin, none other than the controller of the navy— himself, in turn, the devoted servant of that wide-seeing, sagacious first lord of the Admiralty, Viscount Melville.[13] Byam Martin ran the Navy like a fiefdom. But he was dependent on Melville's patronage and protection and, with equal measure, on inspired loyalty from men such as Hall.

Hall brought touches of the exotic to the Navy's Lakes Service. An Irishman of untraceable lineage, he had been promoted rapidly owing to the possibilities of the sword in war. From the little we know about his campaigning in Spanish inshore waters and Sicilian locations he seems to have been a heroic figure, a brave warrior, and a skilled commander in small-boat operations, flotilla tactics, and amphibious, joint operations. Whatever his political connections Hall, Knight Commander of St. Ferdinand and of Merit, and sometime post captain and brigadier general in service of the king of Naples, seemed just the sort of generalissimo to run the intended 1815 campaign in Canada, assuming the war were to last into that year.[14]

As Commissioner of the Lakes of Canada, Hall arrived too late to make any difference in the war. From his headquarters at the Kingston naval dockyard he did double duty in regard to all aspects of naval vessels, including construction and repair, while also superintending all victualling and attending to all matters related to naval stores.

Commodore Hall's letters to London show frankness touched with political verve. Sharply critical of the government of Upper Canada, for to his way of thinking the colony deserved better military as well as civil administration, Hall pushed the limits of propriety in advising his superiors on the means of Canadian defense. "These Lakes will be a Millstone round our Necks & indeed the Colony is scarcely worth the Expense," he told Byam Martin. Had he wished, Byam Martin might have removed Hall there and then—on grounds of partisan commentary unworthy of one of HM's naval officers. No insubordination was intended, for a genuine reanalysis was under way about how to defend Canada. Hall was not alone in this pessimistic view.

Other senior naval officers conversant with the defense problems of Canada regarded the project of defending British America as impossible if not asinine. Admirals Richard Graves and David Milne, respectively the previous and incoming commanders in chief of the North America Station, to which the Great Lakes Command was appended, held equally trenchant views about the costs of defending Canada and were abhorred by the sums the government intended to spend on the making of canals, roads, and wharfs. Milne, who advised Melville and Byam Martin specifically on the matter, told Melville that in a few years the ships kept on the Lakes of Canada would be decayed. Melville's reply was that they only intended to keep up the frames of what could be a revitalized naval force. "I cannot help thinking it would be better for this country if we were quit of Canada altogether," confided Milne to a kinsman. And, he added, "I shall have a very laborious duty to perform when I get to Halifax, the station is so extensive, and a large establishment to be kept up at

Bermuda."[15] Even the secretary of state for war and the colonies, Earl Bathurst, seemed at a loss as to how to act with respect to Canadian defense. Milne's advice was to cut losses: "If we are to keep up our establishment there and be ready to act against the Americans, the expense will be so enormous that the country cannot afford it. . . . There will arise many disputes, the Americans claiming islands and water passages that it is impossible for us to grant without throwing our frontier, particularly the Niagara one, quite open to them. . . . From what I have seen it would be lucky for this country to be well rid of it. It is certainly a fine country, but too distant for us to defend against so powerful a neighbour."[16]

The admiral did not win this argument. Politics were deflecting strategy, and imperial motives were supplanting defensive capabilities. Professional military opinion, based on fundamentals of military geography and on past war experience, were being set aside for the necessity of defending Canada against a resurgent United States. As with Milne so with Hall. Thus, in dealing with Hall's "write-off" suggestion, Byam Martin put the matter carefully to Melville that "there are points touched upon [in Hall's letters] which are foreign to our present relative situation [to the United States]." Again, when Hall preached to Byam Martin that if the British minister in Washington, Charles Bagot, whom Hall distrusted, made new arrangements with the U.S. government that interfered with the Navy's obligations, the controller advised the first lord that there was a necessity to consult and advise as required. No officer commanding British ships on the Great Lakes wanted to be exposed by diplomatic shifts that would leave him high and dry, so to speak.[17] Hall particularly disliked the thought that Bagot in Washington was calling the shots.

In touchy circumstances such as these, Byam Martin smoothed passage of measures for effecting what the British Ministry termed "the Peace Establishment" on the Great Lakes. These measures, to which credit to Hall is due, brought into existence what was called somewhat incorrectly in later days "the undefended border," in effect, on the Canadian side, a hand of iron in a glove of velvet.

Hall's major worry remained how to defend Lake Erie and Lake Huron, likely to be tomorrow's battleground. Hall inherited problems of his predecessors, and he was familiar with how the past conflict had been waged on the Lakes. In the course of that affair the British had pinned great expectations on Lake Erie as the first line of naval defense. In a future war command of Lake Erie would be the means of checking any American encroachments. But after 1815 British military planners, with grim realization that they could not offset American naval power on that particular body of water, turned increasingly to amphibious operations and flotilla defense as preferred measures for Canadian security.

The future of naval defense and offensive military operations hinged on Penetanguishene. "Penetanguishene Harbour on Lake Huron," Hall reported glowingly to London,

> possesses every requisite for construction & protection: It is far removed from any American Settlement & by building ships there of a light draft of water that will admit of descending into Lake Erie by the River St. Clair we shall not only oblige them to keep up their Squadron of Lake Erie but also in the event of War turn their whole attention to the protection of their Michigan Territory along which they are now establishing a chain of Posts. These posts, small & divided through an immense tract of country, must fall to the savages if encouraged by a floating force on Lake Huron; if suffered to remain unmolested they are sure to cut us off from our Indian alliance, but they have their effect, particularly on detached Posts.[18]

Not only did Penetanguishene possess a defensive or protective value, conveniently distant from the complexities of Lake Erie defense, it had an offensive merit requiring some American military response. Penetanguishene would pin down American strategy. "By calling the whole attention of the Americans in that Quarter to the protection of their Michigan Territory, " Hall explained, eloquently, "we prevent the invasion of the upper parts of the Province." He went even further by saying that Penetanguishene could be means of promoting peace by engendering the means of internal American dissension. In his words, "By removing the sources of exasperation from Lake Erie during Peace, the fermentation excited in the public mind opposite will cease, & they will probably quarrel among themselves."[19]

Northward, therefore, ran the course of the Canadian empire. Shifting the field to northern waters became Hall's credo. His intention was to do so at Penetanguishene by the spring of 1817.

Hall's mind always shifted to the geopolitical. Lake Huron would be the next inland sea to be quarreled over, he reasoned. There the destiny of interior lands and waters would be determined. "It is evidently on Huron that we must play our next game," Hall advised the controller of the navy, "by drawing them [the Americans] far from their resources, & striking at their new & scattered settlements, encouraging & letting loose Indians amongst them. You will say perhaps that this is a *savage idea,* but alas! every sentiment of humanity is forgotten in the advantage or glory of our Country, and really the Americans of the Lakes are worse than savages." Admittedly the narrows at River St. Clair posed navigational problems. However, he noted with a touch of self-assurance, its annoying narrowness could be overcome: "But these are difficulties that we have to contend with in European Warfare & can always be surmounted."[20]

Most pressing was the need for men-of-war. The Army could have two of the four transport vessels then available, said Hall. Perhaps the *Sauk* and *Huron* would be enough, "but for God's sake don't let us hazard the honour of our flag in such miserable things." "At all events," he concluded, "we can build everything at Penetanguishene if it is desirable that a part [of the fleet] immediately descend to Lake Erie." New warships were needed, he said, "as the first blow on these Lakes will be everything."

In the summer of 1816, as we have seen, the lords of the Admiralty fixed on Penetanguishene as the Navy's new base of operations. Shipbuilding there was a priority. They ordered the naval establishment at Nottawasaga River be removed to Penetanguishene and sent out the requisite instructions.[21] They also suggested that the War Office erect immediately some military works to protect the establishment. Accordingly, an officer of the Royal Engineers was sent to report.

As of 1816 the Navy's intended assets for the Lakes Service called for the *Champlain,* a fifth rate, to be on Lake Champlain with a complement of 135. Lake Ontario was to have the *Montreal,* likewise a fifth rate with 135 men, the sloop *Star,* and the sloop *Netley,* bearing 80 and 45 men, respectively. On Lake Erie, the largest vessel then was the *Confiance,* captured by Lieutenant Worsley, and not to be confused with the old *Confiance* that had a disastrous sixteen-day career in the late war on Lake Champlain. This schooner had been elevated on the books to a fifth rate, so that, as Commodore Hall's advice explained, she might be commanded by a post captain, that is to say, a captain who had been officially "posted," or listed, as such. That way the Admiralty could have a senior officer on Lake Huron or Lake Erie as required. With the celebrated *Confiance* was a trio of schooners—*Surprize, Sauk,* and *Huron*—each with thirty men. On Lake Huron the key vessel for the interim was the schooner *Tecumseth* with 48 men, rated as a sloop so that she might carry a commander. The *Newash,* another but smaller schooner, was to have a complement of 37.

In short, in those days of uneasy peace the lords of the Admiralty placed their faith in ten vessels of the smallest class of warships. It was a navy of schooners. What counted most to their ways of thinking were sea officers of experience and ability. If either of the two vessels wearing the pendant of the senior naval officer on Erie or Huron were lost, others were to be substituted. The Admiralty was dead set that the mistake of the Battle of Put-in-Bay would have no repetition: enough trained seamen were to be available. The Admiralty, in fact, warned against existing practices of offering bounties to raise necessary numbers for the Lakes Service. Their lordships concluded that sailors were to be sent out from England, in drafts as required, a policy that remained in effect for as long as the Royal Navy had ships stationed in Canadian waters. In making this decision, the Admiralty looked disapprovingly on taking volunteers from merchant ships and transports for the Lakes Service: that would do for the Fleet, they opined, where such men could become hardened sailors capable of firing guns efficiently. With an eye to past experience at Put-in-Bay, their lordships determined on a fighting force of respectable skill. What was lost in size of fleet might be won in martial abilities.

Hall showed rare strategic genius in devising Canada's lake defenses in the Old Northwest. He wisely judged Britain's ability to defend Canada by weighing American means to wage a future war. As Moltke put it, one must meet the mind-set of the enemy. Hall saw American capabilities as considerable and growing. At the commencement of war, advised Hall, three grand objects would engage British attention—Sackets Harbor, the naval and military depot on Lake Ontario; Presque Isle, naval depot on Lake Erie; and Fort Gratiot, at the head of River St. Clair. Sackets Harbor was fast becoming a powerful, populated base of operations. There it would be hard to winkle out the Americans without considerable losses. Presque Isle, though burdened by a bar at the entrance that necessitated loading vessels outside, was vulnerable, for it could be destroyed early on, by a vigorous army and navy force. It was a superb target for the four gunboats being built on Lake Erie, each drawing but four feet and carrying three long 24-pounders. Hall imagined that these could sweep across the lake and enter Presque Isle at will. With a warrior's true mind, Hall also imagined that by using four of the six available companies of the regiments posted at Niagara, Burlington, and York "a dash may be made at Presque Isle, and the American Ships (which may be fairly supposed to have not Guns on board inside the Bar) destroyed." Burlington, being built up as a depot, Hall envisioned as the means of supplying Lake Erie via the Grand River.

The British foresaw the capture of Fort Gratiot as necessary in any successful plan. An ancient fort known as Fort St. Joseph had dominated the water route between north and south when the territory was being contested by French and

British. Fort Gratiot, built in 1814 by the United States Army on the same site as the French original, was erected to protect the area from the natives and the British. Fort Gratiot in British hands, Hall argued, would not only ensure British communication with Lake Erie but also cut off all supplies for American posts on Lake Huron, "and secure to us the friendship of all the Warlike Tribes that inhabit the Forests and Coast between St. Clair and Michigan which according to a report recently made by Major John Long, an American engineer, 'breathe a rancorous spirit and hostility to the American name.'" A company of soldiers, reasoned Hall, ought thus to be stationed at Penetanguishene, which could be reinforced by way of the Ottawa River, the customary route of North West Company supply canoes. Eleven or twelve days only would elapse in the sending of supplies from Montreal.[22] Hall recommended that salt provisions and biscuits—then the solid fuel of the Navy, so to speak—be made up in smaller than customary casks weighing seventy pounds, so that they could be shipped in canoes. He noted that there was no use in sending bread in bags as experience had shown that it had been shaken to dust before it reached Kingston. A second company of soldiers, sent from Montreal to Penetanguishene, could be used with the first for a strike against Fort Gratiot, "and as it is but a contemptible stockade, a dash may be made at it with fair prospects, and filling it with Pork and Rum for the Indians we should soon have a formidable force about it."[23]

Fort Gratiot, that military choke point, remained Hall's strategic target. It guarded the narrows of River St. Clair, as mentioned, and the river had only nine feet of water and a current of six knots. Because the river there measured only a mile wide Hall imagined that the American garrison would fire a hail of musket shot at any would-be attackers. Hall's predecessor, Sir Edward Owen, thought that a good heavy brig similar to the *Queen Charlotte* [of the late war] would do well against Detroit and Fort Gratiot, but Hall realized such a vessel would draw too much water. "If you mean to confine them to Huron it is all very well," concluded Hall. All outlying posts depended on communications that passed Detroit and Fort Gratiot. Thus an offensive action against the latter, if successful, would mean that Michilimackinac's supplies soon would be cut off: "If the Tree is girded the Branches must soon die. . . . No time however is to be lost in having a depot of Military as well as Naval Stores at Penetanguishene and Blockhouses should be immediately thrown up there and at the mouth of the Grand River."[24]

Nothing less than a revolution in the military arrangements for the defense of Canada would do. Guns were extraordinarily expensive even if blockhouses could be erected at trifling expense. All guns had to be shipped from Quebec and Kingston, and had to come through the War Office's Ordnance Department. Hall wanted naval control over the guns used on this frontier. "Does a ship filling out at Plymouth send for her guns to Woolwich?" he asked. Naval guns should be shipped at naval expense. He added a number of other items to his shopping list of requisites: annual reports of Canadian military posts, more knowledgeable Army officers who knew about western frontier defense, and a reduction of troops kept at Niagara and their dispersal at various places of future need. A sure supply of seamen would be needed for the Great Lakes, and he warned the lords of the Admiralty against the admiral in Halifax sending ships to sea to cruise for American men-of-war all the while ignoring the worrying needs of the Lakes Service.

There would be no more battles of Put-in-Bay. Future war on the Lakes would be that of small expeditions and flotillas. Hall saw the gunboat as means of defense and attack. A number of gunboats with eight seamen and four gunners in each would suffice for Lake Erie and elsewhere in the interior. What was needed were seamen to supplement the soldiers there, who Hall noted a little maliciously now knew how to row bateaux. Again, all depended upon the state of American preparations: "Everything may be attempted against Militia, and the Americans cannot organize regular Troops very easily." Readily supplied across the bridge between Lakes Ontario and Erie by a road to be built, places like Turkey Point and Fort Norfolk and, farther west, Amherstburg could be made secure and provisioned as required. Even so, the north shore of Lake Erie had proven to be a poor coast for a sailor's refuge, and at the Deep Hole near Fort Norfolk, a breakwater was needed in a place where shallowness otherwise prohibited anchorage. The passage by way of Lake St. Clair was tedious and uncertain.

The administrative structure to defend the western rim was also put in place at this time: thirteen clerks, coopers, laborers, and others based on York, Holland Landing, and Nottawasaga River ("the shipping place"), all connected in turn to a deputy assistant commissary general, a clerk, and one officer at Penetanguishene. These fifteen personnel, regarded as indispensable according to Governor Sir John Sherbrooke, who estimated the annual cost of this establishment at £2,830, were satisfactory to Hall. His biggest worry was a proposed cutback in the commissariat, which would reduce an establishment that was already ruinous, and he told his superior that such a cut "seemed vengeful." "I fear I have tired you with Canadian politics," he closed his last letter to Byam

Martin on Canadian defenses, adding, "I shall conclude by begging my best respects to Lady Martin and you."[25]

In the face of declining expenditures and changing trans-border politics, the defense of Upper Canada remained a daunting prospect to Commodore Hall. So was it to the Admiralty. Future hopes were pinned upon flexible response and ingenious use of small men-of-war and supply routes through the Canadian bush. If the United States could command the Great Lakes in the next war, as history had shown, imperial forces must fight on terms selected by them and in ways for which they must prepare.

Another no less pressing reason existed to complete the hydrographical surveys: the Treaty of Ghent included provision for a commission to recommend final solution to the water boundary through the Great Lakes. In such circumstances completing the Lake Erie survey became an urgent matter. The northward shift of hydrographic inquiry—to Lake Huron, St. Marys River and Lake Superior—had equal if not greater requirement for securing the trade and the native alliances of the north. When Surveyor Owen was recalled to England, his trusted assistant Bayfield, then a twenty-two-year-old lieutenant, assumed the task of surveyor on the Lakes. He did so exactly at the time the establishment was being run down and all larger vessels paid off or laid up in ordinary. Thus, whereas Owen had conducted inquiries from the schooner *Huron,* Bayfield did his duty in unimaginably puny craft no larger than a cutter, working by day in extremes of heat and cold, sleeping by night in buffalo robes under the boat's mainsail rigged up as a tent ashore. The boats were *Troughton* and *Ramsden,* named for English instrument makers. The duties were onerous. Swarms of mosquitoes, searing summer weather, tempestuous gales, and heavy seas added to the legion of difficulties facing these imperial measurers. And he could have wished for better instruments. "The Rocky shores of Lake Huron have so shook our Time Keepers," he complained bitterly, "that in their present state they are useless, and indeed the whole of our Instruments, from having seen 8 years of hard service are nearly in the same state, my own sextant is the only instrument fit for service."[26]

Bayfield, who with Midshipman Philip Collins completed the Lake Erie survey in 1818, shifted that year to Lake Huron. Based on Penetanguishene, Bayfield systematically went about ascertaining the shape, size, and situation of some six thousand islands, flats, and rocks. He examined a shore broken into deep bays and coves. By the time Bayfield wound up his survey in 1822 no fewer than twenty thousand islands had been placed on the plans and charts of Lake

Huron. In 1823 Bayfield shifted his field of activity once again, this time to Lake Superior, where he worked for two seasons. There even the North West Company pretended to have little knowledge of the lake. Gradually the work neared completion. Draft plans of River and Lake St. Clair, Detroit River, St. Joseph Channel, St. Marys River, and plans of Penetanguishene and other harbors were filed in the Hydrographical Office of the Admiralty. Many were engraved by the Hydrographical Office under authority of the Admiralty. In short, by the late 1820s the bulk of the secrets of these immense inland seas and passages were disclosed for all to use.[27]

For a century afterward, American as well as Canadian mariners relied on Bayfield's charts. U.S. as well as British boundary commissioners had access to Admiralty charts, which were looked upon by the Americans as authoritative and not in need of revision. When the boundary was being determined upon by the commissioners, British hydrographical information formed the scientific basis of agreement, though the two sides might quarrel upon which channel was most suitable as the international boundary. Not until 1844 did the Corps of Topographical Engineers, responsible for U.S. Lakes Survey, bring plans forward for extensive map making. That year Washington instructed Capt. W. G. Williams, based at Buffalo, then at Detroit, to survey American waters of the Great Lakes. Green Bay and the Straits of Mackinac were prime requirements, and Williams in the vessel *Ark* pressed his inquiries there before going on elsewhere, and the great charts of 1852 showed his office's steady progress. The opening of the Soo Locks in 1855 required preliminary surveys.[28] By 1860 these lakes had shed all semblance to wild artistry of the charts of the French era: now all lakes, bays, and harbors were known and principal navigational hazards fixed on charts and described in *Sailing Directions*. Never were there enough lighthouses and channel markers, equally applicable nowadays, but Bayfield's work, and that of his counterpart Williams, were precursors to safe navigation and commercial prosperity.

IX

~

The End of Fighting Sail
TODAY'S HISTORY TRACKS

Today Lake Huron and Georgian Bay are great sailing seas for yachtsmen, and the tonnage of vessels carrying sails far exceeds those of distant days of the War of 1812. Only in our mind's eye can we imagine those trusty little brigs and topsail schooners that wore flags of their respective countries: the famous victory brig *Niagara* with which Perry carried the British fleet at Put-in-Bay; the doughty Detroit-built *Nancy,* pride of the North West Company and workhorse of empire; or the remarkable surveying schooner *Huron,* which bore two hydrographic surveyors of notable memory, Owen and Bayfield. To be sure, there were many other vessels of the age of fighting sail, American and Canadian, all of which played out roles on the upper Great Lakes at an urgent time in international affairs, of war and of uneasy peace.

These days it seems but a dream. Still, at Discovery Harbour, on the northeastern margin of the town of Penetanguishene, Ontario, you can see three look-alikes—one a schooner man-of-war, another a typical North West Company trading schooner, the other a small schooner or Durham boat—lying at the wharf, adjacent to the Province of Ontario's fine tourist attraction which commemorates the War of 1812 in these northern waters. At one time it was called the Historic Naval and Military Establishments, partly in deference to the fact that both Navy and the Army kept separate establishments there. Today it has a new name. Discovery Harbour, so called, exists in all its diminutive splendor. There you can go back in time, imagining what it must have been like to see oxen dragging shipbuilding timber from the forest, or sawers working away in the pits with their long saws, or shipwrights fashioning a new hull on the ways, or a blacksmith hammering away, making new fittings for the masts and yards. In fact, a whole establishment is in the remaking, including store-houses, shops, cooperage, bakery, hydrographic surveyor's chart office, and even the assistant surgeon's dwelling. It is all, it is Navy and empire in minia-ture with a good nod at the social history of the times.

In its day Penetanguishene never ranked as a great naval establishment. There was nothing of a Halifax or Gibraltar to it. At the height of its influence, 1820, the base was headquarters to a sizable flotilla of more than twenty ves-sels. It supplied the British posts at Drummond Island. It housed more than seventy personnel, including officers and their families besides sailors, soldiers, and civilian workers. But even at this time it never boasted sufficient resources as supplied it from London, Montreal, and Kingston to give it much material strength. Its buildings were wooden (some log cabins were along the North American model, others were clapboard sided). And only one stone building stood there at midcentury, a War Department structure known as the Officers' Quarters.[1]

Penetanguishene, naval base and garrison, was the runt of the litter of impe-rial bases, so to speak, always at the mercy of forces beyond its control. "It is in a sad state," complained Commo. Robert Barrie, there in 1819 to inspect its prospects. "We have here two lieutenants, half a dozen seamen—and as many shipwrights to look after two rotten schooners and some boats. The expense of conveying salt provisions and stores to this little out of the way place is nearly equal to a strong dockyard."[2]

Expensive it indeed was—and isolated. Yet this too gave it its influence: its greatest strength was in its rather secluded and safe anchorage, which was snug and secure, and far away from the military power of the United States that could press north from Lake Erie if and when it wanted to. The place, observed Commodore Barrie, had agricultural potential: "The country here-abouts is in a perfect state of nature but only requires settlers to produce everything, for the land and climate are excellent." To this he added, "The ground is so rich that the old farmers have taken sixteen crops of corn run-ning from the same field without once manuring the ground—they say that manure would spoil the crop."

Two of HM vessels that sailed from Penetanguishene were named by the British for their allied Indian commanders. The *Tecumseth*, named for the famous Indian leader, was built at Streets Creek opposite Navy Island, Upper

Canada, in 1814. She was sister to the *Newash,* named for an Ottawa chief, fashioned at the same yard and completed near Niagara Falls shortly after war's end.

The two sister schooners were constructed under direction of Henry Kent, along with 120 artificers, and were completed in four months. Each measured seventy feet on deck, with a beam of more than twenty-four feet. Each was designed to carry a pair of 24-pounder long guns, powerful weapons given the dimensions of the gun-carrying platform. These guns were mounted on circle pivots, one on the bow and the other amidships. Each carried two 32-pound carronades, one on each quarter. Each had accidents when first sailed, and accordingly they were then rigged as brigantines (with square sail on foremast replacing the schooner headsails).

Tecumseth and *Newash* had brief lives, though not without excitement, when the frontier was still hot in Canadian-American relations and boarding and searches were the order of the day. The *Tecumseth,* for example, with Kent as her first captain, chased the *Julia* into the mouth of the Detroit River, firing on her in pursuit. This brought charges of piracy against the British but the situation was eventually soothed over.[3] Later, the *Tecumseth,* this time commanded by Lt. W. Head, was employed transporting provisions for the Commissariat Department from Fort Erie to Amherstburg and Drummond Island. She was registered as "sloop of war" and thus rated to be a flagship. In 1817 her sister, *Newash,* was rerigged as a brigantine. The reason for this is due to the inefficiency of the topsail schooner rigging in the working of the gaff foresails in a squall or coming about.

Another British vessel, the crack schooner *Huron,* was an American-built craft. She was formerly the USS *Ohio,* constructed at Cleveland in 1810. As noted, she was taken 12 August 1814 in a daring cutting-out expedition by the British at Fort Erie. The *Huron* became Surveyor Owen's command, and he had found her capable of beating against strong northwesterlies with very heavy seas.[4] It was the *Huron* which accompanied the *Sauk* in 1815 running supplies from Nottawasaga River to the garrison at Drummond Island. She was shifted to Lake Erie in 1816 for similar duties to supply the new northern post. These were prosaic tasks, shared by all the vessels kept at Penetanguishene, and whether ferrying supplies or delivering commanding officers and men, the *Huron* was a handy vessel and good sailer.

As a good example of Great Lakes schooner design, it may be useful here to give some particulars of the *Huron,* given in 1817 at the time of her survey at

British Schooner *Huron*

Gun deck length	53 feet, 11 inches
Keel for tonnage	44 feet, 3 5/8 inches
Breadth extreme	17 feet, 3 1/2 inches
Depth in hold	8 feet, 0 inches
Weight	65 59/94 tons
Light draft, fore	4 feet, 6 inches
Light draft, aft	6 feet, 0 inches
Number of men	30
Number of guns	Gun deck 1 24 pounder, 1 24-pounder carronade

Fort Erie. This trusty workhorse of empire on the upper lakes has dimensions of stoutness and strength.[5]

Another man-of-war, HMS *Sauk,* likewise a veteran of the lakes, rose from the stocks at Niagara River, above the falls, in 1809. An American merchant schooner, she served in the U.S. Navy until captured by a British boarding party in August 1814. A contemporary illustration of this fine craft by Lt. Adam Gordon Kenmure, dated 15 September 1815 and now held in the Royal Ontario Museum in Toronto, for many years provided the only record of a lakes schooner constructed in pioneering days, that is until the discovery, in 1975, of the *Hamilton* and *Scourge,* the so-called Ghost Ships of the War of 1812, in southwestern Lake Ontario. The *Sauk* carried two guns, as did the *Huron,* and was likewise a workhorse of empire on the upper Great Lakes.

We find these vessels in the historical record but their progress across time and space is not easily traced. They were workhorses of empire, showing the flag in all ports of call from Fort Erie to the Mouth of the Grand River then west to Amherstburg and Malden, and upriver again to Detroit and opposite the new U.S. post Fort Gratiot. Some of them sailed to the bottom of Georgian Bay and into the tricky-to-enter mouth of the Nottawasaga River, there at the depot to take on supplies, chiefly flour and pork, for distant Drummond Island and its garrison. There were, too, messages and instructions to be carried to Sault Ste. Marie and after Drummond Island returned to American hands to Fort St. Joseph on St. Joseph Island. *Tecumseth* and *Newash* ferried supplies and provisions from Fort Erie, Amhertsburg, and Nottawasaga to the new base and arsenal, Penetanguishene. In June 1817 they made their last run together. On the second of that month Captain Owen had arrived at Nottawasaga with orders to lay up *Tecumseth* and *Newash* "in ordinary" at Penetanguishene. The British demilitarization was under way, even in advance of the Rush-Bagot Agreement (not formally ratified until 28 April 1818). On the eighteenth they dropped anchor at Penetanguishene with their last cargo of stores. The next two weeks were spent discharging their stores into the storehouse, lowering guns into their holds, unbending sails, unstepping masts, taking down rigging and warping each vessel into its final anchorage in the bay. On 30 June 1818 the pendant was handed down and the crews of both vessels took up lonely but safe residence on Dobson's (Magazine) Island. *Tecumseth* was taken out of ordinary in 1819 and used to convey two hundred men of the 68th Regiment from Penetanguishene to Drummond Island and to return with the detachment of the 70th Regiment stationed there. Sir Peregrine Maitland, governor of Upper Canada, likely made the return voyage to Drummond Island. In September the expected recall of the Drummond Island garrison was ordered, and *Tecumseth* was pressed into duties once again. Inasmuch as she could carry a maximum of one hundred men and baggage at a time it is certain that she made double return passages to Drummond Island in 1819. Thereafter *Tecumseth* and *Newash* nearly disappear from the record.[6] *Tecumseth* joined *Newash* in being placed "in ordinary," nearly a death sentence.

The deep cold of a Penetanguishene winter and the humid warmth of a Lake Huron summer played havoc with the planking and decking of these men-of-war. Maintenance requirements always outstripped resources. A similar situation existed on Lake Erie. In 1820, the *Huron* and the *Sauk*, surveyed at the Grand River Naval Depot, were found defective from the bad timber used in their construction and the subsequent invasion of dry rot. Repairs were ordered. Even so, in the survey of 1830 the *Huron* and *Sauk* were again found rotten to the water line and suspected of being in the same state underwater. Like the *Confiance* and *Surprize*, which were also then disclosed as "very rotten," the *Huron* had seen last days. An interesting two-decade career under two flags had been her lot. Penetanguishene became a graveyard. The *Tecumseth*, for example, was paid off in 1819 and by 1827 was found "completely rotten."

In those years after the ends of the War of 1812 and of the French and Napoleonic Wars, economy became the order of the day. This was the peace dividend of the times. Reductions in military establishments seemed commonplace everywhere in the British Empire, save in Canada where the British government were devoting considerable sums to upgrading defense arrangements through canals and fortifications. If the Canadian provinces could not be defended by naval power alone, as 1812 had revealed and the peace arrangements with the Americans had required, then new means had to be adopted to put military muscle into the western heartland of British America if and when required.

To those naval officers witnessing savage reductions of the naval establishment on the Great Lakes as well as at Halifax the matter was always one of confusing duality. For, on the one hand, successive flag officers would like to have had more naval units at their disposal, considering the multifarious duties required, including fisheries protection and showing-the-flag. Often, on the other, despair was shown by these men, for they feared that their superiors, and their political masters in turn, did not understand the circumstances of "the man on the spot." As Rear Adm. David Milne explained in a private letter to an associate,

> [The] Ministry are so much alarmed [by costs and inflation] that they are reducing the expense of the Navy as much as possible. All the frigates are to be taken from the Newfoundland station, and some of the ships from me, and the vessels on the lakes of Canada are to be paid off and only a very few men left to take charge of them. I told Lord Melville [First Lord of the Admiralty] I hoped he would go a step further and abandon them altogether; it is such an enormous expense to this country; and we cannot keep Canada if the Americans declare war against us. . . . And while we keep possession of Nova Scotia, Canada would be of very little use to them.[7]

Milne's worries were shared by others. Restraint became the order of the day, and conservative, even reactionary, politics were a given. A fighting machine, such as the Royal Navy had been for a generation, was being reduced to the extensive peacetime duties of the Pax Britannica, when Britannia ruled the waves and, when necessary, waived the rules. Young lieutenants, hopeful of rapid advancement in the service, now had to accept other duties, including Arctic surveying, if they were to get the attention of their superiors. Cutting back the Great Lakes establishment and that of the North America, Newfoundland, and West India commands damaged morale and increased the rates that seamen deserted to the United States. One young officer, in 1816, lamented the decline of the establishment at Quebec and Bermuda, the disgraceful, ragged appearance of British tars owing to being given no pay abroad, and the miserable state of the ship in which he was serving. "Nothing can exceed the disgust which every officer of every rank expresses of this wretched Peace-establishment, & more than one or two have *said* that they will not stand it many months." He concluded, "What they will *do* I cannot tell, but . . . I cannot help entertaining *some* hope that they may be driven home to escape the misery of commanding one of His Majesty's ships on such a reduced & degraded establishment."[8]

The Army was likewise crippled by economies. After Waterloo the standing force suffered cheeseparing on a grand scale. Wellington did all he could to keep the Army an effective, fighting establishment. Regiments were taxed with duties at home and abroad. Upper and Lower Canada needed protection, as did Nova Scotia and New Brunswick. Bermuda and Jamaica needed garrisons, artillery, and engineers. A "little Englander" could claim, with justification, that Britain maintained garrisons "on every rock in the ocean where a cormorant could perch." The War Office groaned under its responsibilities. Wellington never tired of warning about the domestic and foreign problems facing the British. "We have never, up to this moment," he said in almost his last speech in the House of Lords, "maintained a proper peace establishment. That is the real truth. I tell you that for the last ten years you have never had in your army more men than enough to relieve the sentries on duty in your stations in the different parts of the world."[9]

Britain's drive to economy was strong, but so too was that of her late enemy. The United States emerged from the conflict a naval power. Her merchant ships were seen in almost every ocean and major port. And with such newly stated global reach she had a young and powerful navy. Those arresting victories over the British in the single-ship duels, as in the total capture of the enemy's fleet at Put-in-Bay, had announced to the American public that they were a naval power. The ship-to-ship encounters, writes Christopher McKee, "put the American people and the nations of the Atlantic and Mediterranean worlds on notice that a highly professional new naval force was cruising the oceans." Nothing of the sort could have been said of the U.S. Navy in 1793, for then it had neither warships, nor commanders, nor dockyards. But in consequence of the 1812 war a new professional officer class had developed, and this had profound implications for the post-war years.[10] And for the better management of the service a Board of Navy Commissioners was put in place.

The War of 1812 enhanced the prestige of the U.S. Navy. Perry's remarkable victory, the success of American arms on Lake Champlain, the long litany of gains by American privateers, the rout of the British Army at New Orleans— all these, to say nothing of the single-ship encounters so glorious to the

American viewpoint, exalted the greatness of the U.S. Navy, and even gave it the legendary penumbra of victor over the world's greatest naval power. Students of history, and of sea power in particular, have been more cautious in their assessments. The war at sea accentuated the value of cruiser commerce raiding, *guerre de course*.[11] For three-quarters of a century, until the 1890s, these philosophies dominated American thought and legislation. Even before the War of 1812 ended, American statesmen and advocates of sea power were urging the necessity of capital ships, in order that the American seaboard would not be held hostage to enemy blockade. More seventy-four-gun ships, heavy frigates, and sloops-of-war were called for; and if they could not be kept in commission, they could be held in reserve for time of need and emergency. In April 1816 Congress passed a six-year program calling for the building of nine seventy-four-gun ships-of-the-line, twelve forty-four-gun frigates, and three steam-driven "batteries," the latter for purposes of port defense. Soon distant stations were developed: the Mediterranean in 1815 to protect commerce and punish the Barbary pirates; the Pacific in 1821 to protect American commerce and "show the flag"; the West India in 1822 to guard against pirates and irregular "privateers"; and the Brazil, or South Atlantic, East India, Home, and African Squadrons in later years. The 1816 legislation "for the gradual increase of the Navy" did not yield enough protective power for a burgeoning maritime power such as the United States was becoming.

Against such overabundant power as the Americans were acquiring, both at home and abroad, the British were hard-pressed to maintain their frontiers in British North America. The tally for defense continued to mount. Costs for the building of the great defense canals never flagged. Little Englanders would champion the abandoning of such imperial obligations, and there was talk of empire as being a millstone round the neck of the Mother Country. In 1837 and 1838 rebellions in Upper and Lower Canada gave added credence to the argument that it was time to forsake the colonies. At the very least, Canada should be placed in such a position as better to get on in its relations with the United States. The movement toward relaxing trade restrictions advanced steadily, and Britain permitted the American merchant vessels to do business in British West Indian ports. And try as much as the Royal Navy might, on official instructions, the American fishermen could not be kept out of the waters from Labrador south to Nova Scotia. And on Lake Erie the U.S. naval command kept a sizable fleet: the brigs *Niagara* and *St. Lawrence,* the prize ships *Detroit* and *Queen Charlotte,* the prize schooner *Lady Prevost,* the prize brigs

Hunter and *Caledonia,* the schooners *Amelia* and *Porcupine,* and the pilot boat schooner *Dispatch.*[12]

In such circumstances as these, British diplomacy had to do double duty: to protect imperial interests in North America on the one hand, and to do so without giving offense to the United States government on the other. And given the fiscal parsimony of the times empire had to be continued "on the cheap."

From Penetanguishene naval base sailed various brigs, schooners, and Durham boats which showed the White Ensign on these northern waters. This diminutive fleet was never of sufficient force to satisfy its senior naval officer. It was never tested in war, and played very much the role as a counterweight to what might happen. The Royal Navy in that age won most of its battles riding at anchor. Penetanguishene's job was to serve the fleet and to watch the American forces, and to spring into action as required. Whether or not it would have been able to deal with the potential enemy in combat will never be known. The changing circumstances of international affairs was reducing the chances of war on this station.

By midcentury only a memory remained of Penetanguishene naval base. Indeed, early historians of this part of Ontario pondered why the British should ever have established a fortified port in that out-of-the-way spot. One whimsically suggested that the answer might be found on the general ground that "they do those things better in France." Another, author of *Smith's Canada,* a broad-brush treatment, wryly suggested in 1852 that Penetanguishene was "probably from being the safest place in the Province to keep out of danger, and as being the place least likely to be invaded in case of hostilities." To this he hastened to add, "The absurdity of the affair appears at length to have struck the authorities, and the establishment had been broken up, and the place shorn of its honors."[13] The place was so remote that the rest of Canada "might have been lost and won several times over before the commander in that remote spot could be made aware that his services were in request." By that time, a steam gunboat, HMS *Midas,* was laid up there, and Penetanguishene's future seemed relegated to that of a depot or colony for pensioners, who were to be settled on small portions of the Government Reserve.

In 1828, as part of the withdrawal of the British garrison from Drummond Island, seventy-five families of the voyageurs followed the garrison to Penetanguishene. These Canadians remained fiercely loyal to the Crown, says their historian, for they were battle-scarred veterans of Michilimackinac, St. Joseph's, Sault Ste. Marie, "and other sanguinary points during the war of 1812." One of the voyageurs recalled that Sgt. Santlaw Rawson of the 68th Regiment hauled down the British flag at Drummond Island. "After performing this somewhat disagreeable duty, he remembers Lieutenant Carson handing over the keys to the U.S. officers, when they shook hands all round in most cordial manner." The embarkation took place 4 November 1828. Troops, stores, Indian agency supplies, and various items were loaded into the hired brig *Wellington* and the small and cramped schooner *Hackett*. November was a poor month to sail this body of water. Sailing toward Penetanguishene they met a fierce storm and the schooner was wrecked on Fitzwilliam Island. In any event, the voyageur families made Penetanguishene and environs their home, many settling in Tiny Township, Simcoe County, Tiny being one of Queen Victoria's dogs. These families placed a distinct stamp on the settlement in and around Penetanguishene. To this day their proud descendants honor the remarkable and patriotic activities of their forebears—and maintain a vibrant community that is part of a unique Franco-Ontarian population. From a cedar swamp they built a fine town with defined social and religious characteristics.[14]

Then, as in the days of the war, Penetanguishene was supplied overland by way of Holland Landing and the Nottawasaga River. In 1830, however, all of that changed, for the colonial government opened a portage between the Indian reserve stations of Orillia and Coldwater. From Coldwater, water access could be made to Gloucester Bay at Waubaushene, the old bateau building place of the war. Until the Northern Railway was opened to Collingwood, on Lake Huron, this portage and access remained the sole route of communication to and from, as Scottish empire-builder and poet John Galt termed it, "the most inland Canadian military post from which waved the meteor flag of England."[15]

Explorer John Franklin of the Royal Navy was there, too, and had this to say about this lonely station:

> Penetanguishene is the most northerly of our naval stations, and the key to Lake Huron. At the close of the war they were preparing to build a frigate of thirty-two guns, but its construction was deferred when the peace was concluded, and the establishment was then reduced. We have found, however, very comfortable quarters in the house of the lieutenant commanding. There are a lieutenant of the army with his wife, and a surgeon and his wife stationed here; these form a social party and cause the time to pass very pleasantly. . . . I do not think, however, that either you or I would relish such a secluded life. If we could convey our library, it would be the very place for me to get through it.[16]

Penetanguishene became a naval backwater. It had in those sunset years, it is true, a resident collector of customs. But there was so seldom an arrival by water that one officer who held the post, Capt. John Moberly, a retired Royal Navy officer, confessed upon demand that eleven years had elapsed since he had made an entry in the port log. Much of the activity was on shore, and the place had a grist and saw mill, a Roman Catholic church and an old Anglican church halfway between the village and the disheveled government establishment at the naval yard and garrison. Fishermen took a great number of sturgeon in the bay, and from it isinglass was made for export.

In 1832 the post witnessed a considerable reduction, and on 15 March of that year the Navy issued instructions that all vessels and naval stores were to be sold at auction. Listed for sale were the *Tecumseth*, schooner, 175 tons; *Newash*, brigantine, 175 tons; *Bee*, gunboat, 41 tons; *Wasp*, gunboat, 41 tons; *Mosquito*, gunboat, 31 tons; three bateaux, one 32-foot cutter, two 32-foot gigs; one whale boat; one jolly boat; and one 19-foot gig. Except for the *Tecumseth* and *Newash* all the others had been built at Penetanguishene after its founding as a naval yard.

For one reason or another the folks of Penetanguishene took no interest in the rotting warships, which seemed to offer no potential for the making of a living on Lake Huron. The vessels attracted no bidders at auction; they remained unsold. Local citizens and others bought up quantities of stores. But the vessels lay rotting and unattended. Gradually they settled into the bay. It was, in all, a sad end to this doughty little mosquito fleet of the Royal Navy on the upper Great Lakes.

Like the gunboats of yesteryear, the base itself, and its buildings, fell into abject destitution and ruin. "The only remains of all the warlike demonstrations of former times are a sloop sunk and rotting in the bay, and a large stone-building at the entrance, called the 'Fort,' but merely serving as barracks for a few soldiers from the garrison at Toronto," wrote traveler Anna Jameson in 1834.[17]

Meanwhile, at Grand River Naval Depot on Lake Erie, the vessels had fallen into neglect and disuse. *Sauk* and *Huron* and four gunboats ended their days there and sank or were broken up. These declines, at Penetanguishene as at Grand River, were mirrored in the general reduced state of the Navy. The number of officers and sailors was reduced from about fifty-five hundred in 1816 to four thousand in 1822. Additional demands called for the "peace establishment" to be put even lower. In 1834 the Royal Navy's command on the Great Lakes ceased altogether on grounds that "the political motive . . . for keeping the Commodore on the Lakes would appear to My Lords to have ceased, as well as every naval object." The Admiralty could not match any imagined U.S. naval buildup, and orders were sent to Commodore Barrie to pay off the HM schooner *Cockburn* at Kingston, strike his broad pennant and reduce the naval bases under his command, and repair to England. At sunset 30 June 1834, this was accomplished, closing the ancient base of British naval operations on the Great Lakes.[18] (It is a matter of record that this command had to be revived in 1838 when the service was called upon to suppress the rebellion in Lower Canada and to provide protection against Hunters Lodges attacking from Oswego and elsewhere on American soil.)

For about two decades British line regiments kept the watch at Penetanguishene. There they guarded the northern gateway of Upper Canada from American attack and, in theory at least, prepared to spring into action to fulfill the promise of Commodore Hall's post-1814 design to take out the Americans at Fort Gratiot and elsewhere. At one time or another some distinguished regulars would mount the guard, parade regimental colors, and conduct ceremonial duties. Penetanguishene was the western rampart of imperial defense keyed on Quebec, Montreal, Kingston, and York. The size of the garrison depended on the state of Anglo-American relations (and fear of war). Always, however, the regiments were the finest, among them the Royal Berkshires (the 66th Regiment of Foot, who later gained renown at the Khyber Pass in the Afghan War of 1848), the Hindoostan Regiment (76th Regiment of Foot), and the Warwickshires. A fine church, St. James'-on-the Lines was built in 1836. "Lines" is an old military term referring to the military lines that connected York with Penetanguishene. This small frame-built structure of the Church of England was built with locally raised funds and imperial contributions. It was seen, as the commanding officer, Lt. F. L. Ingall of the 15th Regiment, put it, in 1836 "so highly necessary and advantageous to the Officers and soldiers composing this remote garrison." A rector of St. James's-on-the-Lines, George Hallen, credited Captain Moberly as founder of the church.[19]

The Great Lakes was also run down as an American military zone. In 1824, for instance, war planners decided that it was expedient to dispose of all stores belonging to the Navy at its yards on Lake Ontario, Lake Erie, and Lake Champlain, which could not be moved advantageously to the Atlantic or could not be stored. All public vessels except two ships of the line on the stocks at Sackets Harbor were to be sold.[20] With the northern border with Canada apparently secure there seemed less immediate need to keep a large standing naval force. Protection of the seaboard of the United States by suitable warships, the improvement of the naval infrastructure of the United States (by the building of two dockyards in 1827), and the construction of harbor and port fortifications were seen as the requisite measures for American naval defense. Thus, while the cry went up for more capital ships the statesmen of the age were content with inshore or littoral defense requirements, at the same time expanding the Navy as required to protect U.S. commerce, political interests and prestige "on distant station."[21]

In the continental interior United States government policy turned on the issue of regulating trade between whites and natives. This was based in the "commerce clause" of the Constitution, and empowered Congress to regulate commerce not only with foreign nations but with several states and "with the Indian tribes." Congress adopted a licensing system under the intercourse act of 1790 to regulate trade with Indians. Enforcement of this rested increasingly with the War Department. In 1806 the office of superintendent of Indian trade was established within the War Department, and under this until its demise in 1822 was supervised the factory trading system.[22] This put the purchase, transfer, and sale of native goods in the hands of agents. Indian policy was closely tied up with government monopoly of commerce. To further tighten the strings of influence, government intended to bring the natives to ground, to *pacify the tribes.*

In Michigan Territory, the energetic Governor Lewis Cass, that veteran of frontier warfare, lawyer, soldier, and experienced legislator, set about after the Ghent Treaty to pacify the tribes. His intention, born of necessity and experience, was to bring lasting peace to the frontier. His object was to make this old trading and warring zone safe for settlement. By using military contractors for rations distribution and friendly natives to influence hostile ones he arranged for treaty councils when and where required. In 1822, he had forts erected—at Saginaw, Lake Huron, to guard against Chippewa raiders, and at Sault Ste. Marie to protect northern trading Americans and their families. At Sault Ste. Marie Ermatinger's establishment, probably at Nolin's former post, was expropriated by the American military as a spot to erect their fort. For years garrisons were kept there and elsewhere. Cass also reorganized the militia. He ordered the cutting of military trails. Meanwhile he energetically sought to quell native resistance by signing treaties of peace and friendship. At Spring Wells, near Detroit, on 8 September 1815, peace was granted to all tribes represented. No land cession occurred in this instance but a general peace was proclaimed, bringing an end to nearly a decade of frontier unease.

Elsewhere government Indian "factories" were opened to regulate the trade at certain controllable locations. An Indian treaty was signed at Fort Meigs, on the Rapids of the Miami River, in 1817. At Sault Ste. Marie, opposite from the North West Company post, Cass signed a treaty in June 1820 with the Chippewa, confirming their permanent fishing rights in the river and their camping privileges there. That same year the St. Martin Islands, near Michilimackinac, were ceded by Indians, ensuring American control. Elsewhere, Cass or his agents systematically went about the business of pacification: at Chicago, 1821; Prairie du Chien, 1825; and Fond du Lac, 1826. The public lands of Michigan now were sold, and from western New York, Ohio, and Indiana, but especially from New England, settlers arrived in a steady number. The state legislature convened in 1836, and after some delays admission to the Union was effected on 26 January 1837.[23] In Ohio the pattern was similar: in 1817 a treaty was signed with many tribes, with the exception of the Miamis, ceding much of the northwestern portion of the state. In Illinois, at Edwardsville in 1819, the Kickapoo signed for a reservation forever in the Territory of Missouri. In Wisconsin, in 1829, at Prairie du Chien, the Americans concluded their treaty with the Chippewa, Ottawa, Potawatomi, and Winnebago. "So the treaties were executed at last," wrote a U.S. agent, "and a passage had been acquired across the country from Lake Michigan to the Mississippi." To this he added: "South of the Wisconsin [River] the Indians now own only reservations, which as soon as the white people settle on all the ceded lands, will be sold to us, and the Indians will retire above the Wisconsin, or cross the Mississippi, where the bear, beaver, the deer, and the bison invite them."[24]

And so the removal and pacification continued. Tecumseh had warned of this. Jefferson had talked about the Indian salvation being in private property in land, not an unending public domain of Indian lands. "In this way alone," he had told them, "can you ensure the lands to your descendants through all generations, and that it shall never be sold from under your feet."[25] The reservation became homeland, replacing expanses of forest lands, marshes, lakes and prairie.

Nowadays Penetanguishene is recovering its history, kept quiet since the days of the War of 1812. Documentary research in Admiralty, War Office, and Colonial Office files are yielding new particulars about its history. Archaeology, too, is making great strides in uncovering the past. It was long known that a naval slipway existed at Penetanguishene, for its remains still sit above water. Archaeological discoveries in the 1970s revealed footings of a long, narrow shed, measuring thirty by sixteen feet, the principal feature of which was a pair of long rails, like railway tracks, designed to hold a cradle upon which a vessel could be hauled up an incline and out of the water, or the reverse. Sturdy oak rails eleven feet apart were fastened to oak beams supported in turn by columns of pine "sleepers." Its extensive cribwork had been put in carefully, then filled with rock ballast. The whole had been neatly designed and precisely measured to underwater contours.[26]

Penetanguishene, and Discovery Harbour, now boasts a heritage fleet. HMS *Tecumseth* is considerably larger than her namesake. She is the great tall ship of Penetanguishene and has sailed to Chicago on a tall ships rendezvous. Her sail and rigging plan is based on John Fitcham's classic *Masting and Rigging of Ships* (1829). Based at Discovery Harbour, too, is the replica of HM schooner *Bee,* forty-three feet in length, and 40 65/95 tons.[27] With sister ships *Wasp* and *Mosquito,* built at Nottawasaga River, these small schooners, sometimes referred to at the time as Durham boats, were gunboats. They had various duties, hydrographic, diplomatic, and imperial. They had been built without strong timbers and decks and could scarcely carry a gun in safety. By 1827 *Bee* needed repairs, and her sister ships were described as "completely rotten." Today the replica of the *Bee,* launched at Penetanguishene in 1984, with distinctive yellow-striped hull, costumed crew, and suit of sails, is a colorful reminder of the British Navy's presence in those waters. From time to time these vessels are joined by the *Perseverance,* once kept at Fort William on Lake Superior and acquired from Old Fort William in Thunder Bay in 1990. She is molded on the schooner destroyed, as we have noted, in the falls of Sault Ste. Marie at the hands of American forces in 1814.

Taken altogether it is a tidy little fleet, much dedicated to the history of the 1812 war on the upper Great Lakes as well as to shipbuilding and shiphandling in those remarkable days. Ashore visitors will find the King's Wharf, the dockyard, quarterman of shipwright's office, and clerk-in-charge's office and house. They will also find sailors' barracks and guardhouse, assistant surgeon's house,[28] the commanding officer's house, the kitchen, hydrographic surveyor's house, fort adjutant's house, and original officers' quarters. A number of structures, including King's Wharf Theatre, Bayfield's Centre, Chandlery, and Captain Roberts' Table, complete the shore establishment. Beginning in August 1998 a reenactment of the so-called Battle of Georgian Bay helped revive the spirit of the War of 1812.

As for Nottawasaga River, where the schooner *Nancy* met her fiery end, it has nowadays taken on a different character than in the days of the northern war. Country highways and roads now criss-cross the lush landscape of this heartland of Ontario agriculture. The old pathways of the 1812 warriors, though hard to find, can be located with a little diligence. For instance, historical plaques advise the passersby of a war all but forgotten. Willow Creek Depot, Glengarry Landing, and Schooner Town can be visited by the motorist.

Not far from the Nottawasaga River exit is Nancy Island Historic Site in Wasaga Beach Provincial Park (at one time called the Museum of the Upper Lakes). In summer tourist season the place, known generally as Wasaga Beach, swarms with cottagers and fun-seekers. The heritage attraction, well worth a visit, is a lively re-creation of the *Nancy* affair billed locally as "a tale of flame and vengeance": it boasts a fine museum holding military artifacts of the event, a splendid model of the doughty schooner, and various displays of the conflict.

Visitors to the river mouth (about half a mile east of Nancy Island, which stands in the middle of the Nottawasaga River) will see how secretive is the entrance and, too, how defensive the American commodore, Sinclair, must have been as he viewed from his flagship *Niagara* the surf pounding on the fair, white and shoaling sands of Wasaga Spit. He could have seen the topmasts and rigging of the *Nancy.*

For years the schooner's charred bones lay in the river, gathering sand and silt. In 1911 Toronto journalist, historian, and ship buff C. J. H. Snider found the just-visible hull. At least one American 24-pounder roundshot was discovered nearby, and in 1928, 114 years after the event, the first Nancy Museum was opened. In 1934 a great model of the famous schooner was completed, with Snider playing a leading role.[29] The actual bones of the *Nancy,* her below-the-waterline remains, can be seen in a climate-controlled chamber in the Wasaga Beach complex. In 1968 a museum, theater, and lighthouse were built, the architectural features of the museum and theater inspired by sails straining against winds. In 1978 management of the *Nancy* site became the responsibility of Wasaga Provincial Park. In later years the possibility was raised that the *Nancy* as found and rescued might actually have been another such vessel of the same name, sometimes called *New Nancy,* built for the New North West Company, or XY Company, in 1801–2. But this has never been substantiated. We do know that the Navy stripped the original *Nancy* of her ironware, using these precious parts for maintenance of other vessels. Therefore, further detective work may close the case.

Today as yesterday the mouth of the Nottawasaga retains a wild and enchanting appearance. The prevailing winds can drive a vessel in difficulty ashore. The beach is largely unchanged in configuration since 1812. As for the Nottawasaga River it is now largely cleared of debris, the river channel is now larger (at about one hundred yards), and the channel is made safer, marked by navigational markers courtesy of the Canadian Hydrographic Service and Coast Guard.

In Erie, Pennsylvania, is to be found Commodore Sinclair's flagship for his 1814 cruise, USS *Niagara*. This brig is best remembered—indeed, will always be lauded—as Perry's flagship during the Battle of Put-in-Bay. By 1820 the *Niagara*, which had been built with unseasoned timber, had deteriorated badly and was sunk in Misery Bay, Erie, to preserve her. One hundred years after the battle, in 1913, the remains of this historic vessel were raised. The main timbers, especially those of the keel, were found well preserved. A detailed plan of the ship could not be found. Rebuilt at that time, and rebuilt or repaired again (most recently in 1990), she is now the commissioned flagship of the Commonwealth of Pennsylvania, calling her birthplace, Presque Isle (now Erie), her home port. Her main mast stands one hundred feet, and on the fighting deck are eighteen carronades, or smashers, and two long guns as bow chasers.[30] Perhaps this is not the original or same armament as in the famous battle, or for her Lake Huron cruise. She is symbolic for two reasons: one, the well known, victory over Barclay and the British Navy at Put-in-Bay; two, her little known action at Nottawasaga Bay which resulted in the destruction of HMS *Nancy*. In her time the *Niagara* covered herself with glory, and those who have sought to preserve her as a living piece of history deserve the gratitude of every serious student of Great Lakes history. She, though not original, is the only floating survivor of the Age of Fighting Sail on the inland waters.

Looking back on the War of 1812 on the upper Great Lakes we can see how narrow was the imperial achievement, how close the Americans had come to taking Lake Huron and destroying Canadian trade on Lake Superior. By the narrowest margin a full victory had been denied to U.S. forces. Put-in-Bay had been a remarkable triumph, a conclusive victory for the U.S. Navy. It fulfilled every tenet of Mahan's naval strategy: command of the sea acquired in battle, with the full fruits of victory being bestowed upon the victors. The British Army under Procter had been caught on an exposed frontier at the Maumi and Sandusky Rivers. Tecumseh and his gallant supporters could not offset the prevailing American military might. The imperial forces were thrown back into the Upper Canadian bush, where they perished. The Right Division was reduced to a shambles. Procter's fortunes had rested with Commodore Barclay. Once British sea power had collapsed, Procter, out on a limb, could not survive. History has mistreated him.

Once triumphant on Lake Erie, the U.S. Navy could flood its power northward into Lake Huron. Navigational difficulties beset Commodore Sinclair here, for he could not come to grips with Canadian shipbuilding capabilities safely holed up at Matchedash Bay. Nor could he deal with the transhipment of stores by bateaux from Nottawasaga. The Canadians moved where the Americans could not, protected as they were by the secrets of their Laurentian Shield which skirted the eastern shore of Georgian Bay and the northern waters (and North Channel) of Lake Huron. Above Sault Ste. Marie, also, the Americans could not press. Destroy the North West Company post there they could, but that is all. They attempted a blockade, or patrol, of Nor'Wester lines of communications. In doing so they were caught napping, and two of their splendid schooners fell to Lieutenant Worsley's seasoned skills. Imperial forces showed inventiveness in fighting this war in northern waters, using the practices of military deviousness, or inventiveness, out of necessity. They took Michilimackinac at the outset of the war, and did it by surprise. They launched a far-distant campaign for the control of the Upper Mississippi River's Prairie du Chien, and did so with complete success. They continued to be a thorn in the side of U.S. territorial governors, particularly Governor Cass of Michigan.

Thus, although sea power could exert a prominent role in the affairs of Lake Erie and all waters above—Lake Huron, Georgian Bay, Lake Michigan, and Lake Superior—in those waters and adjacent lands a small-boat war, of schooners, bateaux, and canoes, resulted. Part of the reason for this was the limitations placed on navigation by the shallows and rapids of the St. Clair River. In addition, the skills of the American men-of-war, so brilliantly displayed at Put-in-Bay, were not demonstrated in Lake Huron and Georgian Bay. Caution, even timidness, characterized Sinclair's actions. Lack of alertness was a feature of commanders of the *Scorpion* and *Tigress*. The U.S. Army as it fought its Lake Huron campaign could not retake Michilimackinac, even though it had been in garrison there for many years before 1812 and possessed local knowledge. A British and Indian force, small in number though decided in purpose, dealt a telling blow against the amphibious forces under Crogan at Michilimackinac. Without adequate artillery support, or gunfire from naval units, an assault against a carefully prepared, though small number of defenders was impossible of success. In the end, imperial forces kept control of the trade of Lake Huron and maintained the Indian alliance, despite the overabundant power of the U.S. Navy and U.S. Army. Another year of fighting might have changed all that.

The misfortunes of the U.S. Navy on Lake Huron and Georgian Bay (as opposed to their victory on Lake Erie) did not reflect the fighting capacity of that service generally. American ships and sailors won the respect of British statesmen, and even Royal Navy officers, if grudgingly, showed respect for their opposites. A young lieutenant in the Royal Navy, Michael Scott, paid a remarkable tribute to what he called "those damned Yankees." "I don't like Americans," he wrote in 1832, "I never did, and never shall like them. . . . I have no wish to eat with them, drink with them, deal with, or consort with them in any way; but let me tell the whole truth, *nor fight* with them, were it not for the laurels to be acquired, by overcoming an enemy so brave, determined, and alert, and every way so worthy of one's steel, as they have always proved."[31]

Commodore Yeo, in reflecting on the War of 1812, wrote that the Royal Navy and the British Army had learned the necessity of full and close cooperation, and that as of that date their situation of the Lakes had improved by the exertions of both arms of the state. He was aware, too, that American ignorance, and the impolicy of their plans, had kept them from greater success, even victory. The disunion of their commanders, Sinclair and Croghan would be a case in point, had been a critical factor. So, too, had the mistaken confidence the Americans placed in the attachment of the Canadians to the American cause.

As for the British, Yeo pointed out that their difficulty in maintaining a naval force on the Lakes was due to lack of sites for suitable shipbuilding in such convenient positions as would make easy the transport of stores and supplies. There was, besides, an insufficiency of transport on the River St. Lawrence which was so much exposed to fire from American riflemen on its banks. For his superiors he offered some advice. He pointed to the need for a very large military and naval establishment to maintain Upper Canada in the future. Kingston in particular should be made a strong frontier town. He recommended a communication between Montreal and Kingston by an alternate waterway, a back door access so to speak, via the Ottawa and Cataraqui Rivers; in doing so he foreshadowed British imperial and military logic accepted after 1825, which led to the building of Canada's notable military canals.[32] By fortifying Kingston and Montreal, as Yeo and others realized, the Canadian provinces might be made safe from future American raids. In time millions of pounds sterling were invested by the British government in Canadian defenses, for if sea power could not be projected inland then armies could be sent by canals or kept in Martello towers and garrisons as counterweights to American military dominance in North America.

In effect, the War of 1812 registered a balance of power in North America, for although the British could command the Atlantic approaches to the continent and blockade the Americans at will, they could not maintain a preponderant force on the Great Lakes. Lake Ontario might be kept in their control, against heavy obstruction from the Americans from Oswego and Sackets Harbor. But in waters above Niagara a British-controlled inland seas was an impossibility. Land power had outflanked sea power. In such circumstances as these, Canadian security after 1815 rested in an equipoise established at Ghent and retained by British and American diplomats after the war. It took a generation to cool the heated passions. Military and naval forces on both sides were not partial to making easy the successes of the former enemy. It was a reluctant peace. As for Canadian patriotism, it was handed the highest trump card, and fear of American invasion cast a long shadow over the affairs of British North America and further shaped the nature of national and imperial loyalties.

As to Tecumseh and his supporters, as to the Indian allies of McDouall and McKay who fought in the Michigan and Wisconsin campaigns, their story is all the more tragic. They could not sustain their independence or political vitality. Succor from British governors was replaced by indifference. Indian military support was no longer needed, and as Anglo-American peace became more assured as the century advanced after 1812 so did the influence of native peoples diminish in the official minds of the Canadian and British policy makers. In the United States, similarly, the Indians were cast aside militarily and were even seen as a detriment to the consolidation of the republic in western lands. Put-in-Bay was symbolic of the U.S. Navy's inland power, and all adjacent lands soon came under the sway of the enlarging United States. But the defense of Upper Canada, so dearly bought by imperial forces, deflected the American frontier southward, intensifying as it did the pressures upon any remnants of Tecumseh's warriors and statesmen.

The War of 1812 had larger implications than the taking and holding of Michilimackinac, the escape and destruction of the *Nancy,* or the proceedings of amphibious expeditions intent on securing some distant post in the forested wilderness. It was the last of the northern frontier wars of North America. The struggle on these warpaths echoes down through the years, bringing with it the sounds of ship cannon and field artillery, of landing parties and Indian escorts. Bringing it to mind may seem on the romantic side, but in its own way it marked the close of an era going back to the first English and French colonizers arriving on the eastern seaboard of America. By the time this course of empire had reached the upper Great Lakes, the drama was reaching its ultimate conclusion, and in it sea power and amphibious force played out their conspicuous parts with memorable effect.

APPENDIX A

MILLER WORSLEY'S LETTER REPORTING ACTION AGAINST THE U.S. NAVY

H.M. Schooner *Confiance*
Nottawaysaga, Lake Huron,
October 6th, 1814

My Dear Father:—

I have this moment received yours of the 20th March which you sent out by Edmond. I can assure you that I write by every opportunity but the distances are so great and the letters often miscarry so that must be the reason you have not received any . . .

No doubt you will be astonished to hear that I have got command on Lake Huron which is about seven hundred miles farther inland than Lake Ontario. On my arrival on this lake I got a schooner called the *Nancy* mounting 3 guns and 24 men. I had not possession of her more than ten days when I received information that an American Squadron was on the Lake. I took my schooner up this River and built a Block House and put my guns into it to defend her as I expected an attack, which was the case, as I was getting my last gun into it.

The enemy force consisted of a 20 gun Brig and three schooners mounting each a long 24 pounder with 450 soldiers. I however contended with them for my vessel from nine A.M. till four P.M. with my three guns, 24 seamen and 10 Indians. Finding my little crew were falling all round me, I immediately formed a resolution to blow both up, which I did, made my escape with the rest of my little crew through the woods to the great astonishment of the enemy.

We walked that night with our wounded and dying 36 miles before we came to any house. We lost everything we had except what we stood upright in. On my arrival at this house [Fort Willow] which had stores in etc. for the Island Michilimackinac which Island I had to supply with stores and provisions, I waited two days and then made my mind up to go on to it in open boats the distance of 380 miles.

This I did and arrived safe in six days within 40 miles of it when to my great astonishment and regret I saw two of the enemy's Schooners at anchor in a narrow passage that I had to pass called the Detour. Only having two boats and 18 seamen with few arms and knowing the enemies schooners each had a long 24 pr. and forty men I put my men into an Indian canoe and passed them in the night with the intention of applying to the Officer at Michilimackinac for a few soldiers, that I might cut them out.

He complied with my wishes, I returned and finding only one, at night I boarded and took her with the loss of two killed and seven wounded. She proved to be the American Schooner *Tygres* mounting a long 24 pr. and 40 men. They had 4 killed and 3 thrown overboard and drowned and five wounded.

She informed me the other schooner would be back next day therefore I remained at anchor and sent my prisoners away and prepared to attack her. The following morning she hove in sight I directly cut my cable and ran down to her, boarded her and took her after a sharp resistance.

She proved to be the American Schooner *Scorpion* mounting a long 24 and a long 12 pr. We had two wounded, the enemy had 2 killed and 4 wounded. Thus you see after a series of hardships I have got two schooners both finer vessels than the *Nancy* and providentially escaped unhurt.

I shall once more be able to make a trip to this Island with provisions before I shall lay my vessel up for the winter it being out of my power to navigate this Lake after the 1st of November it being covered with ice and so very cold that you can scarce show your nose out.

In case you should be at a loss to know the importance of keeping this Island, it is the key for the North West Fur Trade and a head post of the Indians Warriors who are a fierce race of men. I must now conclude having letters of service to write and the time short. You will see my dispatches in the paper. . . .

M. Worsley

Source: *War Log of the Nancy,* xlvii–xlviii.

APPENDIX B

MILLER WORSLEY'S APPEAL TO THE KING

Isle of Wight
13th April 1831

Sir

In venturing to address your Most Gracious Majesty [William IV], I hope it will not be considered too great a liberty for a subject to take and that your Majesty will be pleased to pardon my doing so under this impression I am induced to lay my case before your Majesty when I feel confident it will meet with that indulgence your Majesty bestows upon all classes of your subjects. In stating my case it is necessary to inform your Majesty that I have been in your Majesty's Royal Navy twenty eight years, fifteen of which I have held the rank of Commander, that during the last War I was in the Battles of Trafalgar, Copenhagen, Flushing and Basque Roads, that I was employed in taking a party of seamen over land from Halifax to the Lakes in Canada in the winter of 1812 and 1813, that I was in four general actions with the American squadron on Lake Ontario, that I was appointed to the Command of your Majesty's Naval Force on Lake Huron by Sir James Yeo the Commander in Chief as a mark of distinction for the manner in which I conducted your Majesty's Ship *Princess Charlotte* in the attack and taking of the town and fort of Oswego on Lake Ontario, after my Captain was wounded that I was obliged to destroy your Majesty's Schooner *Nancy* which vessel I commanded, to prevent her falling into the Enemy's hands, after defending her five hours, against a superior force, whereby I lost all my clothing, time keeper, nautical instruments together with two hundred pounds of money, that with the remnant of my Crew I crossed Lake Huron in an open boat exposed to great hardships and privations of every description having only what we could shoot or catch by fishing to subsist upon. That after three weeks exposure to the above mentioned hardships, and within 40 miles of my destination Michilimackinac I captured after a severe action two American Schooners of 4 guns each. . . . I was afterwards appointed to the Command of your Majesty's Brig *Star,* by Sir Edward Owen, the Commander in Chief on the Lakes, which vessel I paid off at Kingston, Upper Canada, at the close of the American War, since which period I have not had the honour of being employed in your Majesty's Royal Navy. That I have a wife and a Family who depend solely on my exertions for their support, and that my expected applications for employment have not been attended with success. I therefore most humbly beg that your Majesty will be graciously pleased to take my case into your Royal consideration—and should your Majesty deem my services worthy of employment be graciously pleased to command it.

I have the honour to be, Your Majesty's Most Obedient, Most Humble and devoted Subject.

Miller Worsley, Commander Royal Navy
Source: Admiralty Papers, 1 / 2728, CapW20.

NOTES

ABBREVIATIONS

Add. MSS	Additional Manuscripts, British Library, London
Adm.	Admiralty Papers, PRO
AO	Archives of Ontario, Toronto
BL	British Library, London
CO	Colonial Office Papers, PRO
Cruikshank	Ernest A. Cruikshank, "An Episode of the War of 1812: The Story of the Schooner *Nancy*"
DAB	*Dictionary of American Biography*
DCB	*Dictionary of Canadian Biography*
DICD	*Documents Relating to the Invasion of Canada and the Surrender of Detroit, 1812*, ed. Ernest A. Cruikshank
Dudley	William S. Dudley, ed., *Naval War of 1812: A Documentary History*
Marshall	John Marshall, *Royal Naval Biography; or Memoirs of the Services . . .*
MHC	*Michigan Historical Collections*
NAC	National Archives of Canada, Ottawa
NMM	National Maritime Museum, Greenwich, London
Niles	*Niles' Weekly Register* (Baltimore)
PRO	Public Record Office, Kew, England
RMC	Royal Military College of Canada, Library, Kingston, Ontario
War Log	*Leaves from the War Log of the Nancy, Eighteen Hundred and Thirteen, with Comments by C. H. J. Snider*
USNA	United States National Archives
WO	War Office Papers, PRO
Wood	William Wood, ed., *Select British Documents of the Canadian War of 1812*
WHC	*Wisconsin Historical Collections*

INTRODUCTION

1. Quoted in Gregory H. Nobles, *American Frontiers: Cultural Encounters and Continental Conquest* (New York: Hill and Wang, 1997), 101.
2. On the causes of the war, see J. C. A. Stagg, *Mr. Madison's War: Politics, Diplomacy, and Warfare in the Early American Republic, 1783–1830* (Princeton: Princeton University Press, 1983); Reginald Horsman, *The Causes of the War of 1812* (1962; reprint, New York: Octagon Books, 1972); and Reginald Horsman, "On to Canada: Manifest Destiny and United States Strategy in the War of 1812," *Michigan Historical Review* 13, no. 2 (1987): 1–24.
3. Quoted in Carl P. Russell, *Guns on the Early Frontiers: A History of Firearms from Colonial Times through the Years of the Western Fur Trade* (Berkeley and Los Angeles: University of California Press, 1957), 53.
4. Quoted in Alfred L. Burt, *The United States, Great Britain, and British North America: From the Revolution to the Establishment of Peace after the War of 1812* (New Haven: Yale University Press, 1940), 305–6.
5. J. G. Simcoe to Henry Dundas, 2 June 1791, CO 42/316.
6. Simcoe to Henry Dundas, 23 February 1794, in R. Louis Gentilcore and C. Grant Head, *Ontario's History in Maps* (Toronto: University of Toronto Press, 1984), 58–59.
7. On this, the correspondence of Hawkesbury and Grenville is instructive. See G. S. Graham, ed., "The Indian Menace and the Retention of the Western Posts," *Canadian Historical Review* 15 (1934): 46–48. Lord Hawkesbury to Lord Grenville, 17 October 1794, enclosing Observations by Isaac Todd and Simon McTavish on the Indian Trade, GD 8-152 and 8-346, Chatham Papers, BL.
8. Or alliances, for the British maintained formal arrangements with different tribes and tribal groups. On this, and the obligations of alliances, see Colin G. Calloway, *Crown and Calumet: British-Indian Relations, 1783–1815* (Norman: University of Oklahoma Press, 1987), 4–5.
9. Quoted in Richard White, *The Middle Ground: Indians, Empires, and Republics in the Great Lakes Region, 1650–1815* (Cambridge: Cambridge University Press, 1991), 484.
10. Capt. A. Gray to Gen. Sir George Prevost, 13 January 1812, *MHC* 15 (1909): 70–72, also *DICD;* Fred Landon, *Western Ontario and the American Frontier* (Toronto: Ryerson, 1941), and Donald Creighton, *The Empire of the St. Lawrence, 1760–1850* (Toronto: Macmillan Company of Canada, 1956), 166–80.
11. "Ideas on the Defence of the Canadas, Grounded upon our Present Strength, and such Resources in Men, as the Population of the Two Provinces May Offer," by Noah Freer, Captain and Quarter Master Generals Office, Quebec, 8 May 1812, MU8559.2, AO.

12. Tiger Dunlop, *Tiger Dunlop's Upper Canada* (Toronto: McClelland and Stewart, 1967), 23–24.

13. Quoted in Fred Landon, *Lake Huron* (Indianapolis: Bobbs-Merrill, 1944), 71.

14. A full discussion of this is given in David Curtis Skaggs and Gerard T. Altoff, *A Signal Victory: The Lake Erie Campaign, 1812–1813* (Annapolis: Naval Institute Press, 1997), chap. 1.

15. Theodore Roosevelt, quoted in Herbert Richmond, *Statesmen and Sea Power* (Oxford: Clarendon Press, 1946), 251.

16. M. M. Quaife, "The Royal Navy of the Upper Lakes," *Burton Historical Collection Leaflet* 2, no. 5 (May 1924): 49–64.

17. Quoted in Landon, *Lake Huron,* 71.

18. Quoted in C. P. Stacey, ed., *Introduction to the Study of Military History for Canadian Students* (Ottawa: Queen's Printer, 1953), 66.

19. Quoted in Bert Hubinger, "Little Wasp, Big Sting," *Naval History,* July–August 1994, 30.

20. *Niles* 3, no. 26 (27 February 1813): 403–4.

21. He called on the governor of Kentucky to supply the effective men. Harrison to Gov. Meigs, 6 August 1813, in ibid., 4, no. 26 (28 August 1813): 420.

22. Duke of Wellington, "Memorandum [on the defense of Canada]," 31 March 1841, WO 1/537, pp. 75–106, WO.

CHAPTER 1. THE ROWBOAT WAR

1. James P. Barry, *Georgian Bay: The Sixth Great Lake* (Toronto: Clarke, Irwin, 1978).

2. Walter Havighurst, ed., *The Great Lakes Reader* (New York: Macmillan, 1966), 179. Also Reuben Gold Thwaites, "Story of Mackinac," *WSC,* 1898, and *Encyclopedia Britannica,* 11th ed., 255–56.

3. David A. Armour and Keith R. Widder, *At the Crossroads: Michilimackinac during the American Revolution* (Mackinac Island, Mich.: Mackinac Island State Park Commission, 1978), 3.

4. Ojibwa call themselves *Anishinabe,* "original man." Helen Hornbeck Tanner, *The Ojibwa* (New York: Chelsea House, 1991), contains a fine historical survey. Diamond Jenness, *The Indians of Canada,* 7th ed. (Toronto: University of Toronto Press, 1977), 277–83. *Handbook of Indians of Canada* (Ottawa: King's Printer, 1913), 96–97.

5. Armour and Widder, *At the Crossroads,* 175–83.

6. Ibid., 188.

7. Quoted in Walter Havighurst, *Three Flags at the Straits: The Forts of Mackinac* (Englewood Cliffs, N.J.: Prentice-Hall, 1966), 109–10.

8. Duke of Portland to Lord Dorcester, 19 November 1794, CO 43/10.

9. *DCB* 5:713–14.

10. This account of Roberts's campaign is based on his letters to E. Baynes (adjutant general, Quebec) and to Brock, both 17 July 1812. The latter contains, as enclosures, the Capitulation and its Supplement. William Wood, ed., *Select British Documents of the Canadian War of 1812*, 3 vols. (Toronto: Champlain Society, 1920–28) (hereafter cited as Wood, followed by volume and page number or volume, part, and page number), 1:432–36. Also John Askin Jr. to D. Claus, 18 July 1812, ibid., 436–37.

11. Wood 1:24.

12. John Askin Jr., quoted in John Abbot, Graeme S. Mount, and Michael J. Mulloy, *The History of Fort St. Joseph* (Toronto: Dundurn, 2000), 85.

13. Sir Alexander Mackenzie, *Voyages from Montreal . . .* (London, 1801), xxxvii.

14. Capt. W. H. Merritt's Journal, in Wood, vol. 3, pt. 2, 549.

15. He did not escape the censure of historians. See, however, the sympathetic treatment in J. Mackay Hitsman, "Sir George Prevost's Conduct of the Canadian War of 1812," in *Canadian Historical Association Annual Report for 1962* (Ottawa: Canadian Historical Association, 1963), 34–43.

16. Edward Channing, *A History of the United States,* vol. 4, *Federalists and Republicans, 1789–1815* (New York: Macmillan, 1917), 467–68; also *DCB* 5:714.

17. On the business consequences of the war, at Michilimackinac, see Ida A. Johnson, *The Michigan Fur Trade* (1919; reprint, Grand Rapids: Black Letter Press, 1971), chap. 7. Also Gordon C. Davidson, *The North West Company* (1918; reprint, New York: Russell & Russell, 1967), 133–35, 139–43. Gabriel Franchère, introduction to *Journal of a Voyage on the North West Coast of America during the Years 1811, 1813 and 1814,* ed. W. Kaye Lamb (Toronto: Champlain Society, 1969).

18. Prevost to Lord Liverpool, 18 May 1812, in Kate Caffrey, *The Twilight's Last Gleaming: Britain vs. America, 1812–1815* (New York: Stein & Day, 1974), 303–9.

19. In this episode six soldiers from Amherstburg in a bateau, under command of Lt. Charles Frederick Rolette (a veteran of Trafalgar as well as the Nile), boarded *Cayahoga Packet* in the Detroit River and ordered her into Amherstburg's anchorage. Thirty Americans were made prisoner by this daring action. Return of Prizes, Lake Erie, in *DICD*, 232; on Rolette, *DHCNF* 2:57–59.

20. Journal of Charles Askin, 15 August 1812, Wood 1:538.

21. Brock to Liverpool, 29 August 1812, Wood 1:508.

22. William F. Coffin, *1812: The War and Its Moral: A Canadian Chronicle* (Montreal: John Lovell, 1864), 202.

23. *DCB* 5:795–801, quotation at 799. Much has been written about Tecumseh; however, for the specific purposes of this analysis I have depended upon John Sugden,

Tecumseh's Last Stand (Norman: University of Oklahoma Press, 1985), David R. Edmunds, *Tecumseh and the Quest for Indian Leadership* (Boston: Little, Brown, 1984), and Sandy Antal, *A Wampum Denied: Procter's War of 1812* (Ottawa: Carleton University Press, 1997).

CHAPTER 2. THE BATTLE OF LAKE ERIE

1. Brock to Governor-General, 2 December 1811, quoted in Ernest A. Cruikshank, "The Contest for the Command of Lake Erie in 1812–13," in *The Defended Border: Upper Canada and the War of 1812,* ed. Morris Zaslow (Toronto: Macmillan, 1964), 84.
2. Gen. John Armstrong to William Eustis, 2 January 1812, quoted in ibid., 87.
3. Hickman to Elliott, 8 January 1813, in "Capture of the British Brigs Detroit and Caledonia," 12th Cong., 2d sess., no. 99, all in *American State Papers Naval Affairs* (Washington, D.C.: Gates and Seaton, 1836), 1:282–84. Elliott's report of proceedings, 9 October 1812, is in William Dudley, ed., *The Naval War of 1812: A Documentary History,* 2 vols. to date (Washington, D.C.: Naval Historical Center, 1985, 1992) (hereafter cited as Dudley, followed by volume and page numbers), 1:328–31. See also William M. Fowler Jr., *Jack Tars and Commodores: The American Navy, 1783–1815* (Boston: Houghton Mifflin, 1984), 215, and Abel Bowen, comp., *The Naval Monument, Containing Official and Other Accounts of All the Battles Fought between the Navies of the United States and Great Britain during the Late War* (Boston: A. Bowen, 1816), 253–55.
4. Chauncey to Perry, 20 January and 15 March 1813, Dudley 2:419–20.
5. Ibid.
6. David Curtis Skaggs, "The Battle of Lake Erie," in *Great American Naval Battles,* ed. Jack Sweetman (Annapolis: Naval Institute Press, 1998), 66.
7. Usher Parsons, *Battle of Lake Erie: A Discourse, Delivered before the Rhode-Island Historical Society . . . February 16, 1852* (Providence, R.I.: Benjamin T. Albro, 1853), 5.
8. Here I have relied heavily on John K. Mahon, *The War of 1812* (1972; reprint, New York: Da Capo Press, 1991), 90–91.
9. Warren to R. H. Barclay, Adm. 1/503, B1448, pp. 178–79, PRO (sources from PRO hereafter cited as Adm. followed by number).
10. Robert Holden Mackenzie, *The Trafalgar Roll: Containing the Names and Services of all Officers of the Royal Navy and Royal Marines who participated in the Glorious Victory of the 21st October 1805, together with a History of the Ships engaged in the Battle* (London: George Allen, 1913), 225. Memorandum of the Services of Captain Robert Barclay, Adm. 9/4, no. 1241. Other particulars are to be found in

John Marshall, *Royal Naval Biography; or Memoirs of the Services* . . . (London, 1831) (hereafter cited as Marshall, followed by volume, part, and page number), vol. 3, pt. 1, 186–87.

11. Prevost to Bathurst, 21 April 1813, quoted in Thomas Malcomson and Robert Malcomson, *HMS Detroit: The Battle for Lake Erie* (St. Catharines, Ontario: Vanwell Publishing, 1990), 24.

12. Barclay court-martial record, Wood 2:298.

13. Barclay to Yeo, 1 June 1813, Adm. 1/5445, fols. 73–74.

14. John B. Hattendorf, ed., *Mahan on Naval Strategy* (Annapolis: Naval Institute Press, 1991), xxix.

15. Barclay to Prevost, 16 July 1813, Long Point, Dudley 2:544–45.

16. Barclay to Yeo, 5 August 1813, off Presque Isle, Dudley 2:546–47.

17. Prevost to Yeo, 14 September 1813, copy, Adm. 1/2737, CapY2, 8–9.

18. Quoted in Malcomson and Malcomson, *HMS Detroit*, 86.

19. David C. Bunnell, *Travels and Adventures of David C. Bunnell during twenty-three years of a Seafaring Life, containing an Accurate Account of the Battle of Lake Erie, under the command of Com. Oliver H. Perry, together with ten years service in the Navy of the United States, also Service among the Greeks, imprisonment among the Turks, etc.* (Palmyra, N.Y.: Bortles, 1831), 110.

20. Barclay to Yeo, 1 September 1813, Wood 2:267–69; also Dudley 2:551–52.

21. George Bancroft, *History of the Battle of Lake Erie, and Miscellaneous Papers* (New York: Robert Bonner's Sons, 1891), 149.

22. Bunnell, *Travels and Adventures,* 118.

23. Here I have relied on the assessment, and use of Mahan, of Col. C. E. Callwell, *Military Operations and Maritime Preponderance, Their Relations and Interdependence* (Edinburgh: William Blackwood and Sons, 1905), 396.

24. O. H. Perry to Gen. William Henry Harrison, 10 September 1813, and copy of a letter from Commodore Perry to Secretary of the Navy, 13 September 1813, *Niles* 3 (25 September 1813): 60–61.

25. Usher Parsons, M.D., "Surgical account of the Naval engagement on Lake Erie," in Dudley 2:562–64; published in slightly different form in the *New England Journal of Medicine and Surgery* 7, no. 4 (October 1818): 313–16.

26. Bancroft, *Battle of Lake Erie,* 186–87. Historian, diplomat, and Cabinet officer, Bancroft was doubtless exercising some prospects of Anglo-American accord on this occasion.

27. Perry, as reported in *Niles* 3, no. 5 (25 September 1813): 61–66.

28. Howard I. Chapelle, *The History of the American Sailing Navy: The Ships and Their Development* (New York: Norton, 1949), 269.

29. For a beginning to the study of this controversy, see Christopher McKee, "An Aerial View of Put-in Bay: United States Historians Scrutinize a Campaign," in

War on the Great Lakes: Essays Commemorating the 175th Anniversary of the Battle of Lake Erie, ed. William Jeffrey Welsh and David Curtis Skaggs (Kent, Ohio: Kent State University Press, 1991), 87–92.

30. George Inglis to Barclay, 10 September 1813, Adm. 1/504, 387–89.
31. Yeo to Sir George Prevost, 15 November 1813, *Niles* 6, no. 11 (14 May 1814): 181.
32. Yeo to Warren, 14 November 1813, Adm. 1/2737, CapY2, 2–3; also Yeo to Warren, 10 October 1813, Adm. 1/2736, 134–35.
33. Warren to Melville, 9 November 1813, NMM, microfilm A-2076, Melville Papers, NAC.
34. *Niles* 6, no. 11 (14 May 1814): 175; *Naval Chronicle* 35 (1816): 378–79.
35. *Niles* 5, no. 21 (22 January 1814): 351.
36. Barclay to Croker, 13 and 28 August 1814, Adm. 1/1557, CapB386.
37. Court martial documents in Adm. 1/5445. These are printed in Wood 2:289–319; see especially the court's judgment, 308–9 and 318–19.
38. Barclay's Narrative of the Proceedings (as given to the court), 9 September 1814, ibid., 306.
39. Marshall, vol. 3, pt. 1, 186–95.
40. Tecumseh's speech, recorded by Maj. John Richardson and first published in 1842, reprinted in Alexander C. Casselman, *Richardson's War of 1812* (Toronto: Historical Publishing, 1902), 205–6. For a fuller account and analysis of Procter's relations with Tecumseh at this juncture, see Reginald Horsman, *The War of 1812* (London: Eyre & Spottiswoode, 1969), 110–12.
41. [George Procter?], *Lucubrations of Henry Ravelin* (London, 1823), 355–56; reprinted in Carl F. Klinck, ed., *Tecumseh: Fact and Fiction in Early Records* (Englewood Cliffs, N.J.: Prentice-Hall, 1961), 186.
42. Perry's report, 24 September 1813; in *Niles* 5, no. 6 (9 October 1813): 99; also Dudley 2:569; Robert S. Quimby, *The U.S. Army in the War of 1812: An Operational and Command Study* (East Lansing: Michigan State University Press, 1997), 1:274–76. Perry's support for Harrison's land operations and the close harmony existing between the commanders is analyzed in David Curtis Skaggs, "Joint Operations During the Detroit–Lake Erie Campaign, 1813," in *New Interpretations in Naval History: Selected Papers from the Eighth Naval History Symposium,* ed. William B. Cogar (Annapolis: Naval Institute Press, 1989), 121–38, esp. 127–32.
43. The role Kentucky forces played in this action and many others in the war is explained in a number of works, prominent of which is James Wallace Hammack Jr., *Kentucky and the Second American Revolution: The War of 1812* (Lexington: University Press of Kentucky, 1976).
44. Harrison to Secretary of War Armstrong, 9 October 1813, Dudley 2:570–76. A recent review of this battle is William F. Freehoff, "Tecumseh's Last Stand," *Military History,* October 1996, 30–36.

45. Horsman, *War of 1812*, 114.

46. Quoted in *DCB* 5:799. The Royal Navy named one of its vessels for Newash, as it did for Tecumseh.

47. Procter's conduct as commander and his relationship with Tecumseh are worth greater study than can be given here. See, however, the detailed works Sugden, *Tecumseh's Last Stand,* and *Tecumseh: A Life* (New York: Henry Holt, 1997), and Antal, *Wampum Denied.* On reflection, it seems as if Procter was left "high and dry" and unable to sustain a campaign in such a location, dependent as he was on waterborne support. His military judges, however, gave him very low marks; and historians have followed suit. As for Tecumseh, he and his fellow warriors were undoubtedly acting in the way of self-interest. Who would expect any the less of them? They were also, undeniably, working as allies. They had a longer war to fight (than did the United States against Great Britain); during the War of 1812 the aims of Tecumseh ran on parallel courses with those of the British and Canadians. Worth stressing is the fact that Indians in Canadian territory did not take up the same cause as did Tecumseh and his followers. Their alliance as "HM Indian allies" was longstanding (and predates any arrangements made between the Crown and Tecumseh).

48. A. C. Whitehorn, *The History of the Welch Regiment* (Cardiff, Wales: Western Mail and Echo, 1932), 106. See also Sir John Fortescue, *History of the British Army* (London: Macmillan, 1920), 9:334–36. Historians continue to condemn Procter or, conversely, to rescue his sagging reputation: Richardson, Hannay, and Kingsford, for instance, have varying views on him. Also see previous note.

49. *Wellington's Dispatches,* ed. John Gurwood, 12 vols. (London: John Murray, 1838), 2:525; Sir Charles P. Lucas, *The Canadian War of 1812* (Oxford: Clarendon, 1906), 6–7.

CHAPTER 3. THE NANCY AND HER ESCAPE

1. Kenneth A. Cassavoy and Kevin J. Crisman, "The War of 1812: Battle for the Great Lakes," in *Ships and Shipwrecks of the Americas: A History Based on Underwater Archaeology,* ed. George F. Bass (London: Thames and Hudson, 1988), 178.

2. Quoted in Edward A. Cruikshank, "An Episode of the War of 1812: The Story of the Schooner *Nancy* [with illustrative documents]," *Ontario Historical Society Papers and Records* 9 (1910), reprinted in Zaslow, *Defended Border* (hereafter cited as Cruikshank, followed by page numbers), 75.

3. *H.M.S. Nancy and the War of 1812* (Toronto: Ministry of Natural Resources, 1978), 2.

4. The activities of the *Nancy* for the year 1813 may be followed in *Leaves from the War Log of the Nancy, Eighteen Hundred and Thirteen, with Comments by C. H.*

J. Snider, new ed. (Midland, Ontario: Huronia Historical Development Council, 1958) (hereafter cited as *War Log*). The vessel's log for 1812 and 1814 does not survive.

5. "Mr. David Mitchell, Mr. McCoursall, & a Mr. J. B. Geigier," according to *War Log,* xiii.
6. *War Log,* xix and xxi. Mackintosh to Bullock, n.d., in ibid., xx.
7. Ibid., xxi.
8. Ernest Lajeunesse, ed., *The Windsor Border Region, Canada's Southernmost Frontier: A Collection of Documents* (Toronto: Champlain Society, 1960), 9.
9. Francis Parkman, *France and England in North America* (New York: Library of America, 1983), 1:822–23.
10. *War Log,* xxii–xxix, quotation at xxviii.
11. H. F. Pullen, *The March of the Seamen,* and John R. Stevens, *Story of H.M. Armed Schooner Tecumseth,* Occasional Paper no. 8–9 (Halifax: Maritime Museum of Canada, 1961).

CHAPTER 4. THE WATER RATS

1. Wood 1:112.
2. Russell F. Weigley, *The American Way of War: A History of United States Military Strategy and Policy* (New York: Macmillan, 1973), 51–52.
3. Brian Leigh Dunnigan, *The British Army at Mackinac, 1812–1815,* Reports in Mackinac History and Archaeology Number 7 (Mackinac Island, Mich.: Mackinac Island State Park Commission, 1980), 17. In the first instance, ten men of the Royal Regiment of Artillery and sixty of the Canadian Embodied Militia were suggested to form the relief force. As Dunnigan explains, this was changed to two companies of the Royal Newfoundland Fencible Infantry and a small number of artillerymen plus a lieutenant and detachment of seamen of the Royal Navy.
4. *DCB* 7 (1988): 556–57.
5. A. Bulger, *An Autobiographical Sketch of the Late Captain Andrew Bulger of the Royal Newfoundland Fencible Regiment* (Bangalore, India, 1865), 89.
6. William Kingsford, *The History of Canada* (Toronto: Rowsell & Hutchison, 1895), 8:512.
7. *DCB* 7:556.
8. On river vessels of the Spanish and their patrols as far north as Prairie du Chien, see Abraham P. Nasatir, *Spanish War Vessels on the Mississippi, 1792–1796* (New Haven: Yale University Press, 1968), 37, 40.
9. Louise Phelps Kellogg, *The British Régime in Wisconsin and the Northwest* (1935; reprint, New York: Da Capo Press, 1971), 282, and Edwards quote at 278.

10. John Long, *Voyages and Travels of an Indian Interpreter* . . . (London, 1791), 146, 150–51.

11. La Feuille to Roberts, 5 February 1813, Wood, vol. 3, pt. 1, 250.

12. J. Rolette and others to Roberts, 10 February 1813, Wood, vol. 3, pt. 1, 251–52.

13. Peter Lawrence Scanlan, *Prairie du Chien: French, British, American* (Menasha, Wisc.: George Banta, 1937), 117.

14. His own memorial, a record of achievements, is "Major William Mckay's Account of the Michilimackinac Expedition," M7082, McCord Museum Archives, Montreal.

15. Jean Morrison, *Superior Rendezvous-Place: Fort William in the Canadian Fur Trade* (Toronto: Natural Heritage/Natural History, Inc., 2001), 75.

16. Wood 3:253; atrocities reported in *WHC* 11:260. Kellogg, *British Régime*, 317.

17. Guignon, *WHC* 11:87.

18. Perkins's reply in *WHC* 11:256. McKay's report of proceedings is in ibid. 11:263–70.

19. Reginald Horsman, "Wisconsin and the War of 1812," *Wisconsin Magazine of History* 46, no. 1 (Autumn 1962): 11. This article, based on a full reading of printed documents, mainly in *WHC*, is a thorough review of this military campaign.

20. Kellogg, *British Régime*, 319–20.

21. W. McKay to R. McDouall, 27 July 1814, in *WHC* 11 (1888): 254–71, quotation at 267.

22. McKay to McDouall, 27 July 1814, in Wood, vol. 3, pt. 1, 264.

23. Ibid. in Wood, vol. 3, pt. 1, 257–65. The account of Rock River appears at 264–65. Also in *WHC* 11:254–71.

24. Orders for Graham, *WHC* 9:219, and Graham's report of proceedings, ibid., 226–28.

25. McDouall to Drummond, 26 May 1814, Wood, vol. 3, pt. 1, 272.

26. Ibid.

27. Ibid., 272–73. Gordon Drummond to George Prevost, 16 June 1814, NAC, RG 8, C Ser., 733:10–12.

CHAPTER 5. EAGLE AGAINST THE BEAVER

1. John Armstrong to President, 31 April 1814, in Gilbert Auchinleck, *A History of the War between Great Britain and the United States of America during the Years 1812, 1813, and 1814* (1855; reprint, London: Arms and Armour Press, 1972), 294.

2. Stagg, *Mr. Madison's War*, 390–91.

3. Isaac Chauncey to Jesse Elliott, 1 April 1814, Isaac Chauncey Letter Books, N.Hi., no. 01549.

4. Jones to A. Sinclair, 7 April and 15 April 1814, printed in *The New State Papers Naval Affairs*, ed. K. Jack Bauer (Wilmington, Del.: Scholarly Resources, 1981), 4:337–38 and 338–44.

5. Ibid.

6. Christopher McKee, *A Gentlemanly and Honorable Profession: The Creation of the U.S. Naval Officer Corps, 1794–1815* (Annapolis: Naval Institute Press, 1991), 138.

7. George Croghan to Arthur Sinclair, 1 May 1814, USNA, RG 45, CL, 1814, vol. 3, no. 24.

8. Abandoned in 1822 owing to demilitarization of the Great Lakes but reestablished in 1828 owing to Indian difficulties in Wisconsin Territory.

9. Croghan to Sinclair, 26 May 1814, USNA, RG 45, CL, 1814, vol. 4, no. 46.

10. Jones to Sinclair, 1 June 1814, USNA, RG 45, CLS.

11. Secretary of War to Duncan McArthur, 13 July 1814, Clarence Carter, ed., *The Territorial Papers of the United States*, vol. 10, *The Territory of Michigan 1805–1820* (Washington, D.C.: GPO, 1942), 464.

12. No ship could sail into Lake Superior from St. Marys River, and, in those circumstances, American commanders knew that boat parties could be landed at Sault Ste. Marie, make the short land passage, and then capture North West Company vessels on the lake.

13. Diary of Surgeon Usher Parsons, 1812–14, entries for 13–16 July 1814, Rhode Island Historical Society, Providence.

14. Against Harrison's orders to burn Fort Stephenson and withdraw toward Upper Sandusky he refused. "We have determined to maintain this place, and by Heaven, we will," he told the general. The latter succumbed to his earnest entreaties. Hammack, *Kentucky and the Second American Revolution*, 76.

15. Auchinleck, *History of the War*, 294.

16. Sinclair to Secretary of the Navy, 22 July 1814, off St. Joseph's, USNA, RG 45, CL, 1814, vol. 5, no. 24. See also Croghan to Secretary of War, 9 August 1814, off Thunder Bay (west shore Lake Huron), in Cruikshank, 103.

17. The prize papers for the schooner *Mink* are in USNA, RG 21, Prize Case files for the U.S. District Court for the Eastern District of Pennsylvania, National Archives Microfilm M966, roll 2.

18. Sinclair to Secretary of the Navy, 9 August 1814, Cruikshank, 102–3.

19. On this episode, see J. I. Poole, "The Fight at Battle Hill," in Zaslow, *Defended Border*, 130–42; Wood 2:347–56.

20. Daniel Turner to Sinclair, 28 July 1814, in USNA, RG 45, CL, 1814, vol. 5.

21. *Report on Canadian Archives, by Douglas Brymner, Archivist, 1889* (Ottawa: Queen's Printer, 1890), xxxvii–xxxix.

22. Franchère, *Journal of a Voyage*, 184. See also Johnson, *Michigan Fur Trade*, 119–21. For biographical details on Nolin and Ermatinger, see *DCB* 6:546–48 and 236–37, respectively.

23. See *Perseverance* prize papers, in USNA, RG 21, M966, reel 2.

24. Bernard Fergusson, *The Watery Maze: The Story of Combined Operations* (London: Collins, 1961), 19.

25. Sinclair to Jones, 9 August 1814, USNA, RG 45, CL, vol. 5, no. 78.

26. McDouall to Prevost, 14 August 1814, Wood, vol. 3, pt. 1, 273.

27. Dunnigan, *British Army at Mackinac*, 22.

28. McDouall to Miller Worsley, 28 July 1814, NAC, RG 8, C series, 685:100.

29. Dunnigan, *British Army at Mackinac*, 22.

30. Usher Parsons diary, Rhode Island Historical Society; also Seebert J. Goldowsky, *Yankee Surgeon: The Life and Times of Usher Parsons (1788–1868)* (Boston: Francis A. Countway Library of Medicine and Rhode Island Publications Society, 1988), 76.

31. Details of this battle are based on McDouall to Prevost, 14 August 1814, Wood, vol. 3, pt. 1, 273–77.

32. Ibid., 77.

33. Here I rely on the casualty reports reviewed by Dunnigan (*British Army at Mackinac*, 26).

34. Sinclair to Jones, 9 August 1814, USNA, RG 45, CL, vol. 5, no. 78.

35. Quoted in Marjorie Wilkins Campbell, *Northwest to the Sea: A Biography of William McGillivray* (Toronto: Clarke, Irwin, 1975), 134.

36. *DCB* 7:557.

CHAPTER 6. LIEUTENANT WORSLEY'S LITTLE WAR

1. Theodore Roosevelt, "The War with the United States, 1812–15," in *The Royal Navy: A History from the Earliest Times to the Present,* ed. William Laird Clowes (London: Sampson and Low, 1901), 6:128.

2. *DCB* 6:817–18. Further particulars from Adm. 9/5 no. 1571; Mackenzie, *Trafalgar Roll,* 220, 227.

3. McDouall to Worsley, 28 July 1814, NAC, RG I (C Series), 683:100.

4. Quoted in Elsie McLeod Jury, "U.S.S. *Tigress*–H.M.S. *Confiance,*" *Inland Seas* 28 (1964): 8.

5. Bunnell, *Travels and Adventures,* 123.

6. Fred C. Hamil, *Michigan in the War of 1812,* Pamphlet No. 4 (Lansing: Michigan History Division, Michigan Department of State, 1977), originally published in *Michigan History,* September 1960, 41.

7. Worsley's letter to his father, 6 October 1814, *War Log,* xlvii–xlviii.

8. Enclosed in Sinclair to Jones, 3 September 1814 (see note 9 below).

9. Sinclair to Jones, 3 September 1814, DNA, RG 45, CL, 1814, vol. 6, no. 10 (M125, roll 39).

10. Bunnell, *Travels and Adventures*, 123.

11. Sinclair to D. Turner, 15 August 1814, DNA, RG 45, CL, 1914, vol. 5, no. 102.

12. Quoted in *DCB* 5:818.

13. Miller Worsley, Lieutenant Commanding, to Yeo, 15 September 1814, enclosure in Yeo to J. W. Croker, 12 October 1814, Cap Y5, Adm. 1/2738.

14. Bunnell, *Travels and Adventures*, 124.

15. Ibid., 123.

16. A. H. Bulger to McDouall, 7 September 1814, Michilimackinac, Wood, vol. 3, pt. 1, 279–81.

17. Drummond to Sir E. Owen, 20 June 1815, Adm. 1/2264, 158.

18. Yeo to Croker, 12 October 1814, Cap Y, Adm. 1/2738, and Admiralty minutes of 2 February and 13 and 15 July, 1815, ibid. Marshall, vol. 4, pt. 1, 374.

19. Cruikshank, 88. C. H. J. Snider, *The Story of the "Nancy" and other Eighteen-Twelvers* (Toronto: McClelland & Stewart, 1926), 80.

20. Roosevelt, "War with the United States," 129.

21. President's speech, 20 September 1814, in William James, *A Full and Correct Account of the Military Occurrences of the Late War between Great Britain and the United States* (London: printed for the author, 1818), 2:199.

22. Mark Bourrie, *Ninety Fathoms Down: Canadian Stories of the Great Lakes* (Toronto: Hounslow, 1995), 35.

23. "Court of inquiry into conduct of Stephen Champlin in the loss of US schooner *Tigress* and of Daniel Turner in the loss of US schooner *Scorpion*," USNA, RG 125, vol. 6, no. 207 (M273, roll 7).

24. *National Intelligencer,* 29 July 1815. Also, Bowen, *Naval Monument,* 252–53.

25. Stickney to C. Larned (attorney general, Michigan Territory), 21 January 1815, St. Mary's, Cass letter book 1, printed in Carter, *Territorial Papers* 10:500.

26. Acting Governor Woodridge to Secretary of War, 22 January 1815, Detroit, ibid., 500–503.

27. McArthur to Secretary of War, 6 February 1815, ibid., 503; see also Alec R. Gilpin, *The Territory of Michigan (1805–1837)* (East Lansing: Michigan State University Press, 1970), 65.

28. Ibid., 504.

29. William Caldwell to Colonel James, 1 December 1814, Wood, vol. 3, pt. 2, 733–34.

30. Commo. Sir Edward Owen to Secretary of the Admiralty, 25 March 1815, Adm. 1/2262.

31. A full inventory of these is given in "Prize papers relative to taking of American schooners *Tigress* and *Scorpion*," Adm. 49/10. The two schooners were claimed at Michilimackinac to be valued at four thousand pounds sterling each, and the rest

of the property (tackling, guns, anchors, etc.) at just under eight thousand pounds. However, as a lord of the Treasury minuted, "It has always been the practice to value ships & stores captured at any part of the Globe according to their value in England as far as can be ascertained from the descriptions given" and there the matter rested. Prize money was eventually awarded (in 1820), but the amount cannot have been to the satisfaction of any of the captors.

32. Yeo to J. W. Croker, 12 October 1814, no. 32, Adm. 1/2728. There is a copy of this in Adm. 49/10, p. 14.

33. Dobbs to Yeo, 13 August 1814, copy, Adm. 1/2737, CapY38, 142–47. Theodore Roosevelt, *Naval War of 1812*, . . . new ed. (Annapolis: Naval Institute Press, 1987), 336–37.

34. Yeo to Croker, 26 October 1814, Adm. 1/2737, CapY58, 237–38.

35. Yeo to Secretary of the Admiralty, 14 October 1814, Adm. 1/2737. Yeo to Secretary of the Admiralty, 1 January 1815, Adm. 1/2338.

CHAPTER 7. THE UNEASY PEACE

1. Wellington to Liverpool, 9 November 1814, in *Wellington's Supplementary Dispatches*, 14 vols. (London: John Murray, 1858), 9:422 and 425–26; also Worthington C. Ford, ed., *The Writings of John Quincy Adams*, 7 vols. (New York: Macmillan, 1913), 5:179 n. 2; see also Patrick C. T. White, *A Nation on Trial: America and the War of 1812* (New York: John Wiley, 1965), which reviews British and American documentation leading to the peace of Christmas Eve.

2. Text of the Treaty of Ghent, 24 December 1814 (ratified in Washington, D.C., on 18 February 1815). Auchinleck, *History of the War*, 404–7.

3. Burt, *United States, Great Britain, and British North America*, 374.

4. Quoted in Abbott, Mount, and Mulloy, *History of Fort St. Joseph*, 113.

5. I am obliged to Graeme Mount for this information.

6. McDouall to Forster, 15 May 1815, C 688, 37, NAC; also Wood, vol. 3, pt. 1, 532–36.

7. *DCB* 8 (1985): 112. Wood, vol. 3, pt. 1, p. 533. McDouall warned Bulger (20 February 1815): "Be on your guard as to Mr. Dickson, that insidious, intriguing, dangerous, yet despicable character. . . . I shall ever regret having sent him to you." Bulger Papers, *WHC* 13 (1895): 84.

8. With him he took off all public stores of every description, including the guns captured in the fort, in order that they might be restored to the U.S. government at Michilimackinac. It was impracticable to send these guns to St. Louis, and Bulger advised Governor Clark of this by letter, 23 May 1815. Bulger to McDouall, 19 June 1815, Bulger Papers, *WHC* 13:149–51.

9. Bruce Mahan, *Old Fort Crawford and the Frontier* (Iowa City: State Historical Society of Iowa, 1826), 7. Named for the secretary of war, William Crawford of Virginia. An American "factory" was established there to regulate trade with the Indian tribes.

10. Henry P. Beers, *Western Military Frontier, 1815–1846* (Philadelphia: Upper Darby, 1935), 27. Russell, *Guns on the Early Frontiers,* 303.

11. E. Collier to Commo. Sir E. Owen, 20 July 1815, Adm. 1/2263, 161–62. Also, Owen's correspondence with the Admiralty, 16 October 1815, Adm. 1/2264, esp. 129.

12. Anderson narrative, *WHC* 9 (1909): 203; also Jury, "U.S.S. *Tigress*—H.M.S. *Confiance,*" 12. Proceedings of this vessel can be followed in the captain's log, October 1815–June 1817, Adm. 51/2229.

13. J. J. Bigsby, *Shoe and Canoe,* 2 vols. (London, 1850), 1:296.

14. Quoted in Frank B. Woodford, *Lewis Cass: The Last Jeffersonian* (1950; reprint, New York: Octagon Books, 1973), 94.

15. Ibid., 106. See also Burt, *United States, Great Britain, and British North America,* 382–86.

16. Gilpin, *Territory of Michigan,* 114–15.

17. He had recently been promoted (to commander, 19 September 1815) and was senior naval officer on Lake Erie, arguably one of the most difficult commands on the Great Lakes or anywhere.

18. I do not share A. L. Burt's view that the naval commander was a firebrand. He was doing his job. Burt, *United States, Great Britain, and British North America,* 384–86.

19. Anon., "America and Her Resources," *Naval Chronicle* 40 (1818): 149.

20. Nestor's 30 August 1818 letter, ibid., 202–3. For related views, see ibid., 198–202.

21. Adams to Monroe, 30 March 1816, in Ford, *Writings of John Quincy Adams* 5:555.

22. Quoted in Bradford Perkins, *Castlereagh and Adams* (Berkeley and Los Angeles: University of California Press, 1966), 241.

23. Navy Board to Hall, 29 May 1817, Adm. 106/1998.

24. Sir Robert Hall to Charles Bagot, 4 June 1817, in NAC, Bagot Papers, Canadian Correspondence, 2:112; quoted in Burt, *United States, Great Britain, and British North America,* 394. Throughout, I have relied on Burt's interpretation of the disarmament.

25. Byam Martin, Notebook, Add. MSS 41,404, 29, Byam Martin Papers, BL (hereafter cited as Martin Papers).

26. R. Barrie to Admiralty, 26 August 1819, Adm. 12/193 (Digest).

CHAPTER 8. PENETANGUISHENE

1. Canada, *Sailing Directions, Georgian Bay* (Ottawa: Fisheries and Oceans, 1998), 42–47.

2. See Canada, *Indian Treaties and Surrenders,* vol. 1, *Treaties 1–138* (Ottawa: Queen's Printer, 1891), 15–17. Nowadays the customary spelling is Penetanguishene. In 1798, goods delivered to the natives for this arrangement were valued at £101. The tract of land was "all that tract or space containing land and water, or parcel of ground covered with water, be the same land or water or butted and bounded as follows: —Beginning at the head or South-Westernmost angle of a bay situated above certain French ruins, now lying on the east side of a small strait leading from the said Bay into a larger Bay called Gloucester or Sturgeon Bay; the head or South-Westernmost angle of the said bay being called by the Indians Opetiguoyawsing; thence North 70° West to a bay of Lake Huron, called by the Indians Nottoway Sague Bay, thence following the shores of Lake Huron, according to the different courses and windings of the said Nottoway Sague Bay— Penetangushene Harbour and Gloucester or Sturgeon Bay, sometimes called also Matchedash—to the place of beginning: containing all the land to the Northward of the said line running North 70° West and lying between it and the waters of Lake Huron, *together with the Islands* in the said Harbour of Penetangushene." Two maps of the Indian Purchase at Penetanguishene are found following 26.

3. J. W. Croker to Commo. E. W. C. R. Owen, 18 March 1815, Adm. 2/886.

4. Croker to W. F. W. Owen, 28 March 1815, ibid.

5. T. Hurd, memorandum on state of hydrography, 7 May 1814, enclosure in Hurd to Secretary of Admiralty, 12 October 1816; quoted in Vice Adm. Sir Archibald Day, *The Admiralty Hydrographic Service, 1795–1919* (London: HMSO, 1967), 27–29.

6. Commo. E. W. C. R. Owen to J. W. Croker, 25 November 1815, MG11, 383, NAC.

7. E. H. Burrows, *Captain Owen of the African Survey* (Rotterdam: A. A. Balkema, 1979), 61. Also *DCB* 8:668–73; Paul G. Cornell, "William Fitzwilliam Owen, Naval Surveyor," *Collections of the Nova Scotia Historical Society* 32 (1959): 167–68; and R. F. Fleming, "Charting the Great Lakes," *Canadian Geographic Journal* 12 (January–April 1936): 68–77; Robin Harris, "The Beginnings of the Hydrographic Survey of the Great Lakes and the St. Lawrence River," *Historic Kingston* 14 (1966): 24–39. "W. F. W. Owen's Observations and Journal on the Route from Lake Ontario to Lake Huron by Trent Waters and those of Lake Simcoe," 1817, are in Misc. Papers, vol. 31, Hydrographic Department, Taunton, Somerset.

8. N. Poyntz to Yeo, 19 November 1814, enclosure in Yeo to J. W. Croker, 27 November 1814, Adm. 1/2737, CapY12, 56–59.

9. Various plans and surveys of Penetanguishene, 1794–1851, are listed in Joan Winearls, *Mapping Upper Canada 1780–1867: An Annotated Bibliography of Manuscript and Printed Maps* (Toronto: University of Toronto Press, 1991), 378–80.

10. W. Owen's report of proceedings, to Commodore Owen, 21 October 1815, Adm. 1/2264, 331–26.

11. Commodore Owen to J. W. Croker, 25 November 1815, and Admiralty minute, 6 July 1816, ibid., 262–64 and 124, respectively.

12. Instructions to P. S. Hambly, Acting Commander, 12 October 1815, ibid., 145–60. These relate to Lake Huron. Those for Lake Erie (of the same date) are in ibid., 131–44.

13. Quoted in N. A. M. Rodger, *The Insatiable Earl: A Life of John Montagu, Fourth Earl of Sandwich, 1718–1792* (London: HarperCollins, 1993), 166.

14. *DCB* 5:400–401.

15. Letter of Rear-Admiral David Milne, 1 June 1816, in Historical Manuscripts Commission, *Report on the Manuscripts of Colonel David Milne Home* (London: HMSO, 1902), 169.

16. Letter by Milne, 13 June 1816, ibid., 169–70.

17. Sir Thomas Byam Martin to Lord Melville, 28 August 1817, Add. MSS 41,400, fol. 34, and Hall to Byam Martin, 7 October 1816, ibid., fol. 9, Martin Papers.

18. Hall to Byam Martin, 10 October 1816, Kingston, Add. MSS 41,400, fols. 7–8, Martin Papers.

19. Ibid, fol. 8.

20. Hall to Byam Martin, 7 October 1816, Add. MSS 41,400. fol. 9, Martin Papers.

21. Instructions to Sir Robert Hall, 11 July 1816, enclosure in Admiralty to Rear-Admiral Sir David Milne, 11 July 1816, MLN/33, NMM. Instructions from Lords Commissioners of the Admiralty, 12 July 1816, copy, Adm. 1/2262.

22. Hall to Byam Martin, 11 June 1817, Add. MSS 41,400, fol. 26, Martin Papers.

23. Ibid., fol. 27.

24. Ibid., fol. 28.

25. Ibid., fol. 30; also copy of Paper alluded to in Sir Robert Hall's letter of 10 June 1817, ibid., fol. 38 (sent to Melville, 28 August 1817).

26. Bayfield to R. Barrie, 1 November 1822, Adm. 1/3445.

27. Ruth McKenzie, *Admiral Bayfield, Pioneer Nautical Surveyor,* Miscellaneous Publication 32 (Ottawa: Environment Canada, Fisheries and Marine Service, 1976), and Ruth McKenzie, *Bayfield's Survey Journals* 1:xix. Also MG24, F28, vols. 1 and 2, Bayfield Papers, NAC, which contain correspondence and notes re: Great Lakes survey (see, in particular, "Notes re Survey of the Great Lakes, 1816–25," in MG24, F28, vol. 2, NAC). Although Midshipman Bayfield needed convincing by W. F. W. Owen at Quebec to leave the General Service for uncertain activity and promotion in the Hydrographic Service, Bayfield had more steady promotion and longer service time than the Navy's average. Made lieutenant 20 March 1815; commander, 8 November 1826; and captain, for exertions as a surveyor, 4 June

1834. He attained the rank of admiral. He died at Charlottetown, Prince Edward Island, 10 February 1885, at age ninety. Only James Cook and George Henry Richards approximate his contribution to Canadian hydrographical science.

28. The U.S. contribution to the hydrographic surveying of the Lakes may be traced in Arthur Woodford, *Charting the Inland Seas: A History of United States Lake Survey* (Washington, D.C.: GPO, 1991). For a general discussion of the subject, see R. W. Sandilands, "Hydrographic Surveying in the Great Lakes during the Nineteenth Century," *Canadian Surveyor* 36, no. 2 (June 1982): 139–63. Additional information from C. Patrick Labadie.

CHAPTER 9. THE END OF FIGHTING SAIL

1. Construction for the Officers' Quarters began in 1831 and was completed in 1836. Stone for the walls was cut from nearby Quarry Island and brought to the garrison by hired schooner. In 1856, upon the general reduction of military forces in Canada, the British Army closed down the base, and the lands were turned over to the government of Canada West. In 1859 a boys reformatory was established on the garrison grounds, the Officers' Quarters becoming Warden's Residence. Later the Hospital for the Insane took over the lands and buildings, and in 1952 it was opened as a museum (the 1970s saw restoration of the building to the late 1840s).

2. Robert Barrie to his mother, 14 September 1819, Penetanguishene, SPC MS FC441.B3 A4 1967, 7, Barrie Papers, RMC.

3. Pullen, *March of the Seamen,* and Stevens, *Story of H.M. Armed Schooner Tecumseth,* 25–29, where plans are to be found. Cassavoy and Crisman, "War of 1812," 187.

4. On the *Huron,* see Roosevelt, "War with the United States," 130, and particularly W. F. W. Owen to E. W. C. R. Owen, 21 October 1815, MG11, NAC, ser. Q, vols. 141–42 (now CO 42/171–72), and W. F. W. Owen to W. Bouchier, 31 March 1816, Adm. 1/2266.

5. Given in Robert Moore's "A Statement of the Naval Force . . . 6 June 1817," Adm. 106/1998. Also "Survey of H.M.S. *Huron,*" 8 September 1820, Adm. 106/1999. "State and Condition of H.M. Vessels and Boats belonging to this Establishment," by Michael Spratt, Grand River, 1 June 1830, Adm. 106/2002.

6. Brad Davis, "H.M. *Tecumseth* Research Project," 1979 (copy, Huronia Historical Research Centre, Midland, Ontario).

7. Letter of David Milne, 29 January 1819, Historical Manuscripts Commission, *Report on the Manuscripts,* 172–73.

8. [Lt. W. Edward Parry], "A Letter on Service Conditions in 1816," *Naval Review* 23 (1935): 749–50.

9. This is from his speech on the deficiencies of the army, 15 June 1852. *Parliamentary Debates* (House of Lords), 3d ser., CXII, cols. 728–51.

10. McKee, *Gentlemanly and Honorable Profession,* xi.

11. Particularly critical of American strategic analysis and political lessons were Harold and Margaret Sproat. See their *The Rise of American Naval Power, 1776–1918* (Princeton: Princeton University Press, 1939), chap. 7, "Neglected Lessons of 1812."

12. Capt. A. Sinclair, Report on Erie Station, 24 March 1815, in *The New American State Papers, Naval Affairs,* ed. K. Jack Bauer (Wilmington, Del.: Scholarly Resources, 1981), 2:24–26.

13. William H. Smith, *Canada: Past, Present and Future* (1852; reprint, Belleville, Ontario: Mika, 1974), 2:55. Also *Illustrated Atlas of the County of Simcoe [Belden Atlas, 1881]* (Port Elgin, Ontario, 1970), 11.

14. The story of the migration is given in A. C. Osborne, "Migration of Voyageurs from Drummond Island to Penetanguishene in 1828," *Ontario Historical Society Papers & Records* 3 (1901): 123–66. The resource list of Descendants of the Establishments Organization (Box 1800, Church Street, Penetanguishene, ON LoK 1Po) is to be found in the Penetanguishene Public Library.

15. Ibid.

16. H. D. Traill, *The Life of Sir John Franklin, R.N.* (London: John Murray, 1896), 120.

17. Quoted in Barry, *Georgian Bay,* 46.

18. L. Farrington, "The Decline of Naval Bases on the Lakes of Canada, 1815–1834" (unpublished text, 1955), 29–30, author's collection. Sir John Barrow to R. W. Hay, 3 December 1833, CO 42/245.

19. R. T. C. Dwelly, "St. James' Church, Penetanguishene," *Papers and Records, Ontario Historical Society* 34 (1942): 3–8.

20. This was the advice of the Navy Commissioners' Office to the secretary of the navy, 10 January 1824, in "Naval Peace Establishment," 18th Cong. 1st. sess., no. 239, *American State Papers Naval Affairs* 1:933.

21. See, for instance, Robert Erwin Johnson, *Thence Round Cape Horn: The Story of United States Naval Forces on Pacific Station, 1818–1923* (Annapolis: United States Naval Institute, 1963).

22. One scholar terms the factory system "a noble experiment." Wilcomb E. Washburn, *Red Man's Land/White Man's Law: A Study of the Past and Present Status of the American Indian* (New York: Charles Scribner's Sons, 1971), 60.

23. On Cass, specifically, see *DAB* 2:562–64; also, more generally, Gilpin, *Territory of Michigan,* 115–27.

24. Caleb Atwater, *Remarks Made on a Tour to Prairie du Chien thence to Washington City in 1829* (1831; reprint, New York: Arno Press, 1975), 71.

25. Quoted in ibid., 64,

26. Cassavoy and Grisman, "War of 1812," 188. Also Kenneth A. Cassavoy, B. Penny, and A. Amos, "The Penetanguishene Naval Slip," in *Archaeological Research Report No. 13*, ed. M. Skene (Toronto: Ontario Historical Research Branch, 1980), 153–73.

27. Shirley E. Whittington, "British Naval History in Full Sail at Penetanguishene (H.M.S. *Bee* [1817–31], Her History and Rebirth)," and Steve Killing, "The Designing of HMS *Bee*," *Fresh Water: A Journal of Great Lakes Marine History* 1, no. 2 (Autumn 1986): 17–20 and 21–24, respectively.

28. The position of surgeon was exceedingly important here. "The responsibilities attached to the duty of an assistant surgeon at an outpost in Canada far exceeds any he would be liable to serve on board a ship," wrote Captain Roberts, the commandant. Mr. Clement Todd was assistant surgeon, and in addition to dispensing potions and attending to wounds and other obligations, he spent his spare time in collecting plant specimens. His 1828 paper on medical use plants and soil is considered the earliest record of such observations in Upper Canada.

29. See articles by C. H. J. Snider in *Toronto Evening Telegram*, 25 November, 2, 9, 16, 23 and 30 December 1933, and 6 January 1934. Plans for the *Nancy* are available from the National Museum of American History's "Ship Plan List" (plan number T-86) in their catalogue. Information from Gordon Haffner.

30. Irvin Haas, *America's Historic Ships, Replicas and Restorations* (New York: Arco, 1975), 45–49.

31. *Blackwood's Magazine* 32, no. 146 (August 1832), quoted in Thomas A. Bailey, *A Diplomatic History of the American People*, 5th ed. (New York: Appleton-Century-Crofts, 1955), 159.

32. Yeo to Secretary of the Admiralty, 30 May 1815, Adm. 1/2738. George Raudzens, *The British Ordnance Department and Canada's Canals, 1815–1855* (Waterloo, Ont.: Wilfrid Laurier University Press, 1979); also Kenneth Bourne, *Britain and the Balance of Power in North America, 1815–1908* (London: Longmans, 1967), 33–52. The naval aspect of these matters has yet to be written.

BIBLIOGRAPHY

PRIMARY SOURCES: MANUSCRIPTS

CANADA

ARCHIVES OF ONTARIO, TORONTO

"Ideas on the Defence of the Canadas, Grounded upon our Present Strength, and such Resources in Men, as the Population of the Two Provinces May Offer." By Noah Freer, Captain and Quarter Master Generals Office. Quebec, 8 May 1812. MU8559.2

HURONIA HISTORICAL RESOURCE CENTRE, MIDLAND, ONTARIO

H.M. *Tecumseth* Research Project. By Brad Davis. 1979.

MCCORD MUSEUM ARCHIVES, MONTREAL

"Major William McKay's Account of the Michilimackinac Expedition." M7082.

NATIONAL ARCHIVES OF CANADA, OTTAWA, ONTARIO

Bayfield Papers. MG24, F28, 1 and 2, including, in vol. 2, "Notes re Survey of the Great Lakes, 1816–25."

Colonial Office Papers. Copies of CO 42 series; also assorted C series documents of the Army on the defense of Upper Canada. Copies of Co 43/10, being correspondence re: Jay Treaty implementation.

ROYAL MILITARY COLLEGE OF CANADA, KINGSTON, ONTARIO

Barrie Papers. SPC MS FC441.B3 A4, 1967. Correspondence, 1819–28, re: Penetanguishene, Lake Huron, Great Lakes.

GREAT BRITAIN

BRITISH LIBRARY, LONDON

Chatham Papers. North West Company representations on fur trade and security of Canada, 1794. GD 8-152 and 346.

Martin, Byam. Papers. Add. MS 41,400. Correspondence of Byam Martin, Melville, and especially Commodore Robert Hall on naval defense of Great Lakes, 1815–17; Add. MS 41,404. Byam Martin Notebook, giving state of armament on Great Lakes, etc.

HYDROGRAPHIC DEPARTMENT, MINISTRY OF DEFENCE (N), TAUNTON, SOMERSET

Misc. Papers, vol. 31, "W. F. W. Owen's Observations and Journal on the Route from Lake Ontario to Lake Huron by Trent Waters and those of Lake Simcoe," 1817.

NATIONAL MARITIME MUSEUM, GREENWICH

Milne Papers. MLN/33. Rear-Admiral David Milne's observations on Canadian defense.

PUBLIC RECORD OFFICE, KEW, SURREY

Adm. 1. Various volumes on the Great Lakes, in particular the papers of the commodore and commandant at Kingston, Ontario; also various in-letters from commanders of vessels. Of special interest: Adm. 1/503, Admiral Warren's correspondence with Captain Barclay; Adm. 1/2737, Barclay's narrative given at his court-martial, 9 September 1814; and Adm. 1/5445 (Court Martial documents); also Adm. 1/2736, Commodore Yeo's report to Admiral Warren on loss of HM fleet on Lake Erie; also Adm. 1/2738, Worsley's report of proceedings, capture of *Tigress* and *Scorpion,* American schooners, 1814.

Adm. 9. Service record of Robert Heriot Barclay (vol. 4, no. 1241); service record of Miller Worsley (vol. 5, no. 1571).

Adm. 12/193. Digest of correspondence, 1819.

Adm. 49/10. "Prize papers relative to taking of American schooners *Tigress* and *Scorpion*," complete to closing of file in 1820.

Adm. 106/1998, 1999 and 2002. Statements of naval force.

Colonial Office Papers. CO 42/316, J. G. Simcoe's scheme for Upper Canada security. Also CO 43/10 on Jay Treaty implementation.

War Office Papers. WO 1/537. Duke of Wellington. "Memorandum [on the defense of Canada]." 31 March 1841.

UNITED STATES

NATIONAL ARCHIVES, WASHINGTON, D.C.

RG 21. "Prize case files for the U.S. District Court for the Eastern District of Pennsylvania, being cases of North West Company's *Mink* and *Perseverance.*" Copies are in Naval Historical Center, microfilm M966, roll 2.

RG 45. CL, 1814, vols. 3 and 4. Crogan-Sinclair correspondence 1814. Also vols. 5 and 6, Jones-Sinclair and Turner-Sinclair correspondence 1814.

RG 125, vol. 6, no. 207. "Court of inquiry into conduct of Stephen Champlin in the loss of *Tigress* and Daniel Turner in the loss of *Scorpion*, 1814." Microfilm copy in Naval Historical Center M273, roll 7.

NAVAL HISTORICAL CENTER, WASHINGTON, D.C.

N.Hi. #01549. Isaac Chauncey Letter Books. Containing Chauncey-Elliott correspondence.

RHODE ISLAND HISTORICAL SOCIETY, PROVIDENCE

Parsons, Usher. Papers. "A Diary kept during the Expedition to Lake Erie, under Captain O. H. Perry, 1812–14 by Usher Parsons, Surgeon." Microfilm.

PRIMARY SOURCES: PRINTED MATERIAL

American State Papers Military Affairs. Vol. 1. Washington, D.C.: Gates and Seaton, 1836.

American State Papers Naval Affairs. Vol. 1. Washington, D.C.: Gates and Seaton, 1836.

Bowen, Abel, comp. *The Naval Monument, Containing Official and Other Accounts of All the Battles Fought between the Navies of the United States and Great Britain during the Late War.* Boston: A. Bowen, 1816.

Bulger, A. *An Autobiographical Sketch of the Late Captain Andrew Bulger of the Royal Newfoundland Fencible Regiment.* Bangalore, India, 1865.

Bunnell, David C. *Travels and Adventures of David C. Bunnell during twenty-three years of Seafaring Life, containing an Accurate Account of the Battle of Lake Erie, under the Command of Com. Perry, together with ten years service in the Navy of the United States; also Service among the Greeks, imprisonment among the Turks, etc.* Palmyra, N.Y.: Bortles, 1831.

Canada. *Indian Treaties and Surrenders.* Vol. 1, *Treaties 1–138.* Ottawa: Queen's Printer, 1891.

———. *Sailing Directions, Georgian Bay.* Ottawa: Fisheries and Oceans, 1998.

Carter, Clarence, ed. *The Territorial Papers of the United States.* Vol. 10, *The Territory of Michigan, 1805–1820.* Washington, D.C.: GPO, 1942.

Cruikshank, Edward A., ed. *The Documentary History of the Campaign upon the Niagara Frontier.* 9 vols. Welland: Tribune Office for the Lundy's Lane Historical Society, 1902–8; New York: Arno Press and New York Times, 1971.

———. *Documents Relating to the Invasion of Canada and the Surrender of Detroit, 1812.* Canadian Archives Publications no. 7. Ottawa: Government Printing Bureau, 1912; New York: Arno Press and New York Times, 1971.

———. "An Episode of the War of 1812: The Story of the Schooner *Nancy* [with illustrative documents], *Ontario Historical Society Papers and Records* 9 (1910). Reprinted in *The Defended Border: Upper Canada and the War of 1812,* edited by Morris Zaslow. Toronto: Macmillan, 1964.

Dudley, William, ed. *The Naval War of 1812: A Documentary History.* 2 vols. to date. Washington, D.C.: Naval Historical Center, 1985, 1992.

Dunlop, Tiger. *Tiger Dunlop's Upper Canada.* Toronto: McClelland & Stewart, 1967.

Historical Manuscripts Commission. *Report on the Manuscripts of Colonel David Milne Home.* London: HMSO, 1902.

Lajeunesse, Ernest J., ed. *The Windsor Border Region: Canada's Southernmost Frontier, A Collection of Documents.* Toronto: Champlain Society, 1960.

Leaves from the War Log of the Nancy, Eighteen Hundred and Thirteen, with Comments by C. H. J. Snider. New ed. Midland: Huronia Historical Development Council, 1958.

Long, John. *Voyages and Travels of an Indian Interpreter . . .* London, 1791.

Michigan Historical Collections 15 (1909): Prevost correspondence.

New American State Papers, Naval Affairs. Edited by K. Jack Bauer. Vol. 2, *Diplomatic Activities,* and vol. 4, *Combat.* Wilmington, Del.: Scholarly Resources, 1981.

Niles' Weekly Register. Baltimore, Md.

[Parry, W. Edward]. "A Letter of Service Conditions in 1816." *Naval Review* 23 (1935): 749–50.

Parsons, Usher. *Battle of Lake Erie: A Discourse, Delivered before the Rhode Island Historical Society . . . February 16, 1852.* Providence, R.I.: Benjamin T. Albro, 1853.

Wisconsin Historical Collections. Including Anderson journal, vol. 9 (1882), Bulger Papers, vol. 13 (1895), Dickson and Grignon papers, vol. 11 (1888).

Wood, William, ed. *Select British Documents of the Canadian War of 1812.* 3 vols. Toronto: Champlain Society, 1920–28.

SECONDARY SOURCES

Abbott, John, Graeme S. Mount, and Michael J. Mulloy. *The History of Fort St. Joseph.* Toronto: Dundurn, 2000.

Allen, Robert S. *The British Indian Department and the Frontier in North America, 1755–1830.* Canadian Historic Sites Occasional Papers no. 14. Ottawa: Indian and Northern Affairs, 1973.

Antal, Sandy. *A Wampum Denied: Procter's War of 1812.* Ottawa: Carleton University Press, 1997.

Armour, David A., and Keith R. Widder. *At the Crossroads: Michilimackinac during the American Revolution.* Mackinac Island, Mich.: Mackinac Island State Park Commission, 1978.

Auchinleck, Gilbert. *A History of the War between Great Britain and the United States of America, during the Years 1812, 1813, and 1814.* 1855. Reprint, London: Arms and Armour, 1972.

Bancroft, George. *History of the Battle of Lake Erie, and Miscellaneous Papers.* New York: Robert Bonner's Sons, 1891.

Barnes, James. *Naval Actions of the War of 1812.* New York: Harper & Brothers, 1896.

Barry, James P. *Georgian Bay: The Sixth Great Lake.* Toronto: Clarke, Irwin, 1978.

Bass, George F., ed. *Ships and Shipwrecks of the Americas: A History Based on Underwater Archaeology.* London: Thames and Hudson, 1988.

Bourne, Kenneth. *Britain and the Balance of Power in North America, 1815–1908.* London: Longmans, 1967.

Bourrie, Mark. *Ninety Fathoms Down: Canadian Stories of the Great Lakes.* Toronto: Hounslow, 1995.

Buckie, Robert. "His Majesty's Flag Has Not Been Tarnished." *Journal of Erie Studies* 17 (Fall 1988): 85–102.

Burrows, E. H. *Captain Owen of the African Survey.* Rotterdam: A. A. Balkema, 1979.

Burt, Alfred Leroy. *The United States, Great Britain, and British North America: From the Revolution to the Establishment of Peace after the War of 1812.* New Haven: Yale University Press, 1940.

Caffrey, Kate. *The Twilight's Last Gleaming: Britain vs. America 1812–1815*. New York: Stein and Day, 1974.

Cain, Emily. *Ghost Ships Hamilton and Scourge: Historical Treasures from the War of 1812*. Toronto: Beaufort, 1983.

Calloway, Colin. *Crown and Calumet: British-Indian Relations, 1783–1815*. Norman: University of Oklahoma Press, 1987.

Callwell, C. E. *Military Operations and Maritime Preponderance, Their Relations and Interdependence*. Edinburgh: William Blackwood and Sons, 1905.

Campbell, Marjorie Wilkins. *Northwest to the Sea: A Biography of William McGillivray*. Toronto: Clarke Irwin, 1975.

Casselman, Alexander C. *Richardson's War of 1812*. Toronto: Historical Publishing, 1902.

Channing, Edward. *A History of the United States*. Vol. 4, *Federalists and Republicans, 1789–1815*. New York: Macmillan, 1917.

Chapelle, Howard I. *The History of the American Sailing Navy: The Ships and Their Development*. New York: Norton, 1949.

Clare, C. Winton [R. C. Anderson]. "A Shipbuilder's War." *Mariner's Mirror* 29 (July 1943).

Clowes, William Laird. *The Royal Navy: A History from the Earliest Times to 1900*, vol. 6. 1901. Reprint, London: Chatham, 1997. Contains, as chapter 41, "The War with the United States, 1812–1815," by Theodore Roosevelt.

Coffin, William F. *1812: The War and Its Moral: A Canadian Chronicle*. Montreal: John Lovell, 1864.

Cornell, Paul G. "William Fitzwilliam Owen, Naval Surveyor." *Collections of the Nova Scotia Historical Society* 32 (1959): 167–68.

Creighton, Donald G. *The Empire of the St. Lawrence, 1760–1850*. Toronto: Macmillan, 1956.

Davidson, Gordon C. *The North West Company*. 1918. Reprint, New York: Russell & Russell, 1967.

Day, Archibald. *The Admiralty Hydrographic Service, 1795–1919*. London: HMSO, 1967.

Docker, John T. *Grand River Naval Depot*. Dunnville, Ontario: Dunnville District Heritage Association, 2000.

Dunnigan, Brian Leigh. *The British Army at Mackinac, 1812–1815*. Reports in Mackinac History and Archaeology Number 7. Mackinac Island, Mich.: Mackinac Island State Park Commission, 1980.

Dwelly, R. T. C. "St. James' Church, Penetanguishene." *Papers and Records, Ontario Historical Society* 34 (1942): 3–8.

Edmunds, David R. *Tecumseh and the Quest for Indian Leadership*. Boston: Little, Brown, 1984.

Farrington, L. "The Decline of Naval Bases on the Lakes of Canada, 1815–1834." Unpublished manuscript. 1955.

Fergusson, Bernard. *The Watery Maze: The Story of Combined Operations.* London: Collins, 1961.

Fleming, R. F. "Charting the Great Lakes." *Canadian Geographic Journal* 12 (January–April 1936): 68–77.

Fowler, William M., Jr. *Jack Tars and Commodores: The American Navy, 1783–1815.* Boston: Houghton Mifflin, 1984.

Freehoff, William F. "Tecumseh's Last Stand." *Military History,* October 1996, 30–36.

Gentilcore, R. Louis, and C. Grant Head. *Ontario's History in Maps.* Toronto: University of Toronto Press, 1984.

Gilpin, Alec R. *The Territory of Michigan (1805–1837).* East Lansing: Michigan State University Press, 1970.

———. *The War of 1812 in the Old Northwest.* East Lansing: Michigan State University Press, 1958.

Goldowsky, Seebert J. *Yankee Surgeon: The Life and Times of Usher Parsons (1788–1868).* Boston: Francis A. Countway Library of Medicine and Rhode Island Publications Society, 1988.

Hamil, Fred C. *Michigan in the War of 1812.* Pamphlet No. 4. Lansing: Michigan History Division, Michigan Department of State, 1977.

Hammack, James Wallace, Jr. *Kentucky and the Second American Revolution: The War of 1812.* Lexington: University Press of Kentucky, 1976.

Handbook of Indians of Canada. Ottawa: King's Printer, 1913.

Harris, Robin. "The Beginning of the Hydrographic Survey of the Great Lakes and the St. Lawrence River." *Historic Kingston* 14 (1966): 24–39.

Hatch, William S. *A Chapter of the History of the War of 1812 in the Northwest, embracing the Surrender of the Northwestern Army . . . at Detroit . . . [and] Sketch . . . of Tecumseh.* Cincinnati: Miami Printing, 1872.

Havighurst, Walter. *Three Flags at the Straits: The Forts of Mackinac.* Englewood Cliffs, N.J.: Prentice-Hall, 1966.

———, ed. *The Great Lakes Reader.* New York: Macmillan, 1966.

Hitsman, J. Mackay. *The Incredible War of 1812: A Military History.* Toronto: University of Toronto Press, 1965.

———. "Sir George Prevost's Conduct of the Canadian War of 1812." *Canadian Historical Association Annual Report for 1962,* 34–43. Ottawa: Canadian Historical Association, 1962.

H.M.S. Nancy and the War of 1812. Toronto: Ministry of Natural Resources, 1978.

Horsman, Reginald. *Causes of the War of 1812.* 1962. Reprint, New York: Octagon Books, 1972.

———. "On to Canada: Manifest Destiny and United States Strategy in the War of 1812." *Michigan Historical Review* 13, no. 2 (1987): 1–24.

———. *The War of 1812.* London: Eyre & Spottiswoode, 1969.

———. "Wisconsin in the War of 1812." *Wisconsin Magazine of History* 46, no. 1 (Autumn 1962): 3–15.

Hubinger, Bert. "Little Wasp, Big Sting." *Naval History,* July–August 1994.

Illustrated Atlas of the County of Simcoe [Belden Atlas, 1881]. Port Elgin, 1970.

James, William. *A Full and Correct Account of the Chief Naval Occurrences of the Late War between Great Britain and the United States of America,* . . . London: T. Egerton, 1817.

———. *A Full and Correct Account of the Military Occurrences of the Late War between Great Britain and the United States.* 2 vols. London: Printed for the Author, 1818.

———. *The Naval History of Great Britain, from the Declaration of War by France in 1783* . . . 5 vols. London: Baldwin, Cradock and Joy, 1822–24.

Jenness, Diamond. *The Indians of Canada.* 7th ed. Toronto: University of Toronto Press, 1977.

Johnson, Ida Amanda. *The Michigan Fur Trade.* 1919. Reprint, Grand Rapids, Mich.: Black Letter Press, 1971.

Jury, Elsie McLeod. "U.S.S. *Tigress*–H.M.S. *Confiance.*" *Inland Seas* 28 (1964): 3–16.

Kellogg, Louise Phelps. *The British Régime in Wisconsin and the Northwest.* 1935. Reprint, New York: Da Capo, 1971.

Kingsford, William. *The History of Canada.* Vol. 8, *1808–1815.* Toronto: Rowsell & Hutchison, 1895.

Klinck, Carl F., ed. *Tecumseh: Fact and Fiction in Early Records.* Englewood Cliffs, N.J.: Prentice-Hall, 1961.

Landon, Fred. *Lake Huron.* Indianapolis: Bobbs-Merrill, 1944.

———. *Western Ontario and the American Frontier.* Toronto: Ryerson, 1941.

Lomax, D. A. N. *A History of the Services of the 41st (Welch) Regiment (now 1st Battalion the Welch Regiment) from Its Formation, in 1719 to 1895.* Devonport, England: Hiorns & Miller, 1899.

Lossing, Benson J. *Field-Book of the War of 1812.* 1867.

———. "A Naval Victory of One Hundred Years Ago: The Battle of Lake Erie, Sept. 10, 1813." *Harper's Monthly Magazine* 127, no. 758 (1913): 455–62.

Lucas, Charles P. *The Canadian War of 1812.* Oxford: Clarendon Press, 1906.

Mackenzie, Robert Holden. *The Trafalgar Roll: Containing the Names and Services of all Officers of the Royal Navy and Royal Marines who participated in the Glorious Victory of the 21st October 1805, together with a History of the Ships engaged in the Battle.* London: George Allen, 1913.

Mahan, Alfred T. *Sea Power in its Relations to the War of 1812.* 2 vols. Boston, 1905.

Mahan, Bruce. *Old Fort Crawford and the Frontier.* Iowa City: State Historical Society of Iowa, 1826.

Mahon, John. *The War of 1812.* 1972. Reprint, New York: Da Capo, 1991.

Malcomson, Robert. *Lords of the Lake: The Naval War on Lake Ontario, 1812–1814.* Toronto: Robin Bass Studio, 1998.

———. "War on the Lakes: the Struggle on the Inland Sea, 1812–1814." *Beaver* 70, no. 2 (April–May 1990): 44–52.

Malcomson, Thomas, and Robert Malcomson. "Images of Battle: Peter Rindlisbacher, Marine Artist." *Beaver* 71, no. 3 (June–July 1991): 6–11.

McKee, Christopher. *A Gentlemanly and Honorable Profession: The Creation of the U.S. Naval Officer Corps, 1794–1815.* Annapolis: Naval Institute Press, 1991.

McKenzie, Ruth. *Admiral Bayfield, Pioneer Nautical Surveyor.* Miscellaneous Publication 32. Ottawa: Environment Canada, Fisheries and Marine Service, 1976.

Morrison, Jean. *Superior Rendezvous-Place: Fort William in the Canadian Fur Trade.* Toronto: Natural Heritage/Natural History, Inc., 2001.

Morriss, Roger. *The Royal Dockyards during the Revolutionary and Napoleonic Wars.* Leicester: Leicester University Press, 1983.

Mount, Graeme S. "Drums Along the St. Mary's: Tensions on the International Border at Sault Ste. Marie." *Michigan History* 73, no. 4 (July/August 1989): 32–36.

Mount, Graeme S., John Abbott, and Michael J. Mulloy. *The Border at Sault Ste. Marie.* Toronto: Dundurn, 1995.

Mount, Graeme S., and Michael J. Mulloy. "Rivals and Friends: Hands Across the Border at the Sault." *Beaver* 70, no. 3 (June/July 1990): 48–51.

Nobles, Gregory H. *American Frontiers: Cultural Encounters and Continental Conquest.* New York: Hill and Wang, 1997.

Parkman, Francis. *France and England in North America,* vol. 1. New York: Library of America, 1983.

Parsons, Charles. *Memoir of Usher Parsons, M.D., of Providence, R.I.* Providence, R.I.: Hammond, Angell, 1870.

Perry's Victory Centennial, 1813–1913. Cleveland: Cleveland Commission, Perry's Victory Centennial, 1913.

Pullen, H. F. *The March of the Seamen,* and John R. Stevens, *Story of H.M. Armed Schooner Tecumseth.* Occasional Paper no. 8–9. Halifax: Maritime Museum of Canada, 1961.

Quaife, Milo M. "The Royal Navy of the Upper Lakes." *Burton Historical Collection Leaflet* 2, no. 5 (May 1924): 49–64.

Quimby, Robert S. *The U.S. Army in the War of 1812: An Operation and Command Study.* 2 vols. East Lansing: Michigan State University Press, 1997.

Raudzens, George. *The British Ordnance Department and Canada's Canals, 1815–1855.* Waterloo, Ont.: Wilfrid Laurier University Press, 1979.

Richmond, Herbert. *Statesmen and Sea Power.* Oxford: Clarendon, 1946.

Roosevelt, Theodore. *The Naval War of 1812, or the History of the United States Navy during the Last War with Great Britain to Which Is Appended an Account of the Battle of New Orleans.* New ed. Annapolis: Naval Institute Press, 1987.

———. "The War with the United States, 1812–1815." In *The Royal Navy: A History from the Earliest Times to the Present,* vol. 6, edited by William Laird Clowes. London: Sampson and Low, 1901.

Rosenberg, Max. *The Building of Perry's Fleet on Lake Erie, 1812–1813.* Harrisburg: Pennsylvania Historical and Museum Commission, 1930.

Russell, Carl P. *Guns on the Early Frontiers: A History of Firearms from Colonial Times through the Years of the Western Fur Trade.* Berkeley and Los Angeles: University of California Press, 1957.

Sandilands, R. W. "Hydrographic Surveying in the Great Lakes during the Nineteenth Century." *Canadian Surveyor* 36, no. 2 (June 1982): 139–63.

Skaggs, David Curtis. "The Battle of Lake Erie." In *Great American Naval Battles,* edited by Jack Sweetman. Annapolis: Naval Institute Press, 1998.

Skaggs, David Curtis, and Gerard T. Altoff. *A Signal Victory: The Lake Erie Campaign, 1812–1813.* Annapolis: Naval Institute Press, 1997.

Smith, William H. *Canada: Past, Present and Future.* 1852. Reprint, Belleville, Ontario: Mika, 1974.

Snider, C. H. J. *The Story of the "Nancy" and other Eighteen-Twelvers.* Toronto: McClelland & Stewart, 1926.

———. *In the Wake of the Eighteen-Twelvers: Fights & Flights of Frigates & Fore-'n'-Afters in the War of 1812–1815 on the Great Lakes.* Toronto: Bell & Cockburn, 1913.

Sproat, Harold, and Margaret Sproat. *The Rise of American Naval Power, 1776–1918.* Princeton: Princeton University Press, 1939.

Stacey, Charles P. *Introduction to the Study of Military History for Canadian Students.* Ottawa: Queen's Printer, 1953.

Stagg, J. C. A. *Mr. Madison's War: Politics, Diplomacy, and Warfare in the Early American Republic, 1783–1830.* Princeton: Princeton University Press, 1983.

Stanley, George F. G. *The War of 1812: Land Operations.* Toronto: Macmillan of Canada, 1983.

Sugden, John. *Tecumseh: A Life.* New York: Henry Holt, 1997.

———. *Tecumseh's Last Stand.* Norman: University of Oklahoma Press, 1985.

Tanner, Helen Hornbeck. *The Ojibwa.* New York: Chelsea House, 1991.

Triggs, John R. "Archaeological Investigations at the Historic Naval and Military

Establishments at Penetanguishene." *Annual Archaeological Report, Ontario* 3 (1992): 95–99. Also ibid. 5 (1994): 107–11 and 9 (1998): 83–89.

Weigley, Russell F. *The American Way of War: A History of United States Military Strategy and Policy.* New York: Macmillan, 1973.

Welsh, William Jeffrey, and David Curtis Skaggs, eds. *War on the Great Lakes: Essays Commemorating the 175th Anniversary of the Battle of Lake Erie.* Kent, Ohio: Kent State University Press, 1991.

White, Patrick C. T. *A Nation on Trial: America and the War of 1812.* New York: John Wiley, 1965.

White, Richard. *The Middle Ground: Indians, Empires, and Republics in the Great Lakes Region, 1650–1815.* Cambridge: Cambridge University Press, 1991.

Whitehorn, A. C. *The History of the Welch Regiment.* Cardiff: Western Mail and Echo, 1932.

Whittington, Shirley. "British Naval History in Full Sail at Penetanguishene (H.M.S. *Bee* [1817–1831], Her History and Rebirth)." *FreshWater: A Journal of Great Lakes Marine History* 1, no. 2 (Autumn 1986): 17–20.

Winton-Clare, C. [R. C. Anderson]. "A Shipbuilder's War." *Mariner's Mirror* 29 (1943): 139–48.

Wishart, Bruce. "'A Remarkable Fine Ship': Sir James Yeo and the *St. Lawrence.*" *Beaver* 72, no. 1 (February/March 1992): 12–22.

Woodford, Arthur. *Charting the Inland Seas: A History of United States Lake Survey.* Washington, D.C.: GPO, 1991.

Woodford, Frank B. *Lewis Cass: The Last Jeffersonian.* 1950. Reprint, New York: Octagon Books, 1973.

Zaslow, Morris, ed. *The Defended Border: Upper Canada and the War of 1812.* Toronto: Macmillan of Canada, 1964.

INDEX

ABOUT THE AUTHOR

Born in Victoria, British Columbia, sailor and historian Barry M. Gough has spent much of his life in boats or writing about them. He grew up sailing the waters of the Pacific Northwest, and, like Francis Parkman and Samuel E. Morison, he became a traveler in search of history. In his sloop, based on Penetanguishene, Georgian Bay, he has sailed to many of the locations he describes in *Fighting Sail*, and by land he has visited many other historic sites of the War of 1812.

Educated at the University of British Columbia, the University of Montana, and Kings College University of London, he holds M.A., Ph.D., and D.Lit. degrees, the last for distinguished contributions to imperial and common-wealth history. He is a fellow of the Royal Historical Society, past president of the North American Society for Oceanic History, and past president of the Canadian Nautical Research Society. He has written numerous books on the fur trade, the exploration of North America, and the Royal Navy's involvement with the Northwest coast of North America during the eighteenth, nineteenth, and twentieth centuries. His books have won critical acclaim and garnered numerous prizes.

Dr. Gough is currently professor of history at Wilfrid Laurier University in Waterloo, Ontario. In addition to his research and teaching, he is Archives Fellow of Churchill College Cambridge, and editor in chief of the quarterly journal *The American Neptune: Maritime History & Arts*, published by the Peabody Essex Museum in Salem, Massachusetts.